PLAYS BY

Edward Albee

(DATES OF COMPOSITION)

ADAPTATIONS

EDWARD ALBEE

THE PLAYS

EDWARD ALBEE

VOLUME FOUR

Everything in the Garden
FROM THE PLAY BY GILES COOPER

Malcolm
FROM THE NOVEL BY JAMES PURDY

The Ballad of the Sad Cafe
FROM THE NOVELLA BY CARSON MC CULLERS

THE PLAYS

Atheneum

NEW YORK   1982

Library of Congress Cataloging in Publication Data

Albee, Edward, 1928–
 Selected plays.

  Contents: —v. 2. Tiny Alice. A delicate
balance. Box and Quotations from Chairman Mao
Tse-Tung—v. 3. Seascape. Counting the ways. Listening.
All over.—v. 4. Everything in the garden. Malcolm.
The ballad of the sad café.
 I. Title.
 PS3551.L25A19   1982   812'.54   81-3613
 ISBN 0-689-70616-2 (pbk. : v. 4)   AACR2

EVERYTHING

IN THE

GARDEN

FROM THE PLAY BY
GILES COOPER

TO THE MEMORY OF

GILES COOPER

FIRST PERFORMANCE

November 16, 1967, New York City, Plymouth Theatre

BARBARA BEL GEDDES *as* JENNY

BARRY NELSON *as* RICHARD

ROBERT MOORE *as* JACK

BEATRICE STRAIGHT *as* MRS. TOOTHE

RICHARD THOMAS *as* ROGER

MARY K. WELLS *as* BERYL

WHITFIELD CONNOR *as* CHUCK

M'EL DOWD *as* LOUISE

TOM ALDREDGE *as* GILBERT

CHARLES BAXTER *as* PERRY

AUGUSTA DABNEY *as* CYNTHIA

Directed by PETER GLENVILLE

THE PLAYERS

RICHARD
a pleasant-looking man, 43

JENNY
his wife, an attractive woman in her late thirties

ROGER
their son, a nice-looking boy, 14 or 15

JACK
a neighbor, a pleasant-looking man, about 40

MRS. TOOTHE
an elegantly dressed, handsome lady, 50 or so

CHUCK AND BERYL

GILBERT AND LOUISE

CYNTHIA AND PERRY
friends and neighbors,
very much like Richard and Jenny

THE SCENE

The livingroom and sunroom of a suburban house, a large and well-kept garden visible through the glass doors of the sunroom. This was an old house and the sunroom is clearly an addition to the existing structure, though not jarring.. There is no wealth evident in the set; taste and ingenuity have been used instead of money.

ACT ONE

SCENE ONE

(*Stage empty, sounds of lawnmower (hand) out picture window.* RICHARD *passes window, mowing; stops, mops; goes on.* JENNY *enters room from hall, looking for a cigarette; finds pack on mantel, finds it empty, is about to throw it away, remembers, removes coupons, then is about to throw pack in wastebasket when she spies another empty pack therein, shakes her head, stoops, takes it out, un-crumples it, removes coupons*)

JENNY
(*Shakes her head; under her breath*)
Honestly! (*Louder, but* RICHARD *cannot possibly hear*) You might remember!
(RICHARD *passes window again, mowing;* JENNY *opens glass door, speaks out to him*)
You might remember!
(*He goes on mowing; irritated*)
Richard!
(*He stops*)

RICHARD
(*We really don't hear him*)
Hm?

JENNY
You might try to remember! (*Turns, comes back in, leaving glass door open*)

RICHARD
(*Follows her in, mopping neck with handkerchief*)
I might what?

JENNY
You might remember. (*Leaves it at that*)

RICHARD
(*Thinks*)
All right. (*Pause*) I might remember what?

JENNY
(*Still looking for a cigarette*)
When you throw them away.

RICHARD
(*Considers that*)
Um-hum. (*Pause*) May I go back out now? Somebody's got to get the damn lawn mowed, and I don't notice any gardeners out there waiting for me to tell them what . . .

JENNY
(*Finding every cigarette box empty*)
I've told you two thousand times: well, I've told you *two* things two thousand times: please keep cigarettes in the house . . .

RICHARD
(*Used to it, but airy*)
You're running it.

JENNY
(*Something of the strict schoolteacher creeping in*)
When you finish a pack, do two things—I've told you . . .

RICHARD
—two thousand times—

JENNY
(*Closes her eyes for a moment, goes on*)
. . . first, when you finish a pack, look to see if it's the last one—the last pack . . .

RICHARD
(Bored, impatient)

Yes, ma'am.

JENNY
(Undaunted)

And if it is, put it down to get some more, or tell *me* . . .

RICHARD
(Ibid.)

O.K.; O.K.

JENNY

Whenever you *do* finish a pack, don't forget to take the coupons off. Please? The coupons? We save them?

RICHARD

Did I *forget?*

JENNY

You *always* forget. We smoke these awful things just to get the coupons . . .

RICHARD
(Offhand)

O.K.

JENNY
(After a small pause)

Do you have any?

RICHARD

Coupons?

JENNY
(Not amused)

Cigarettes!

RICHARD
(Feels)
Um-hum. *(Suddenly aware)* Want one? *(Offers her the pack)*

JENNY
(Sees the pack)
Why, you dog! Those aren't . . . What are you—how dare
you smoke *those* cigarettes, those don't have coupons,
you . . . Do you mean I sit in here, ruining my lungs, piling
up coupons, while you're sneaking around . . .

RICHARD
(Giggles at being caught)
Caught me, huh?

JENNY
You little . . . twerp!

RICHARD
(Lighting for her)
Big twerp. Good, aren't they?

JENNY
(Rue)
Yes. *(Pause)* How's the lawn?

RICHARD
Growing.

JENNY
Remember what I told you: watch out for the tulips.

RICHARD
(Exaggerated contrition)
Well, I gotta confess I got carried away, zooming along with
the mower, *(Fast shiver sound)* br-br-br-br-br-br-br-br, mowed

'em down; by the time I got control of myself must have chopped up a good two dozen of 'em. *(Afterthought)* Sorry.

JENNY
(Nods knowingly)
Well, it wasn't funny that time you did. *(More-or-less to her-self)* Honestly, a grown man running a lawnmower through a tulip bed.

RICHARD
(Jaunty and proud)
I rather liked it. Besides, what do you mean, "How's the lawn?" What do you care about the lawn? It could turn into one big dandelion patch for all you'd care so long as it didn't interfere with your hollyhocks and your tulips and your pink Williams, or whatever they are.

JENNY
(Superior, but friendly)
We all do what we're equipped for. Some of us are fit for keeping a lawn cut, and others . . . well, how green is my thumb.

RICHARD
(Looks at it all)
Looks good. Your scrambled eggs are a mess, but you sure can keep a garden.

JENNY
(Sweet-and-sour)
I'm just an outdoor type.

RICHARD
(Kisses her forehead)
Yes. You are. *(Collapses in an easy chair; groans with fatigue)*
OOOOOHHHHhhhhhhhhhhhhh, God!

JENNY

Hm?

RICHARD
(Sincere and sad)
I *wish* we could afford things.

JENNY
(Muted; ironic)
Keep smoking! Save those coupons!

RICHARD
Roger call? He get to school O.K.?

JENNY
Yes, he has three roommates this year, and they're going to
let him have his bike.

RICHARD
(Very young again)
I wish they'd let me have a power mower.

JENNY
Well, you can't have one, so just . . . (Leaves it unfinished)

RICHARD
I am probably the only natural-born citizen east of the
Rockies who does not have a power mower.

JENNY
Well, you cannot *have* one, so let it be.

RICHARD
(Points vaguely around, suggesting the neighborhood)
Alan has one; Clinton; *Mark!* Mark's got one he trades *in*
every . . .

JENNY
(*Surprisingly sharp*)

No!

(*Silence*)

RICHARD
(*To himself*)
Forty-three years old and I haven't even got a power mower.
(*Silence*)

JENNY
Do you want something? Some tea, or a sandwich?

RICHARD
(*Sharp*)

Can we afford it?

JENNY
(*Through her teeth*)

Barely.

RICHARD
(*Gets up, paces; offhand*)
You, uh . . . you want to get a divorce? Get married again?
Someone with money? Somebody with a power mower?

JENNY
(*Weary, matter-of-fact*)
Not this week; I'm too busy.

RICHARD
(*Abstracted*)
You let me know. (*Back to her*) How much?

JENNY

Hm?

RICHARD

How much do you spend? On, on seeds, and manure, and shears, and . . .

JENNY
(Gets up)

Oh, for God's . . .

RICHARD

. . . and, and bulbs, and stakes to hold the damn plants up, and . . .

JENNY
(Angry, but, still, rather bravura)

Plow it up! Plow the whole damn garden under! Put in gravel! And while you're at it, get rid of the grass!

RICHARD
(Shrugs)

Everybody has grass.

JENNY
(Furious)

EVERYBODY HAS A GARDEN! *(Still angry, but softer)* I am willing; I am willing to scrimp, and eat what I don't really want to half the time, and dress like something out of a forties movie . . .

RICHARD
(Regretting the whole thing)

All right; all right . . .

JENNY

. . . and *not* have a maid, and only have my hair done twice a month, and not say let's go away for the weekend . . .

RICHARD

All right!

JENNY
. . . to pay and pay on this god-damned house . . .

RICHARD
(Soft, reasonable, but infuriating)
. . . everybody has a house . . .

JENNY
. . . *and* the bloody car . . .

RICHARD
. . . we need a car . . .

JENNY
. . . *and* Roger's school . . .

RICHARD
(Ire up a little)
When the public schools in this country . . .

JENNY
. . . *and* all the insurance . . .

RICHARD
We die, you know.

JENNY
. . . and everything else! Every money-eating thing!

RICHARD
Don't forget the government; *it's* hungry.

JENNY
I'll do it all, I'll . . . I'll smoke those awful cigarettes,
I'll . . . but I *will* not. I *will* not give up my garden.

RICHARD
(Gentle: placating)
I wouldn't *ask* you to.

JENNY
We live beyond our means, we have no right to be here,
we're so far in the hole you'll have to rob a bank or something, we've . . .

RICHARD
I love your garden.

JENNY
(Quieting down some)
There are some things I will just not do: and first in line is
I will not give up my garden.

RICHARD
No; of course not.

JENNY
I *love* my garden.

RICHARD
Y*es.*

JENNY
The way the florist charges, if we had to buy *cut* flowers . . .

RICHARD
I *know;* I *know.*

JENNY
Now, if we had a greenhouse . . .

RICHARD
A greenhouse!

JENNY

Yes, well, a small one, just enough to raise some orchids
in . . .

      (Sees RICHARD *rise, move off shaking his head)*

. . . Where are you going?

RICHARD

I'm going out to kill myself.

JENNY

But why!?

RICHARD
(Losing control)

Do you know how much a greenhouse costs!?

JENNY
(Getting mad)

I'M TRYING TO SAVE MONEY!

RICHARD
(Dismissing her)

You're insane.

JENNY

Do you *know* how much cut flowers *cost?*

RICHARD
(Mimicking her)

Do you *know* how much a greenhouse *costs?*

JENNY

I am *trying* to save *money.*

RICHARD
(Tiny pause, then)

Then why don't you go to Paris and buy Christian Dior!?
That way you won't have to pay for your dresses.

      (Silence)

JENNY
(Preoccupied)
Do you want some tea? Or a sandwich?
(RICHARD shakes his head; silence)
(A little sad, wistful, but reassuring)
We will have a greenhouse, someday. I'll make it nice; you'll
have a livingroom full of flowering plants; you'll like it very
much.

RICHARD
(Mildly ironic, sad)
Can I have a power mower first?

JENNY
(Nice)
You can have *every*thing.

RICHARD
(Sighs)
That will be nice.

JENNY
(Wistful)
And so can I, and everything will be lovely.

RICHARD
(After a silence)
The thing I don't like about being poor . . .

JENNY
(Correcting by rote)
. . . about not having money . . .

RICHARD
The thing I don't like about being—about not having
money . . .

JENNY
(*A little embarrassed, as if someone might overhear*)
We're not starving.

RICHARD
No, we eat, but if we didn't belong to the, the (*Points out the window*) club we'd eat a lot better.

JENNY
(*Patient agreement*)
Yes.

RICHARD
If we didn't try to live like our friends we might put something away sometime.

JENNY
(*Ibid.*)
Um-hum.

RICHARD
Friends we didn't have, by the way, until we moved here, took this place . . .

JENNY
But *friends*.

RICHARD
Oh, yeah, well, you find them. (*Tossed-off, but sincere*) We don't live right.

JENNY
(*Throws her head back, laughs*)
Oh God!

RICHARD
We don't!

JENNY

Poor baby.

RICHARD
(As if in a debate)
You live in a forty-thousand-dollar house and you have to
smoke bad cigarettes to get the coupons so you can afford a
good vacuum so you can clean it; you belong to the club so
you can pay back dinner invitations from people you
wouldn't even know if you hadn't joined the club in the first
place, and you *joined* the club, *and* learned how to play tennis, because you decided to move into a neighborhood where
everybody belonged to the club.

JENNY
(Noncommittal)
Except the Jews and the tradespeople.

RICHARD
Hm? You're up to hock in your eyebrows . . . (*Realizes
what he has said, tries to fix it, retaining dignity*) . . . *up* in
hock to your . . . *in* hock up to your eyebrows, and why!

JENNY
(Calm, nonplussed)
Because you want to live nicely.

RICHARD

I do?

JENNY
(Eyes closed briefly in martyrdom)
Because *we* do, because we want to live nicely; because we
want to live the way a lot of people manage . . .

RICHARD
Yes; people who can afford it!

JENNY

No! The way a lot of other people *cannot* afford it, and still do. Do you think the mortgage department of the bank stays open just for us?

RICHARD

Look at Jack!

JENNY

Jack is rich! Look at everybody else.

RICHARD
(Pause; glum)

I don't feel I belong anywhere.

JENNY
(Slightly patronizing commiseration)

Awww; poor Richard.

RICHARD

It *does*, by the way.

JENNY
(Very straightforward, even a little suspicious)

What does what?

RICHARD

The bank; the mortgage department; stays open just for us.

JENNY
(Laughs a little)

You don't want a sandwich, or something?

RICHARD
(Preoccupied)

No.

JENNY
(Clear they've had this before)
I'm still able-bodied . . .

RICHARD
(Firm)
No.

JENNY
Lots of wives do it.

RICHARD
No.

JENNY
Just part-time, only from . . .

RICHARD
You may *not* get a job!

JENNY
It would make all the difference in . . .

RICHARD
(Out of patience, now)
No, now! *(Softer afterthought)* I'm not going to have a wife
of mine trying to work at some job, *and* running a house, *and*
looking after Roger when he's home from school . . .

JENNY
Roger is fourteen, he doesn't need any looking after.

RICHARD
No! Besides, he's fifteen.

JENNY
And if I *took* a job, then we could afford a maid, and . . .

RICHARD

I said *no.*

JENNY
(Exasperated)
Well, it wouldn't be taking in laundry, for God's sake!

RICHARD
(Slightly nasty)
No? What would it be?

JENNY
(She, too)
Well, that may be all you think I'm good for . . .

RICHARD
(Voice rising)
I didn't *say* that.

JENNY

Well, you *inferred* it!

RICHARD
Implied; not inferred. And I did not.

JENNY
Yes you did, for God's sake.

RICHARD
I said nothing of the sort.

JENNY
(Snotty, exaggerated imitation)
No? Well, what would it *be?* What could you do? *(Anger)*
Is that all you think I'm good for?

RICHARD
(Trying patience now)
I didn't say that all you could do was take in laundry; I
merely meant that . . .

JENNY
(Starting to cry)
I'm sorry you think so badly of me.

RICHARD
(Eyes to heaven)
Oh, for Christ's . . .

JENNY
(Sniffling; the whole act which is not an act)
I'm sorry you think that's all I'm good for. I *try* to help you;
I try to run a decent house . . .

RICHARD
It's a *lovely* house . . .

JENNY
. . . and bring up your son so he won't be some . . . some
ruffian . . .

RICHARD
. . . *our* son . . .

JENNY
I try to *look* nice; I try to take care of myself, for *you*, for
your friends . . .

RICHARD
What, what is this everything *mine* all of a sudden! Most of
the time it's yours; all yours!

JENNY
(Real tears again)

I try! I try!

RICHARD

Oh, Lord! *(Comes over, comforts her)* You do a *lovely* job;
you run everything just . . . lovely; you look . . . you look
good enough to eat. *(Snarls, tries to bite her neck)*

JENNY
(Martyr)

Don't, now.

(RICHARD *repeats snarl, bite*)

Just don't!

(RICHARD *moves away*)

Just . . . just go away.

RICHARD
(Pause; subdued)

I didn't mean to . . . say anything to upset you.

JENNY

No, but you *meant* it!

RICHARD
(Anger rising)

I did not *mean* it!

JENNY
(Angry, too)

Then why did you *say* it!!?

RICHARD
(Eyes narrowed)

What?

JENNY
(Cold)
If you didn't mean it, then why did you say it?

RICHARD
I didn't say what . . . you implied that I . . .

JENNY
Inferred!

RICHARD
SKIP IT!
(Silence)

JENNY
(Great soft-spoken dignity)
I was merely trying to suggest that I might be able to help
at the hospital one or two afternoons a week . . .

RICHARD
(Snorts)
And make enough to pay a maid out of that?

JENNY
(Trying to stay calm)
Or open a hat shop . . .

RICHARD
You're mad! You're absolutely mad!

JENNY
(Very sincere plea)
I just want to help?
(Silence)

RICHARD
(With her again; nicely)
I *know* you do. And you do as much as anyone; you do *more*
than your share.

JENNY

No, no, I don't do *anything* to help you.

RICHARD

(Nuzzles)

You do *every*thing.

JENNY

You think I'm worthless.

RICHARD

(To make light of it)

No, I imagine I could sell you for about . . . oh . . .

JENNY

(Won't go along)

You think I'm a drag; I'm not a helpmeet. Lots of women
have part-time jobs, just to help out, it . . .

RICHARD

(Final)

No!

JENNY

(After a silence; sighs)

Money, money, money.

RICHARD

That's how it's always been. That's how it *is*.

JENNY

(Comforting)

You earn more than you used to.

RICHARD

Earn: yes. Taxes. Beware the steady man! Beware the slow
rise through the respectable ranks.

(JACK *appears in the french doors, enters, observes,*
lolls, speaks to the audience; becomes a part of the
action only when he speaks directly to one or
another of the characters)

JENNY

I know; Mother told me I should marry a real-estate specu-
lator.

RICHARD
(*Going to the liquor cupboard*)
Yes; well, well you should.

JENNY
(*One more try*)
So, if I had just a *little* job . . .

RICHARD
(*Looking among bottles*)
No!

JACK
(*To the audience, while* RICHARD *hunts among the*
bottles)
Are they arguing about money? Poor things; they always do.
They're very nice, though. Richard is decent, and Jenny is
. . . good. Damn it; wish she weren't.

JENNY
(*Unaware of* JACK)
What are you looking for?

RICHARD
(*Ibid., not looking up from the bottles*)
The vodka.

JENNY
There's some right there; right there in front of you.

RICHARD

Not *my* kind; not the Polish, only party stuff—American.

JENNY
("Get you")

Oh; well, sorry.

RICHARD

It's empty anyway.

JACK
(To the audience)

You see? That's it. The Polish vod is eight bucks a fifth. That's what makes the difference: taste; and taste is expensive. Poor children. *(A confidence)* I find Jenny *so attractive*. Not that I'm going to jump her, or anything. My letch is in the mind; *is; generally*.

RICHARD
(To JENNY)

Decent vodka is not a luxury.

JENNY

Nor is a greenhouse.

RICHARD

Yes it is.

JACK
(To the audience)

My uncle died and left *me* three-and-a-quarter mill. Which is very nice. Which means *I* can have a greenhouse, *and* the Polish vodka, *plus* the thirty-year scotch, plus . . . never worry—which is the nicest of all, don't you think? *(In the action now)* Hello, children!

RICHARD

Hm?

JENNY
(Piqued and pleased, her reaction to JACK *is always
a combination of maternal and coquettish)*
Oh, for God's sake, Jack!

RICHARD
(His reaction to JACK *is a combination of slight mis-
trust, discomfort, and natural friendliness)*
Well, hello there, Jack.

JACK
(Sees they are a little embarrassed)
Ah, when I am wandering, footsore and loose, where do I
always come? *Here.* And why? Well, for a warm and toasty
welcome. How are you, children?

RICHARD
Poor.

JENNY
Fine!

JACK
Don't go together.

RICHARD
How've you been?

JACK
(Kisses JENNY *on the forehead)*
Stopped by the club to watch the heart attacks, looked in on
the poker game and dropped a couple of hundred. *(To*
JENNY*)* You . . . smell . . . lovely.

JENNY
(Pleased)
Thank you.

JACK

And . . . thought I'd come over the fence and see you two.

RICHARD
(Nice, but an undertone)

I'll bet you'd like a drink.

JENNY
(To cover)

Ummm; me too!

JACK

Love one. Polish vod?

RICHARD
(A look at JENNY*)*

Fresh out.

JENNY
(To RICHARD*)*

Why don't you make us all a nice martini?

JACK
(Clucks; false disapproval)

Drink drink drink.

RICHARD

No vermouth either.

JACK

Such hospitality; I *tell* you.

RICHARD

I'll go get some.

JACK

Perfect! That way I get to be alone with your wife.

JENNY
Oh, Jack!

RICHARD
(To suggest, "If you are, I'll go get some")
You staying long?

JENNY
(Cheerful admonition)
Richard!

JACK
Well, what I thought I'd do is have one final drink with the
two of you. You see, I've settled a quarter of a million on
each of you, and after I had my drink I thought I'd go down
in the cellar and kill myself.

JENNY
Awwwwww.

RICHARD
(A little grim)
You ought to do it somewhere else; we might have trouble
getting the money if . . . *(Leaves it unfinished)*

JENNY
(Playing the game)
Yes . . . they might . . . *you* know . . . ask questions.

JACK
(To the audience)
He's right there, you know. Good mind. *(Back into action)*
Oh. *(Pause)* Do you think? Yes; well, all right. I'll just have
the drink, then.

RICHARD
(Slight, uncertain pause)
O.K. *(Pause)* Well, I'll go get some.

JACK

Go, bucko; go.

JENNY
(Giggles)

Oh, honestly, Richard; I'll be all right.

JACK

You have a faithful wife, Richard; never fear. *(To the audi-ence)* He has, too. She's rare; she's a good woman.

RICHARD
(Moving to exit, through hallway)

I know; it's the only kind I ever marry.

JACK
(Genuine surprise)

You been married before?

RICHARD
(Surprise)

No. I was just . . . *(At a loss for words)* . . . it was just a . . . something to say. *(To* JENNY*)* You, you want any-thing? At the store?

JENNY
(Shakes her head)

Unh-unh. Hurry back. Oh! Cigarettes!

RICHARD
(About to exit; a little bitter)

Which kind?

JENNY
(A giving-up sigh and smile)

The ones we like. Hurry, now.
*(*RICHARD *exits)*

JACK
(To the departed RICHARD*)*
By-ee! *(To* JENNY, *almost Groucho Marx)* Quick! He'll be
fifteen minutes even at a dog trot! Where's the guestroom?

JENNY
(Laughs)
Oh, come on, Jack! Besides, you aren't even a guest.

JACK
(Seemingly surprised)
No? What am I?

JENNY
A . . . uh . . . a fixture.

JACK
Something from the neighborhood? Bothersome Jack, here-
he-comes-again-probably-drunk-and-time-on-his-hands-so-why-
not-waste-everybody-else's-afternoon-while-he's-at-it?

JENNY
Mnnnnn.

JACK
(To the audience)
Am, too. Like that, I mean. Time, time. God, the ambition
you have to have to overcome good fortune. I haven't *got* it.
(Back to JENNY*) Let* me paint your picture.

JENNY
(Cheerful, but it's clear they've had this before)
No.

JACK
Won't cost you a penny.

JENNY

No.

JACK
(To the audience)
I'm not a bad painter. Flattering portraits of the rich? *(Back to* JENNY*)* What is it, then?

JENNY
I . . . just want to be different.

JACK
(Mild lechery)
Oh, you *are*, Jenny.

JENNY
Every, every house I go into, every time Richard and I go out, there it is! Sybil, Grace Donovan, Junie, Mrs. what's-her-name, Beachcomber, or something; *over* the mantel, badly framed, the lady of the house; your portrait.

JACK
(Axiom)
Ladies *like* to be painted, *I* paint ladies, ladies hang pictures.

JENNY
(Apologetic)
It isn't proper.

JACK
(Brief laugh)
Tell 'em in Newport; put me out of business. *(Digging)* Besides, I bet I make more money in three good months up there than Richard does in a whole . . .

JENNY
Oh, *money!*

JACK
(Waits a moment; quietly, smiling)
Yes? Money?

JENNY
I just don't . . . I don't want to look at myself, that's all.

JACK
(Very elegant)
If I were you . . . I would. *(Normal tone)* What's the matter, love?

JENNY
Oh . . . *(Very sincere, even plaintive, for a joke)* Would you do it, Jack? Go down in the cellar? I mean, leave Richard and me a quarter of a million each and then go kill yourself somewhere? I mean that nicely.

JACK
I'd do almost anything for you. *(Afterthought, but not flip)* Unless it got in the way of what I wanted to do for me. *(JENNY laughs ruefully)* What is it, puss?

JENNY
(Not going to talk about it)
Tired. Just . . . tired.

JACK
Want a shoulder to cry on?

JENNY
Nope; just a quarter of a million and an easy mind.

JACK
(Shakes his head knowingly)
Wouldn't help. Money's hungry, lonely, wants more of itself. Stay poor; you're better off.

JENNY
(Snorts)

Crap!

(The doorbell rings; JENNY *goes toward the hallway)*

JACK

Really; you are.

JENNY
(Going)

You'd *know*.

JACK

I *watch*. (JENNY *has gone;* JACK *addresses the audience)* I
have; it *does*; money always wants more to keep it company.
And a little money is a dangerous thing. Don't aim for a
million: that's the danger point. If I were to *die* . . . I
wouldn't leave them a quarter of a million each. Bad. *I'd*
leave 'em the whole damn three. As a matter of fact, that
isn't a bad idea at all. With three mill plus, they wouldn't
have to worry. I think I'll do it. Yes; consider it done. *(Considers)* I am *healthy*, though. They might not get it till it's
way too late. Still . . . consider it done.

JENNY'S VOICE
(From the hallway)

No, of course not, don't be silly.

*(*JENNY *appears, followed by* MRS. TOOTHE)*

MRS. TOOTHE
(Entering)

I *should* have phoned before just appearing at your door, but
I thought that on . . . Ah, this must be your husband. How
do you do, I'm Mrs. Toothe, and your wife has been kind
enough to . . .

JENNY
(A little laugh)
Oh, no, this isn't Richard—my husband, I mean . . .

MRS. TOOTHE
Ah. Well.

JENNY
(A little lame)
This is just . . . Jack.

MRS. TOOTHE
(Extends her hand to JACK*)*
No matter. How do you do, just the same.

JACK
(Takes hand, does curt little formal bow)
Mrs. Toothe.

JENNY
(Lame, and embarrassed by it)
Jack was just . . . passing by.

MRS. TOOTHE
(Noncommittal)
A friend of the family; of course.

JENNY
Yes.

JACK
(To MRS. TOOTHE*)*
Not at all: a secret admirer of lovely Jenny. I only come
round when Richard's out. We have a signal—panties on the
laundry line.

JENNY
Jack!

MRS. TOOTHE

How divine!

JENNY
(To MRS. TOOTHE; *embarrassed and furious at being)*
There isn't a word of truth to what he says. There isn't a
word of truth to *anything* he says, *ever.*

JACK
(Still to MRS. TOOTHE)
White panties if we've got one hour, yellow if we'll have to
hurry, pink for those special occasions . . .

JENNY

Jack! Please!

JACK
(Shakes his head, sadly)
I must confess it, madam, I am only what she says: a friend
of the family . . . dropping by. Damned attractive, though.
Wish it were true.

MRS. TOOTHE
(Pleased and sympathetic)

Ahhhh.

JENNY
Why is everybody standing? Please sit down, Mrs. . . .
uh . . . Toothe.

MRS. TOOTHE
(Sits)

Thank you.

JENNY
Jack, don't you think you should be . . . ?

JACK
(Makes it obvious he has gotten the signal)
By gum, I must be moving on! Different lines, more panties.
There is no rest for the wicked in the suburbs. Mrs. Toothe,
it's been . . .

MRS. TOOTHE
A great pleasure. And don't get your signals mixed.
*(JENNY accompanies JACK to the doors to the gar-
den)*

JACK
Tell Richard I'll be back for that martini another day. *(Sotto
voce)* Who is she, your fairy godmother?

JENNY
Will you go?

JACK
(Pecks her on the forehead)
Bye. *(To the audience, a wave before quick exit)* Bye.
(JACK has gone; JENNY returns to MRS. TOOTHE)

JENNY
You mustn't believe a thing Jack says, Mrs. . . . .

MRS. TOOTHE
(A hand up to silence her)
Oh, really. I can tell a lover from a friend.

JENNY
(Maybe even a little offended)
Oh? How?

MRS. TOOTHE
(Laughs)
Because in this country they're very seldom the same.

JENNY

You're English.

MRS. TOOTHE

Yes. Very.

(*Small silence*)

JENNY

Would you like some tea . . . or a drink?

MRS. TOOTHE
(*Very efficient*)

No thank you; this is business. Strictly business.

JENNY
(*Pause*)

Oh?

MRS. TOOTHE

I'm told you need a job?

JENNY
(*Somewhat confused*)

Who, who told you that?

MRS. TOOTHE
(*Airy*)

Oh, one of your friends. A woman.

JENNY
(*Curious, still puzzled*)

Oh? Who?

MRS. TOOTHE

No matter. Am I mistaken?

JENNY
(A *little ill-at-ease*)
Well, no . . . that is, I *was* thinking about getting a job . . .

MRS. TOOTHE
Yes, well, I thought so.

JENNY
Not a . . . a career, you understand, just something . . .

MRS. TOOTHE
. . . part *time*, something to bring a little extra money in.

JENNY
Well, yes; you know how it is: my son's away at school, and
I have the spare time. Besides, one can always use money,
can't one?

MRS. TOOTHE
(*Looking about, noncommittally*)
Yes; one can.

JENNY
These days, with taxes, and the private school . . .

MRS. TOOTHE
Oh, yes; yes; quite. What does your husband do?

JENNY
(*Uncomfortable, as if being interviewed*)
Well, he . . . he's a research chemist, and . . .

MRS. TOOTHE
. . . and that, as so many good things, pays less than it
should.

JENNY
(*Protecting* RICHARD)
Well, he doesn't do *too* badly; I mean . . .

MRS. TOOTHE
(The laugh again)
Of course not! But, still; you would like a job.

JENNY
*(Looks to the hallway, guilty—*RICHARD *might come back)*
Well, yes; one . . . one likes to feel useful.

MRS. TOOTHE
(Looking into her handbag)
Yes; useful. *(She takes out a thick bundle of bills, shows them to* JENNY*)* Money. *(*JENNY *just looks at it, her mouth falling open a little)* For you. *(Makes to give it to her)*

JENNY
Yes, but . . . *(Laughs a little, astounded)*

MRS. TOOTHE
(Nods her head)
Yes, money. For *you*. A thousand dollars. Here, take it.

JENNY
(Withdrawing a little from it)
Well, no, I . . .

MRS. TOOTHE
Count it if you like. Here; a thousand dollars. *(Tries to force it on her)*

JENNY
(A little panicked)
No!

MRS. TOOTHE
Very well. *(As calm as can be; rises, goes with the money to the fireplace, throws it on the burning logs)*

JENNY
*(Reflex, runs to the fireplace, almost puts her hands
into the fire, makes a little yell; straightens up, holds
on)*
Oh—I think you'd better go, Mrs. Toothe.

MRS. TOOTHE
(Enigmatic smile)
Not yet. Let's begin again. *(She takes another bundle of
money from her handbag, makes as if to throw it in the fire;
JENNY holds out her hand; MRS. TOOTHE quietly hands her
the money, resumes her seat; JENNY stays standing)*

JENNY
(Never taking her eyes off MRS. TOOTHE)
You're quite mad.

MRS. TOOTHE
No. Very rich.

JENNY
(Looks at the money, almost weighs it)
Look, you . . . you can't just . . . *give* me money like this.
I can't just . . . take money from you.

MRS. TOOTHE
(A little laugh)
You have. It's yours. Isn't there something you'd like to buy?
For yourself, for . . . what is his name? . . . Richard?

JENNY
People can't just give people money. I want to work.

MRS. TOOTHE
Good then. That's an advance of salary. You can work for
me.

JENNY

But I haven't *said* I'd take a job at *all*. Richard is *very* much
against it, and . . .

MRS. TOOTHE
(Daring her to refuse)
I was told you needed money.

JENNY

Yes, but Richard wouldn't approve of anything like this,
and . . .

MRS. TOOTHE

Like what? *(Indicates the money)* Wouldn't he approve of
that?

JENNY
(Looks at the money in her hands)
I'm sorry; I didn't mean to be rude, but it's all so vague,
isn't it? And . . . and so unexpected.

MRS. TOOTHE
(Shrugs)
It's a job.

JENNY
(Nervous laughter in her voice)
Well, you'll have to tell me what it *is*. I mean, money isn't
everything.

MRS. TOOTHE

No? What isn't money? Here we are; this house is money,
that garden, that lovely garden, those clothes you're wearing,
it's all *money*, isn't it?

JENNY

The job?

MRS. TOOTHE
What are your husband's hours?

JENNY
He leaves at eight and gets home from town at seven-thirty,
but . . .

MRS. TOOTHE
Very good. *You'll* come in town, four afternoons a week,
from one to five, say. You'll come to my address—lovely
street: psychiatrist's office, doctors . . .

JENNY
Is this a . . . uh . . . a receptionist's job?

MRS. TOOTHE
Receptionist?

JENNY
Making, making appointments, and so on?

MRS. TOOTHE
I make appointments. For *you*.

JENNY
(Tiny pause)
For me? Who with?

MRS. TOOTHE
Clients.

JENNY
(Innocent)
What *for?*

MRS. TOOTHE
For a hundred dollars.

JENNY

No, I mean . . . A hundred dollars?

MRS. TOOTHE

More, sometimes—if they're generous.

JENNY

But these clients . . . who are they?

MRS. TOOTHE

Some businessmen, some visitors. All gentlemen; all rich.

JENNY
(The knowledge is there but not admitted yet)
What . . . exactly . . . what exactly would I do . . . for
this money?
    (MRS. TOOTHE *laughs lightly;* JENNY's *jaw drops with
    the admission; pause)*
    (JENNY *picks up the bundle of money, holds it out
    to* MRS. TOOTHE; *even, hard)*
Get out of my house.
    (MRS. TOOTHE *does nothing;* JENNY *drops the money
    on the table)*
I'll call the police.

MRS. TOOTHE
(As calm as anything; a little superior)
Whatever for?

JENNY
(Quivering)
You know what for!

MRS. TOOTHE
(Smiles)
I've said nothing.

JENNY
You know what you've suggested!

MRS. TOOTHE
(Shrugs)
That you make money.

JENNY
THAT WAY!

MRS. TOOTHE
You have a friend who does.

JENNY
Who!

MRS. TOOTHE
Oh, no; we're very discreet.

JENNY
(Through her teeth)
I don't believe you, not a word! People around here wouldn't
do that sort of thing; you don't realize; you don't know what
we're like.

MRS. TOOTHE
(Unconcerned)
Have it your way.

JENNY
One of the tradespeople, maybe; you're thinking of someone
like that.

MRS. TOOTHE
I'm thinking of a friend of yours; a very nice woman with a
lovely house, who keeps it nicely—much more nicely than
this, by the way—a woman who has no more worries about
money, who is very happy. So could you be.

JENNY

You're a filthy woman! IT'S DISGUSTING!!

MRS. TOOTHE
(Very calm)

Nothing is disgusting, unless one is disgusted.

JENNY

YOU'RE EVIL!!

MRS. TOOTHE

Yes, yes . . .

JENNY

I'LL TELL THE POLICE!

MRS. TOOTHE
(Stands up, stretches a little)

Good. Then perhaps they'll arrest me.

JENNY

I hope they put you in prison!

MRS. TOOTHE

Yes, well, they probably will, and then I shall admit everything.

JENNY

Everything?

MRS. TOOTHE

Yes, how you approached me, and we discussed it, but the terms didn't suit you. The *money* wasn't enough.

JENNY

THAT'S NOT TRUE!

MRS. TOOTHE

Perhaps not. I think it would be believed, though. By enough
people.

JENNY

GET OUT OF HERE!

MRS. TOOTHE
(Takes a calling card from her handbag)
Here is my card; address; telephone; let me know what you
decide.

JENNY
(Change of tone; almost tearful)
Please? Please go?

MRS. TOOTHE

No police then; good. *(Sees* JENNY *will not take the card, puts
it down next to the bundle of money on the table)* Don't telephone me before ten, though, please. I *do* like my sleep.

JENNY

Please? Go?

MRS. TOOTHE
(Smiles)
I'll see myself out. It's been very nice to meet you. *(Looks one
final time at the garden)* What a lovely garden. Do you have
a greenhouse?
(Smiles, exits, leaving JENNY *standing in the center
of the room)*
*(*JENNY *looks after* MRS. TOOTHE *for a long moment,
not moving. Then she looks down at the table
whereon sit the bundle of money and* MRS. TOOTHE's
*card. She picks up the card, reads it, moving her lips,
then, with a grimace, rips the card in half and, as if
she were carrying feces, takes it over to a wastebasket*

and drops it in. She comes back to the table, stares at the money, picks it up, looks at it with detached fascination; doesn't know quite what to do with it; finally, rather firmly, puts it in desk drawer, locks drawer, keeps key, starts toward french doors, looks back at locked drawer, goes, stands at french windows looking out)

RICHARD'S VOICE
(From the hallway)

Hell-oo-oo. *(He enters, with a paper bag of liquor)* Oh, there you are. And who the hell was *that* tripping down our path, that bit of old England? "How do you do?" she . . . Where the hell *is* he—Jack?

JENNY
(Sort of vacant)

Oh. Hi.

RICHARD
(Puts liquor down, starts taking bottles out of bag)

Well, who *was* she—your fairy godmother?

JENNY
(Some alarm)

My what?

RICHARD

The woman; the lady. Who was she?

JENNY
(Still preoccupied)

Oh. Mrs. Toothe.

RICHARD

Mrs. what?

JENNY

Toothe; Toothe.

RICHARD

You're kidding. Where's Jack?

JENNY

It's a perfectly proper English name. *(Pause)* I guess. Jack?
He *went.*

RICHARD

Figures. Send me out to buy up the liquor store and off he
goes.

JENNY

It was *your* idea to go.

RICHARD
(A little cross)

Who *was* she?

JENNY

Mrs. Toothe? *(Tosses it off)* Oh . . . committee; wants me
for the hospital.

RICHARD

Free? Or pay?

JENNY
(Pause; casual)

Pay.

RICHARD

No!

JENNY
(Pause; softly)

All right.

RICHARD
(Looks at the liquor)
Well, with all your rich guests gone, there's just us for drinks.
What do you want . . . a martini?

JENNY
(Very sincere)
Yes, I think that would be *nice*.

RICHARD
O.K. *(Starts to make one; the ice is already there)*
You know what Tom Palmer said the other day?

JENNY
*(Preoccupied, and not exactly unpleasant, but not
pleasant either)*
No, I don't; I didn't see Tom Palmer the other day. What did
Tom Palmer say?

RICHARD
(Looks up at JENNY *for a moment, quizzically, then
back to his work)*
He said Jack was at the club, at the bar . . . soused as
usual . . .

JENNY
Jack isn't always drunk.

RICHARD
(A little annoyance)
He's always drinking.

JENNY
(Dogmatic)
That does *not* make him *drunk*.

RICHARD
I am merely repeating what Tom Palmer said.

JENNY

Tom Palmer's an old woman.

RICHARD

(Quite annoyed)

I do *not* want to argue!

JENNY

All right! *(Contrite)* I'm sorry, darling. *(Pause)* You're a good, decent man and I love you.

RICHARD

(Grudging)

Well, you're a good, decent woman, and I love you, too. As a matter of fact, I shall give you a house-special martini to show you how *much* I love you.

JENNY

Oh, I would like that.

(She comes for her drink, takes it from him, they put arms around each other, move toward the sofa; he kisses her on top of her head)

RICHARD

I think you smell even nicer than Jack does.

JENNY

(Purring)

When have you smelled Jack?

RICHARD

Than *Jack* thinks you smell.

JENNY

Oh.

(RICHARD tries to nip her neck)

Ow! Now stop that; I'll spill my martini.

(They sit on the sofa, relax)

RICHARD
(*A little bitter*)
You want to know something really funny?

JENNY
I don't *think* so. What?

RICHARD
I was in the liquor store . . .

JENNY
That's a riot.

RICHARD
Hush. I was in the liquor store, and Grady, who owns it, do
you know what he told me?

JENNY
No; what?

RICHARD
He's getting a second car? Not trading one in; getting a
second car.

JENNY
So?

RICHARD
Guy who owns a crummy little liquor store can have two
cars? And we have to get by with . . .

JENNY
Did you bring the cigarettes back with you?

RICHARD
Hm? (*Gets them out*) Oh; yes; here.

JENNY
(Takes one; so does he; he lights them both)
I wonder which kills more people: liquor or cars?

RICHARD
Well, when you put them together it's pretty good. What's
for dinner?
(Pause)

JENNY
Let's go *out* for dinner.

RICHARD
Where?

JENNY
(Expansive)
Let's . . . let's go to Le Cavalier.

RICHARD
(Snorts)
You must be out of your mind.

JENNY
No! Let's!

RICHARD
It'll cost twenty-five dollars each. After a drink, the wine,
it'll cost twenty-five each!
(Pause)

JENNY
(Cautiously)
I've got some money.

RICHARD
(Half hearing)
Hm?

JENNY

I said, *I've* got some money.

RICHARD
(Vaguely interested)

How?

JENNY
(Very offhand)

Oh, I've . . . put a little aside out of household. I keep a little bit each week.

RICHARD
(Mildly)

Well, I'll be damned.

JENNY

Come on; let's go out; it'll do us good. Let's go to Le Cavalier. Let's live it up.

RICHARD

Let's pretend we can afford it?

JENNY

Sure! Come on; it'll do us both good.

RICHARD

You ingenious thing. How much have you got?

JENNY

Oh . . . enough. Come on now.

RICHARD

You clever girl. *(Rises)* I'd better wash up. Really? You have enough?

JENNY
(Rises)

Yes. Better put things away in the garden before you get
cleaned up.

RICHARD

Right. *(Moves to the french doors)* You very clever girl.
(Goes outside)
> (JENNY *sees he is out of sight; goes slowly to the
> desk, unlocks the drawer, takes out the bundle of
> money, strips off several bills, puts them on the
> table, hesitates a moment, as to reconsider, then
> puts the rest of the money back in the drawer, locks
> it again, keeps the key. Stands for a moment; looks
> at the wastebasket, lifts it onto the table, takes the
> two halves of* MRS. TOOTHE's *card out, fits them to-
> gether, looks at the card.* RICHARD *pokes his head
> inside;* JENNY *doesn't flinch or try to hide the card,
> knowing that* RICHARD *either can't see it or won't ask
> what it is)*

RICHARD

Jenny?

JENNY

Hm?

RICHARD
(Sort of wistful)

Darling? How much does a greenhouse cost? You know . . .
a little one?

JENNY

Why?

RICHARD

I just wondered.

JENNY
(Looks up)

Quite a bit.

RICHARD

I just wondered. *(Returns outside)*

JENNY
(Looks at the card again, shakes her head; some rue)
Quite a bit.

CURTAIN

SCENE TWO

(Six months later; scene the same; early afternoon; RICHARD *at the desk, paying bills; shakes his head occasionally, despair. Sound of front door opening, closing.* JENNY *comes in, with bundles)*

JENNY
(Cheerful)

Hello.

RICHARD
(Glum)

Hello.

JENNY

On Saturday you're supposed to rest; why aren't you out working in the garden?
(RICHARD *laughs glumly)*
Or, or just . . . lying around?

RICHARD
(Wan smile)

Paying bills.

JENNY

Oh. *(Puts bundles down)* It figures, doesn't it: I go to the store and I forget half of what I want.

RICHARD

Didn't you make a list?

JENNY

Of course; I *got* everything on the list; I just didn't remember
to put everything *on* the list.

RICHARD

Like what?

JENNY

Like what? Like . . . like root beer, and extra milk, and
stuff for cookies, and . . .

RICHARD

What for?

JENNY

We have a son. Right?

RICHARD
(Preoccupied)

Um-huh.

JENNY
(Pause)

He's coming *home* today!

RICHARD
(Puzzlement, pleasure)

Roger? Today? Coming home?

JENNY
(As if he were addled)

Yes. Vacation.

RICHARD

Well, I'll be damned.

JENNY

Mmmmmmm. And cornflakes and stuff, I suppose.

RICHARD

No camp this year.

JENNY

Hm?

RICHARD

No camp this year. For Roger. No camp. Can't afford it.

JENNY
(Noncommittal; her mind on something else)
Oh. Really?

RICHARD

Really.

JENNY
(Making her list)
Well, afford or not, I thought it'd be nice if he was around
here this summer. Get to know him.

RICHARD
(Adamantly grousing)
Well, nice or not . . . necessary.

JENNY

Help *you*, help *me* . . .

RICHARD

While you're at it, get some more envelopes.

JENNY

There *are* some.

RICHARD

No, just that . . . that paper thing goes around them.

JENNY
(Notes it down)
All right. He can help you in the garden.

RICHARD
Mmmm. Or maybe we can get him a magazine route.

JENNY
(Mild disgust and indignation)
Really!

RICHARD
Well, you're so keen for everybody to be working around
here . . .

JENNY
He's just a child!

RICHARD
He's probably going steady already—got some local girl up
at school—probably skips out at night, shacked up . . .

JENNY
(Protesting, embarrassed)
Richard!

RICHARD
Kids grow up early nowadays.

JENNY
Roger is fourteen years old!

RICHARD
Well, if everything's functioning properly, there's no reason
why he can't be getting laid, is there? Besides, he's fifteen.

JENNY
That's enough now.

RICHARD
Well, it's better that than lots of other things.

JENNY
ALL RIGHT!

(Silence)

RICHARD
(Shakes his head, finally, a little sadly, smiles)
I knew a girl once, when you and I were dating—not so as
to say set the alarm for seven, or anything like that, but . . .

JENNY
(A little stony)
Don't regale me.

RICHARD
No; really. And I wasn't in on the good times, 'cause I was
counting on you . . .
(JENNY snorts)
and you met her, I think, but I won't tell you who she was,
cause she still is . . . but she had the reputation as a proper
put-out . . .

JENNY
(Some bored annoyance)
Please, Richard.

RICHARD
No. More than proper: something of a dedicatee, guest bedrooms at parties, drawing blood, literally . . .

JENNY
Let the poor woman alone.

RICHARD
(Slight edge)
I'm not touching her. (Silence) I was planning, though, to
compare her to you.

JENNY
(Sarcastic)

Really.

RICHARD

To your ad*van*tage.

JENNY
(Dripping irony)

Oooohhhh.

RICHARD

Socially—by which I mean out of bed, which is a euphe-
mism for trash heaps and coal bins—you'd think she was the
Queen Mother. Staid? She practically used the royal We. So
proper; you'd never know.

JENNY
(Not nice)

And what does that have to do with me?

RICHARD

Oh. It came up when I said Roger was probably going steady.

JENNY

Getting laid is what you said.

RICHARD

Same difference.

JENNY

Tell *that* to the sociologists.

RICHARD

They know. And I said Roger was probably going steady and
you came on all funny and red and . . .

JENNY

I didn't see any need for you to shout the house down,
and . . .

RICHARD
(Angry)
Who's going to hear? The footmen?

JENNY

Don't you yell at me!

RICHARD
(Pause; shake of head; laugh-whimper)
All I wanted to do was say you're such a funny, silly, wonder-
ful little . . .

JENNY

Nuts.

RICHARD

You are! You're a good wife and you're nice in bed, but
you're funny and . . . prim.

JENNY

Prim!?

RICHARD

Yes! Prim!

JENNY

I'm *sorry.*

RICHARD

And then I thought about, uh, what's-her-name, who came
on like the Queen Mother, and how she was ridiculous and
you were just a little silly about it, and . . . *(Mumbles)* aw,
for Christ's sake, forget it. *(Pause)* I was just trying to pay
you a *comp*liment! I was *try*ing to be *nice!*

JENNY
(Thinks about it, dismisses his reasoning)
I don't see why you brought her up in the *first* place.

RICHARD
(Frustrated anger)

NEITHER DO I!

(Silence)

JENNY
I suppose I could learn a few dirty jokes, or start telling
people about a couple of your peculiarities when it comes
to . . .

RICHARD

Forget it!

(Silence)

JENNY
(Trying to hold back a smile)
Who was she?
(RICHARD pouts, shakes his head)
Come on; who was she?

RICHARD

No, no.

JENNY
(Tickles him a little)

Oh, come on!

RICHARD
(Happier)

No; now, stop it.
*(She tickles more, he grabs her, they wrestle, gig-
gling, a little on the sofa, playing, ending in a kiss,
then another, which prolongs, is far more serious)*

JENNY

Unh-unh; not now.

RICHARD

Ooooohhhh . . .

JENNY

No; Roger'll come in, and . . .

RICHARD

Well, he'll be able to tell his friends we're still alive.

JENNY

Now, come *on. No.*

RICHARD
(*Leans back; sighs*)

All right.

JENNY
(*Pause*)

Who was she?

RICHARD
(*Shakes his head*)

Unh-unh. I promised.

JENNY
(*Eyes narrowing*)

Who?

RICHARD

Myself. Self-discipline.

JENNY
(*Disentangling*)

Oh, honestly!

RICHARD

Well, a little doesn't hurt.

JENNY

(*Looking at herself in the mirror, appraisingly, approvingly*)
Did you see the paper today?

RICHARD
(*Preoccupied*)

Mmmmm.

JENNY

They had an ad.

RICHARD
(*Back to the desk*)
What are they doing, giving away money? I can sure use some, if they . . .

JENNY
(*Still appraising*)
No, for a greenhouse, all-aluminum frame, curved glass . . .

RICHARD
(*Slams a sheet of paper down*)
For Christ's sake, Jenny!
(*Pause, as she looks at him, a little haughtily*)
I just finished telling you Roger isn't going to camp this year because we can't afford it, and . . .

JENNY
(*Slight airy contempt*)
Oh, money-money-money.

RICHARD
Yes. Money. (*Shows bills*) Oil. The car. Con Ed—the bastards. An estimate on the attic—the leak.
(*Doorbell rings*)

JENNY

Doorbell.

RICHARD
(Back to work)
Yes. Why don't you get it?

JENNY
(Tiny pause)
Why don't you?

RICHARD

Hm?

JENNY

Why don't *you* get it?

RICHARD
(Slight whine)
Because I'm working, darling; can't you see I'm . . .

JENNY

What if it's for you?

RICHARD
(Slight bewilderment)
Then you can tell me who it *is*. Or *what*.

JENNY
(Pause, hesitation)
Oh. Yes, that's true.
(Doorbell again)

RICHARD
(Throws pen down, gets up, goes out)
Oh, for God's sake!
(Maybe, offstage, we hear RICHARD saying "Yes?"

and then "Oh, O.K." While he is offstage JENNY
moves about the room a little, practicing unconcern.
RICHARD *re-enters, with a small package: brown*
paper, wrapped with twine, lots of stamps, special
delivery, etc.)

JENNY

Who was it?

RICHARD
(Looking at package, with some curiosity and dis-
taste)
Package.

JENNY

Oh, for me?

RICHARD

No. For me. *(Shakes it, looks at it again)*

JENNY
(Pause)

Well. *(Pause)* Open it.

RICHARD
(Putting it down on the table, stares at it, hands on
hips)
Wonder what it is.

JENNY
(Little laugh)

Well, open it and see.

RICHARD
(Picks it up again, looks it over)
Special delivery, doesn't say where from.

JENNY
Well, open it, for heaven sakes.

RICHARD
(Tries to break twine, can't)
It's . . . tied up so . . .
*(Takes a pocket knife, saws through twine, begins to
unwrap. JENNY keeps a distance. RICHARD reveals
contents. Slow awe in movements)*

JENNY
(Trying for unconcern)
What, what *is* it?

RICHARD
(Wonder)
Jenny! Look!

JENNY
Hm?

RICHARD
Jenny! It's money!

JENNY
It's what?

RICHARD
IT'S MONEY!!

JENNY
(Feigning disbelief and childish pleasure)
Money. It's money?

RICHARD
(Subdued; awe)
Jenny; it's money. It's a great deal of money.

JENNY
(Taking a step closer)
Well, for . . . for heaven sake.

RICHARD
Jenny, it's ten-dollar bills, wrapped in packages of five hundred dollars each.

JENNY
(Beautiful bewilderment)
Well . . . how *much?* How much *is* there?

RICHARD
(Starts counting, aloud then silently)
One, two, three, four, five, six, seven, eight, nine . . .

JENNY
(During his counting. Pauses between)
How . . . how incredible. I've . . . How absolutely incredible.

RICHARD
And wait . . . Here are hundred-dollar bills. One, two, three, four . . . *(Slight confusion)* Forty-nine hundred dollars.

JENNY
(Some confusion)
Forty-nine?

RICHARD
Jenny, there's almost five thousand dollars here. Four thousand, nine hundred dollars. Jenny! Four thousand, nine hundred dollars!

JENNY
Well, that's incredible! Not five thousand?

RICHARD
(Sudden suspicion something's wrong)
I don't get it.

JENNY
Aren't you . . . aren't you pleased?

RICHARD
(Wry comment on her word)
Pleased!? I don't know whether I'm pleased or not.

JENNY
(Still not near the money)
Is it real? Is it real money?

RICHARD
(Looks at a bill)
Yes; of course it's real: real used hundred-dollar bills.

JENNY
(A kind of satisfaction)
My God.

RICHARD
But . . . but *why?* I mean, there's no *sense* to it.

JENNY
(A protective step forward)
Yes, but it *is money.*

RICHARD
(Looks at it glumly)
It's money, all right. Too bad we can't keep it.

JENNY
What do you mean?

RICHARD
(*No great enthusiasm*)
I mean we can't keep it. I'll take it to the police.

JENNY
No!

RICHARD
I *have* to, Jenny. There's something wrong here.

JENNY
What!

RICHARD
(*At a loss for words*)
Well . . . I mean . . .

JENNY
It's addressed to you, isn't it? It came special delivery; it's
not as though you *found* it, for God's sake.

RICHARD
Yes, I know, but . . .

JENNY
(*As offhand as likely*)
Well, it seems to me someone wants you to have it. I . . . I
can't think of any other reason for someone to send it to
you.

RICHARD
Wants me to *have* it. Yes, but who?

JENNY
I . . . I don't know. (*Shrugs*) Someone.

RICHARD
Look, it could be something awful like . . .

JENNY

Like what?

RICHARD

Like, like the Mafia, or something, or bank robbers, or . . .
sent it here for safekeeping, and . . .

JENNY
(Laughs gaily)

Don't be ridiculous.

RICHARD
(Thinks about it; subdued)

You think someone *sent* it to me?

JENNY
(The most obvious thing in the world)

Of *course.*

RICHARD

Yes, but *who?*

JENNY

Well . . . maybe . . . somebody you did something for.

RICHARD

Those sort of things don't happen . . . not to *me.*

JENNY

Well, *this* has happened.

RICHARD
(Holds the money out to her; quite childlike)

Don't you want to . . . touch it, or anything?

JENNY

Oh. Yes; of course. *(Goes to him, touches the money, smiles
faintly)* I wonder who sent it to you.

RICHARD

I . . . I don't *know*. There's a man I sit next to on the train a lot. *He* seems very interested in me; older fellow, banker type. Keeps asking me about my work, how I manage. Maybe, maybe he's a millionaire, and maybe he's sort of crazy.

JENNY
(Unlit cigarette out)

Match.

RICHARD

Hm? Oh, yeah. *(Is about to hand her the matchbook, thinks better of it, lights her cigarette)* It could come from somebody like him.

JENNY
(Slightest doubt)

Well, yes, it could.

RICHARD
(Puzzled, a little deflated)

And then again it couldn't. I mean, probably didn't.

JENNY
(Comforting)

Yes. But someone.

RICHARD

Yes. *(Considers, gives her a bill)* Here. For you.

JENNY
(Tiniest pause)

Thank you. You're . . . you're not going to turn it over to the police, then.

RICHARD
(Pause, slight guilt, but bravura)

No, I don't think so. *(Pause)* I guess someone wants me to

have it. Someone *must*. It'd be silly not to keep it. *(Pause)*
Don't you think so?

JENNY
(Nice smile)
Yes. I think so.

RICHARD
I mean, it would be stupid to just . . . throw it away.

JENNY
Yes; it would be. *(Cheerful)* Let's have a drink: to celebrate?

RICHARD
(The sky has cleared)
Yes! Let's.

JENNY
(Moves toward hall)
I'll get the ice.

RICHARD
(Moves toward the liquor cabinet)
Good— And I'll make us a four-thousand-nine-hundred-dollar martini.

JENNY
Super! *(Exiting)* Call it five thousand even; sounds so much
nicer.
    *(JACK enters through the french doors after JENNY
    exits and RICHARD follows)*

JACK
(Sauntering into the room; addresses the audience)
The months turn; people live and die, but I just . . . wander
around. I tell you, there are days when I admit to myself that
I don't think I'm alive—never have been. *Un voyeur de la*

vie . . . that's me. Look on; look in. *(Propounds a great truth, with nothing other than objectivity)* I've never felt really alive. It can't be only the isolation, the isolation of money, do you know? Naw, can't be that. I know lots of people with much more than I've got, and they've been alive . . . killed themselves and everything! Oh, by the way, I did what I said I was going to. *(Nods)* I made my will—remade it, to be technical—and left the whole kaboodle to Jenny and Richard here. Three million plus. I'd better not tell them, though. It's hard enough to like me as it is. I mean, I'm likable and all, but . . . *(Spies the money on the table)* My goodness. *(Speaks loudly, is now in the action)* My goodness! Look at all that money!

> RICHARD
> *(Enters from kitchen)*

DON'T TOUCH THAT!

> JACK
> *(Feigned affront)*

I'm sorry!

> RICHARD
> *(Still stern, advances toward the money)*

Just don't touch it.

> JACK

Well. Shall I go back out and knock?

> RICHARD
> *(Sighs, laughs a little)*

I'm sorry, Jack.
> *(JENNY re-enters, with the ice bucket)*

> JENNY

Here we go, five thousand dollars' worth of ice, an . . . oh. Jack.

JACK
(Sees they are both ill at ease. To audience)
My goodness.

JENNY
(Tiny pause; show of great bonhomie)
Hi!

RICHARD
Join us.

JACK
(Smiles, waiting to have things explained)
O.K.

RICHARD
(To JENNY)
Jack, uh, noticed the money here, and . . .

JACK
(Very pleasantly)
. . . and practically got my head snapped off.

JENNY
Oh. Well; there it is; money.

JACK
(Looks at it)
Did you steal it, or make it in the basement on your own
little press?

RICHARD
Neither, we . . .

JENNY
It arrived; it just . . . arrived.

RICHARD
(To explain further)

In the mail.

JENNY

Yes.

RICHARD
(Ibid.)

Special delivery.

JENNY

Yes.

JACK
(Tiny pause; clearly, there must be more explanation)
Well, that's very nice.

JENNY

Someone sent it to Richard.

JACK

Oh?

RICHARD

Yes.

JACK

Who?

JENNY
Well, we don't know, someone, we figure, who . . . well,
appreciates him. Admires him, maybe.

JACK
You mean you have no idea where it came from.

JENNY

No.

RICHARD

None.

JENNY

Absolutely none.

JACK

Is there a lot? Can I touch it?

RICHARD
(Involuntary gesture to protect money, withdraws it)
Sure.

JACK
(Touches it with one finger, looks at finger)
Perfectly dry.

JENNY

Of course; it's real.

RICHARD
(Sudden, none-too-happy thought)
Jack . . . *you* didn't do this, did you?

JACK

Do what?

RICHARD
You didn't. *You* didn't send us this money, did you?

JACK
(Tiny pause, then a laugh)
Christ, no!

RICHARD
You're sure, because if you did . . .

JACK
I'm sure; I'm absolutely sure. *(To audience)* I didn't, by the
way; I didn't send it to them. *(Back to them)* How much is
there?

JENNY
Nearly . . .

RICHARD
Five thousand.

JACK
Well, that should prove it to you. I never deal in small
amounts.

RICHARD
(Defensive)
It might seem a small amount to *you*, but, to *some* peo-
ple . . .

JENNY
(To change the subject)
Why don't we all have a nice martini?

JACK
Splendid!
    (RICHARD *sets about to make them.* JENNY *straightens
    up the room)*
I didn't mean to ridicule your . . . your windfall.

JENNY
Oh, now . . .

JACK

It's just splendid. *(To the audience)* And damned peculiar too, if you ask me. *(Back into the action)* Well, I *do* hope you're going to give a party.

(RICHARD *and* JENNY *look at one another, enthusiasm first)*

JENNY

Why, yes; we could!

RICHARD
(Hesitating)

Well, I don't think we ought to announce that . . .

JACK

No, just a party for the hell of it. Live it up a little! Get some caviar! Serve champagne! Hire a butler! Give a garden party!

JENNY
(Entranced)

A garden party!

RICHARD
(Giving over to it)

Sure! Why not!

JACK

Sure! Why not! *(To the audience; shrugs)* Why not?

JENNY

What a super idea. When?

JACK

Now.

JENNY

Well, no . . . Next week, and . . .

RICHARD
(Wistful; a little sad)
You know . . . people make plans, and . . .

JACK
No; *now*. This very minute: white heat. Get on the phone.
Give a blow-out; just for the hell of it! *(Gentler)* Do something wild, and out-of-the-ordinary, and . . . the sort of
thing you've always *wished* you could do.

JENNY
Yes! Let's! I'll call . . . who shall I call?

RICHARD
Well . . . Chuck and Beryl . . .

JENNY
(On her fingers; enthusiasm)
Yes, Chuck and Beryl, and Cynthia and Perry, too, of
course . . .

RICHARD
. . . yes . . .

JENNY
. . . and . . . and Gilbert and Louise. Who else?

RICHARD
(Little laugh)
Hey, come on now. Let's not spend it all in one place.

JENNY
Is that enough? Six? Oh, and Jack; *you'll* come, Jack.

JACK
No, my darling; I've got a serious game of backgammon at
the club.

JENNY

. . . oooohhhh . . .

JACK

No; *very* serious. High stakes. Wouldn't miss it for the world.

JENNY
(A colt)

I'll go call. O.K.?

RICHARD
(Amused)

O.K.

JENNY
(To RICHARD)

You figure out what we need, how much liquor and all . . .

RICHARD

Not champagne?

JENNY

Yes! Of course! But some people don't like it. I'll go call.
(Starts out of the livingroom)

RICHARD

What time?

JENNY

Oh . . . six, six-thirty. What is it now?

RICHARD

Four.

JENNY
(Momentary pause)

Oh. *(Resolve)* Well, better hurry. *(As she goes)* Bye, Jack!

JACK

Bye! *(To* RICHARD*)* Does that mean I'm supposed to be gone
by the time she gets back from phoning?

RICHARD
(Merely laughs; hands JACK *his martini)*
Here.

JACK
(Takes it)
Ice-cold, juniper-berried heaven. Thank you.
(We will hear JENNY *faintly from the other room,
talking to people on the phone. We will hear her
enthusiasm)*

RICHARD

She's so excited. Cheers.

JACK

Double. Well, why shouldn't she be? Quite marvelous *getting*
money this way.

RICHARD

Yes.

JACK

No tax, I mean. Tax-free?

RICHARD

Hm?

JACK

Well, you won't de*clare* it, of course . . . and that way
there's no tax.

RICHARD
(He'd never thought of that)
You're right! Free and clear. God!

JACK

And maybe there'll be *more*.

RICHARD
(A *little puzzled*)

More? Why?

JACK

Well, good God . . . if someone's sending you money like
this, why should they stop with one bundle? Maybe you'll
get it every week.

RICHARD
(*Almost blushes*)

Oh, come on.

JACK

No; I mean it!

RICHARD
(*Worried frown*)

Jack, you won't . . . you won't tell anybody about this, will
you?

JACK
(*Jaunty*)

My dearest Richard . . . it'll fly out of mind in thirty seconds. No, of *course* I won't say anything. I don't want to
screw it up for you.

RICHARD

I mean not even casually, or reference to it, you know, at the
club, or . . .

JACK

. . . or when I've had a drink or two? No, Richard; I won't.
I promise.

RICHARD

Thanks.

JACK
(Lolling)
Money is a curious thing, isn't it, Richard?

RICHARD
(Small boy)
I don't know; I've never had too much.

JACK
No: the thing and the symbol. It's a piece of paper, with
ink on it . . . and the ink and the paper together aren't
worth a quarter of a cent—less . . . yet if we didn't have
it, the world would stop.

RICHARD
We could go back to barter.

JACK
Yes, I suppose we could. It's like painting. A stretch of
canvas and some paint. Worth what? Four dollars? Five?
Yet put a value on it. Let *me* do it, and it sells for a certain
sum, or someone else, and ten times more . . . a hundred!
A certain Picasso for half a million? Not a bad painting,
worth it, maybe. Money. How much does a cow sell for?

RICHARD
I don't know . . . two hundred dollars?

JACK
Maybe. Let's say. One Picasso painting for twenty-five hundred cows. All that milk. How many gallons does a cow give
off in a day?

RICHARD
Fifteen?

JACK
(Some astonishment)
Gallons?

RICHARD
No. Quarts. I think I read it.

JACK
O.K. *(Figures in his head)* That comes to . . . fifteen times twenty-five hundred is . . .

RICHARD
You want a pencil and paper?

JACK
(Figures; waves him off)
. . . figuring three hundred and *sixty* days a year, giving the cows holidays off. Thirty-seven-five times thirty-six and carry all those zeros . . . comes to . . . good God! Thirteen and a half million quarts of milk in a year.

RICHARD
You're kidding!

JACK

No; I'm not. Thirteen million and a half quarts of milk in one year.

RICHARD
That's incredible!

JACK
It is, isn't it. How much does milk go for wholesale?

RICHARD
Ten cents?

JACK

No, less. There's all that awful mark-up before it gets to us.
Let's say five cents. Thirteen-five by twenty . . . this is even
more fascinating! Nearly seven hundred thousand dollars a
year for the milk alone!

RICHARD

What are you getting at?

JACK

Which would you rather have? The Picasso or the cows?

RICHARD
(Thinks, shakes his head; genuine)
I don't know. Another drink?

JACK
(Gulps his down, simultaneously shaking his head)
No. I've got to get to the club. Old Digby's waiting, panting
at the backgammon board.

RICHARD

Oh. O.K.

JACK
(Both have risen; stops)
Now that's the *interesting* thing. Old Digby. Do you know
that he's eighty-seven, by the way? He *adores* money . . .
and not as a symbol . . . as a *thing* in itself. I'll bet he's got
sixty million if he's got one, but it's all a *thing* with *him*. It
doesn't become Picassos or cows or . . . anything but just the
paper as paper. Money as money.

RICHARD
(Pause, almost apologetic)
Money *is* money, you know.

JACK
(Apologetic; gentle)

I *know* it is.

RICHARD
(Quietly dogmatic)

It's paying for this house, and a good education for Roger,
and something every once in a while to make Jenny
happy . . .

JACK

I *know; I know.*

RICHARD
(Indicates the money on the desk)

So, when something like *this* comes along . . . well, it
means something.

JACK

I wasn't making fun of you.

RICHARD

Don't tell Jenny, but I might be able to get her some kind of
greenhouse, a small one . . .

JACK

I told you: not a word about anything. Money? *What* money?
I've got to go. *(Starts out french doors)* It just occurred to me
that I don't think I've ever used the front door in this place.
Is it nice?

RICHARD

The front door?

JACK

Mmm.

RICHARD
(He'd never really thought about it before)
Well, *yes* . . . it's all right, I guess.

JACK
I must do it someday.

RICHARD
Jack?
(JACK stops, half out)
Nothing.

JACK
(As RICHARD turns away; to the audience)
He's *right*; and I *wasn't* making fun of him. Money . . . is
. . . money. See you. *(Exits)*

JENNY
(Bounces back in)
Are you two . . . ? Oh. Is Jack gone?

RICHARD
Um-hum.

JENNY
(Sort of breathless)
Chuck and Beryl are coming; they were going to just sort of
sit around; and I got Cynthia and Perry, or I got Cynthia,
rather, and they had to get out of something, but they'll be
here, too, and I'm trying Gil and Louise but their line keeps
being busy, so I'll go back and finish *that* up.

RICHARD
O.K. You want a martini now?

JENNY
No; when I come back. *(As she goes again)* Roger should be
arriving soon. He'll have to take a taxi from the station.

RICHARD

A *taxi!?*

JENNY
(Pauses her flight momentarily)
Yes; a taxi. *(Indicates the money)* Don't you think we can
afford one?

RICHARD
(It sinks in; he laughs sheepishly)
Oh. Hunh! Yes, I guess we can.
(JENNY exits)
*(RICHARD looks at the money, straightens it out;
reaches in his pocket for a cigarette, finds none,
looks around for one. Finds a cigarette box empty,
looks some more)*

RICHARD
(Half calling)
Jenny, where did you put the cigarettes? Never mind, I can
find them.
*(Hands on hips for a moment, pondering. Goes to—
what? a side table, maybe, opens a drawer, looks in,
rummages, suddenly halts, frozen. Puts his hand on
something, slowly brings it out. It is a bundle of
money. He looks at it, looks over to the pile on the
table, looks back at the money in his hand, drops
the new bundle down on a chair, or the sofa, which-
ever is handier, and looks around the room, spies
JENNY's sewing basket—say—and goes over to it;
hesitates just a moment, then opens it, reaches in,
takes out yet another bundle of money which he
regards with a curious intensity as he takes it over
and dumps it down where he put the last. Spies a
box on the mantel and goes to it, opens it, and
comes up with a fistful of money. He lets it fall, like
confetti, all around him)*

JENNY
(Re-enters)

Well, that's done. Gilbert and Louise are coming, too, so that makes . . . *(She stops, sees what he has found)* . . . everybody we asked.

RICHARD
(In a kind of a fog)

Jenny; look. What *is* it?

JENNY

Money, Richard.

RICHARD

But . . . is it . . . is it yours?

JENNY

There isn't time to tell you now, I . . .

RICHARD

Yes. There is. You must.

JENNY

We have so much to do before . . .

RICHARD

Wait! *(Points to the money on the table)* Did you send me that package?

JENNY

Actually, yes . . . well, I *had* to; there was *so* much, and I couldn't think of any way to . . .

RICHARD

Have you been . . . have you been *gambling?*

JENNY
(Jumping on that)

Yes!

RICHARD

Where? On what? Who through?

JENNY

There's . . . there's this man.

RICHARD

Called?

JENNY

What does it matter so long as I've been winning?

RICHARD
(Steelier)

Called?

JENNY

Desorio.

RICHARD

That's a lie.

JENNY

Don't you *talk* to me like that!

RICHARD

Isn't it a lie?

JENNY

Well . . . sort of.

RICHARD

THEN IT'S A LIE!

JENNY
(Shrugs)

Yes.

RICHARD

How much is there here? There's thousands!! Where did you get it?

JENNY
(Defensive)

I didn't *steal* it.

RICHARD
(Steely)

Where did you *get* it!?

JENNY

I earned it.

RICHARD

A job! You've got a job!

JENNY

Sort of.

RICHARD

I *told* you I didn't want you to take a *job*. No! You couldn't have earned this at a job. There's too much! There's thousands of dollars here, and . . .

JENNY

Six months!

RICHARD
(Laughs ruefully and half hysterically)

No, look, darling; look. Tell me. Did . . . did someone leave it to you? Did someone die and you haven't told me?

JENNY

Nobody died. I earned it. *(Slight pause)* In the afternoons.

RICHARD

Look; sweetheart: even if you worked full-*time* you couldn't
have earned *this* kind of money. Come on now; *tell* me.

JENNY
(Miffed and playing for time)
Oh? Really? I guess *not* if all I'm supposed to be good for is
a domestic or something.

RICHARD
(Gritting his teeth)
Where did you *get* it?

JENNY
(Sighs, rattles it off)
I make two hundred dollars an afternoon, four days a week,
sometimes more. I've spent a little on clothes, but there
hasn't been time to *spend* the rest, and . . .

RICHARD
Nobody pays that sort of money! I mean you've no training.

JENNY
You don't *need* any.

RICHARD
(Bewildered, and getting angry at the mystery)
What *do* you need?

JENNY
Where's my martini? You promised me an ice-cold, super-
special . . .

RICHARD
(Grabs her arm)
Now tell me!

JENNY

Ow! Now let go of me!
*(He does; she rubs her arm as they glare at each
other. Subdued)*
There's nothing worth telling.

RICHARD

By God, you tell me or I'll make a bonfire of this money in
the middle of the lawn!

JENNY
(Pleading underneath)
Don't be ridiculous! It's money!

RICHARD

I want to know where it comes from!

JENNY
(Her voice rising, too)
It comes from a job!

RICHARD

What *kind* of a job!?

JENNY
(Wild hunting)
A . . . a receptionist.

RICHARD

For *that* kind of money? *(Snorts-sneers)*

JENNY

It's a very expensive place!

RICHARD

What *sort* of expensive place?!

JENNY

A . . . a doctor's office.

RICHARD

You expect me to believe you sit behind the desk at some
god-damn doctor's office a couple of hours in the afternoon,
and you get two hundred dollars a day for it?! You must
think I'm crazy!!

JENNY

It's a very special and very expensive place!

RICHARD
(A *little fearful, a little disgusted*)

What, what is it, some kind of . . . of abortionist office, or
something?

JENNY

My God, you're disgusting!

RICHARD

Why! I've read in the paper of a man found out his wife
worked for an abortionist, brought him patients, as a matter
of fact.

JENNY

You're disgusting!!

RICHARD

Well, I'm *sorry;* but if you're going to be so damned secretive,
what am I *supposed* to think? Hunh?

JENNY
(*Trapped and furious*)

Think what you like!! (*Quite cutting*) Don't you want the
money?

RICHARD
(Both furious now)
The money's got nothing to do with it!

JENNY
Oh yes it has! You don't think I do it for pleasure, do you?

RICHARD
Do what!? Sit behind a desk!?

JENNY
Yes; sit behind a desk!

RICHARD
What's the name of this place?

JENNY
(Daring him)
No name; just a number.

RICHARD
Yeah? Well, what's the number?

JENNY
It's confidential!

RICHARD
I'm your husband!

JENNY
I'm your wife! Do you tell me everything?

RICHARD
I like being told the truth!

JENNY
How much do you talk about *your* job? To *me*.

RICHARD

It's a dull job!

JENNY

So's mine!

RICHARD

The money isn't! The money isn't so damn dull! Christ! It's
four times what *I* get. *(Contemptuous)* Sitting behind the
desk in a doctor's office . . . sounds more like a high-class
whorehouse!

JENNY

I don't *like* that word.

RICHARD

Whorehouse! Call house! Cat house!
        (There is a silence. JENNY *looks out toward the*
        garden. RICHARD *begins to realize he's hit on it)*
No; look; come on; what is it *really?*

JENNY
        (Looking away; sort of wistful, sad)
Just a place.

RICHARD

A place.

JENNY

Where they pay me.

RICHARD
        (Grabs her arm again)
For God's sake! What do they pay me for!?

JENNY

It's *me* they *pay!* *(Long pause; sort of lost)* Don't you want
the money?

RICHARD
(Lets go of her arm, backs away a little, shakes his head; stuttered, almost laughing disbelief)
I, I don't . . . I don't believe it. I, I don't believe it.

JENNY
(Quite light)
Then don't.

RICHARD
(Backs a bit further away; same confusion)
I, I can't *believe it.* I CAN'T.

JENNY
(Coming toward him; the nicest smile)
Darling, it's going to make such a tremendous difference.

RICHARD
(Laughing mirthlessly at the irony)
Oh, by God it is!

JENNY
(Still happy; occupied)
All the things we've been wanting for years . . .

RICHARD
We!

JENNY
We can have a second car, and . . .

RICHARD
There's no . . . I don't believe this!

JENNY
There's no what?

RICHARD

Room in the garage. (*Incredulous*) How could you *do* such a thing!? (*Pause*) Come on, it *isn't* true, *is* it?

(JENNY *nods, slowly*)

No; is it? Really?

JENNY
(*Dogmatic; impatient*)

It is for *us*; for everything we *want!*

RICHARD
(*Between set teeth; quiet rage, letting it sink in firmly*)

You are my wife; and Roger's mother; and you are a common *prostitute!?*

JENNY

That's a *horrid* way to *put* it.

RICHARD

HOW THE HELL AM I SUPPOSED TO PUT IT!!?

JENNY

I'm not the only *one*, you know. I'm not the only person in the world who . . .

RICHARD

You're the only one who's married to *me!*

JENNY
(*Triste reasoning*)

But it doesn't make any difference to *us*, and . . .

RICHARD
(*Hard*)

Doesn't it? (*Walks over to her, slaps her hard across the face*) Doesn't it? How much do you charge for *that? (She just stares at him, firm but maybe near tears way underneath. So he slaps her again, just as hard)* I said: how much do you charge for that!!

JENNY
(Says nothing, really, maybe a kind of growl-cry as she slaps him back, just as hard as he hit her)

RICHARD
(Cold, after a moment's pause)
Get out. Pack up and get out of here.

JENNY
(Equally cold)

Where!

RICHARD
Anywhere! Or I will. No, by God, I won't! It's my house, I paid for it. I stay here!

JENNY
(Curiously unemotional)
I can't . . . just like that.

RICHARD
I said get out!

JENNY
A lot of things here are mine.

RICHARD
Take them! Take them!

JENNY
(Through her teeth)
You certainly don't expect me to get everything together right now and . . .

RICHARD

I'll send it after you! Just . . . just get out!

JENNY

No, no, you wouldn't. I know *you*: you can never manage anything like that. I'm the one who has to get the movers and arrange everything, and . . .

RICHARD

CRAP!!

JENNY

Well, it's perfectly true. When your aunt what's-her-name wanted her big, ugly breakfront back, you said you'd take care of it, and *weeks* went by and you didn't do a damn thing.

RICHARD
(Quietly, with controlled rage)
Get your things together and get out of this house!

JENNY
(Tired of it all)
Oh, don't be silly.

RICHARD
(Fury and disbelief)
Don't be *what!?*

JENNY

I said, don't be silly. Give me a cigarette.

RICHARD

You god-damn wanton bitch!

JENNY

I am *not* wanton! I told you: it's for the money! The money *you* don't make! The money we *need!* You think I get any enjoyment out of it?

RICHARD

Think!? I, I, I, I. I don't think anything! I *can't!* I'd go
stark raving mad if I thought! Men kill their wives for this
sort of thing!

JENNY
(*Giggles*)

Oh, darling . . .

RICHARD
(*Mocked, becomes uncontrollable*)

You don't think they do? (*Starts toward her with serious
intent*) Read the papers and find out! By God, read tomorrow's papers and find . . .
    (*They are both stopped by the sound of the front
    door slamming.* ROGER *enters, from the hallway*)

ROGER

Hi! I took a taxi; do you have any money?

JENNY
(*As if she'd forgotten all about him and is sorry*)

Roger!

ROGER

The taxi driver says he wants five dollars over the fare because
it was such a long way.

RICHARD
(*Fury turned on driver*)

Oh, he does, does he? W*ell,* I'll fix that son of a bitch.
    (RICHARD *exits, maybe pushing* ROGER *to one side as
    he goes*)

ROGER
(*Looks at* RICHARD'*s exit, confused; back to* JENNY;
genuine affection)

Hi, Mom.

JENNY
(Embarrassed, but covering)
Darling! You're so . . . so terribly early.

ROGER
(Statement of fact)
The train was on *time*.

JENNY
(A little flustered)
Oh? Was it? Well, then . . . our clock must be slow.

ROGER
Must be. *(Goes to a chair, stands on its seat, looks out through french windows over fence.)* How's the tennis?

JENNY
What tennis?

ROGER
(Points)
At the club.
(Angry voices from outside front door)

JENNY
(Looks off apprehensively)
Oh, I . . . I don't pay much attention.

ROGER
Dad been playing? I hope the cab driver doesn't kill him.

JENNY
(Calling off; worried)
Richard? *(To* ROGER*)* Get *down* off that before your father sees you!

ROGER
O.K. . . . *(Jumps down; sees the money)* Wow! Is that money?

JENNY
(*Preoccupied, defensive*)
Yes, now . . . just leave it be.

ROGER
What is it, the sweepstakes?

JENNY
Just . . . don't concern yourself, now.

ROGER
Can I have a bunch?

JENNY
(*Sudden anger*)
No! Now let it alone!

ROGER
(*Hurt, some*)
I'm sorry. (*Heavy-handed irony*) Gee, am *I* glad *I* came home.

JENNY
(*Apologetic*)
Oh, Roger, darling, I'm . . .
(RICHARD *reappears, a little mussed*)

RICHARD
(*Vengefulness and pride*)
I hit him!

ROGER
(*Shy*)
Hi, Dad.

RICHARD
(*To* JENNY, *since she caused it*)
I hit the son of a bitch!

JENNY
(*Quite rebuking*)
Did you say hello to your son?

RICHARD
Hm?

ROGER
(*Shy, pleased*)
Hi.

RICHARD
(*Really sees* ROGER *for the first time; sadness and pride*) Hi.
(*Back to* JENNY; *quiet fury and glee*) I hit that son of a
bitch.

JENNY
(*Quietly desperate*)
Why!

RICHARD
Why!!? He wanted nine dollars. The bastard wanted the
regular fare and five dollars extra because . . .

JENNY
That is no reason to hit anyone!

RICHARD
WHO AM I SUPPOSED TO HIT! (*Less loud, but no less intense*)
Who am I supposed to hit!

ROGER
(*To fill a tiny silence*)
How's the tennis, Dad?

RICHARD
(*To* ROGER)
What?

ROGER
(Intimidated)

Tennis. How is it?

RICHARD
(Confused)

I, I haven't . . . I, I, I, haven't played.

ROGER

Un huh . . .

JENNY

You'll get a lawsuit on us, you know.

RICHARD
(Deflated; embarrassed, even)

I only hit him on the shoulder. We . . . we just scuffled a little.

JENNY
(Pause, disappointment and relief)

Oh.

RICHARD
(A sneer)

Not what I wanted to do.
                    (ROGER *has gone up on the chair again*)

ROGER

Wow! Right in the crotch!

RICHARD

Who! What!

JENNY

Roger, don't use words like that.

RICHARD
(Scoffs)
Oh, Jesus!

ROGER
Serve took a bad bounce, hit him right in the . . . what
word shall I use?

RICHARD
Don't ask your mother, she's too ladylike. *(Realizes where*
ROGER *is)* GET THE HELL OFF THE GOD-DAMNED FURNITURE.
(ROGER *does so)*

ROGER
(Subdued, unhappy)
Sorry.

RICHARD
You think we're made of money?

ROGER
(Defensive, indicates money all over)
It *looks* like it.
(This sets in an embarrassed silence)

RICHARD
(To change the subject)
Did you have a good term?

ROGER
All right.

RICHARD
What's your average? What did you end up with?

ROGER
C plus.

RICHARD

What did you start out?

ROGER

C plus.

RICHARD
(Bitter)

Keep it up: by the time you're eighteen we won't even be able to get you into an agricultural college!

JENNY

Be nice!
    (RICHARD's *mouth drops open, but he doesn't say anything*)
Set the clock right.

RICHARD

It *is* right.

ROGER

It's twenty minutes slow.

RICHARD
(Furious)

Then you set it right!

JENNY

Richard!

RICHARD

Shut up!
    (ROGER *goes to the mantel clock, takes it down*)

ROGER

What do I do?

RICHARD

Turn the knob; turn the god-damn knob!

JENNY

Richard, if you can't be . . .

RICHARD
(Between clenched teeth)

I told you to shut up! *(To* ROGER*)* No! Too far! That's tooo
. . . DON'T TURN IT BACK. *(Disgust, takes the clock, none too
gently, from* ROGER*)* Here; give me the god-damn clock.
NEVER TURN IT BACK! Don't ever turn a clock back!

ROGER
(Flustered, confused)

I'm sorry, I . . .

JENNY

Roger, darling, why don't you take your bag upstairs, and . . .

RICHARD
*(Concentrating, excessively, on the clock; to himself
as well as* ROGER*)*

You *never* turn a clock back; *never.*

JENNY

Why don't you go unpack?

ROGER
(Sullen)

O.K. You've got so much money, I don't see why you don't
go *buy* a clock.

RICHARD

ALL RIGHT!

JENNY

Go unpack and then you can come down and *help* us.

ROGER

You want me to go upstairs, or would you rather I turned around and went right back to school?

RICHARD

GET UPSTAIRS!!

ROGER
(Under his breath)

Christ!

RICHARD

And don't say that!

ROGER
(Standing up to him)
Why not! YOU do! *(Exits)*
(Small silence. RICHARD *hurls the clock down on the floor)*

JENNY
(Calm, displeased)

That helps.

RICHARD
(Intense, pounding his chest with his fingers)
It helps *me!* ME!!

JENNY
(Closes her eyes for a moment; then all business)
I wish you'd make a list of what we need, what liquor we need.

RICHARD
(Stares at her; quietly)

Whore.

JENNY
(Ignores it)
We'll have champagne, but there are always some people
don't like it, and . . .

RICHARD
(Ibid.)
Whore!

JENNY
. . . and so you'd better check. If we're going to have *fresh*
caviar, and I think we should, then I've got to go down **to**
Blaustein's and get some . . .

RICHARD
(Ibid.)
Filthy, rotten, no-good little whore!

JENNY
(Quite savage)
Be quiet! You've got Roger in the house!

RICHARD
(Top of his voice)
I'VE GOT A ROTTEN, FILTHY WHORE IN THE HOUSE!

JENNY
(Tiny pause; continues quietly)
Now make a list. They'll be here in about an hour . . .

RICHARD
(Laughing in disbelief)
A party! We're going to have a party!

JENNY
(Level)
Yes; we are.

RICHARD
(The tears that finally come, tears of rage and de-
spair, are incipient; we notice what is coming by a
quivering in the voice)
What, what shall we do? Make the announcement? Break
it to the neighborhood? Tell them to tell their friends where
they can go to get it? Hunh?

JENNY
Make a list.

RICHARD
Hunh? Is that what we should do? Is it? Whore? *(Tears*
nearer now)

JENNY
You can phone for the liquor, but we have to know what we
need.

RICHARD
(Tears even nearer)
Or, or maybe they already know. Maybe . . . maybe Chuck
and Perry and Gil . . . do they . . . do they know already?

JENNY
List.

RICHARD
L, l, list? We . . . all, all right, we need . . . *(Crying com-*
mences now) v, v, v, vodka, and . . .

JENNY
(Gentle)
American or Russian?

RICHARD
(Looks up; pleading)
Both?

JENNY

Both, then.

RICHARD

. . . and . . . and . . . sc, sc, sc, scotch, and . . . bourbon,
and . . . (*Full crying now*) . . . and gin, and . . . gin,
and . . . gin, and . . . (*The word* gin *takes a long time
now, a long, broken word with gasps for breath and the attempt to control the tears*) . . . g—i—i—i—n, and . . .
    (*Final word, very long, broken, a long howl*)
G——i——i——i——i——n——n——n——n.
    (*Curtain falls slowly as the word continues*)

ACT TWO

(Set the same; one hour later. RICHARD alone on stage, sitting facing out at audience. It might be interesting if he looked the people in the audience right in the eye, but absently, seeing them, but thinking of something else. No attempt to set a new convention (with RICHARD), but it will give quite a few people an interesting sensation)

(JENNY enters, followed by ROGER, both laden with glasses, etc.)

JENNY
(Pleasantly incredulous)
What are you *doing?*

RICHARD
Hm?

JENNY
What are you *doing?* Roger, put those over there and be careful you don't break them.

ROGER
(Embarrassed at being warned)
O.K.

JENNY
(Puts her things down)
I asked you what you thought you were doing. You've got guests coming over in about ten minutes, and . . .

RICHARD
(Ugly but quiet; a threat of explosion)
What am I supposed to do?

ROGER
(Breaks a glass)

Damn!

JENNY

Oh, Roger . . .

RICHARD

That's right! Break the house up!

ROGER

It's only a glass, for God's sake, it . . .

RICHARD

We're not made . . . Do you know how much those things cost?

ROGER
(Standing his ground)

No. How much?

RICHARD
(To JENNY)

How much do they cost?

JENNY

Well, they're new, and . . .

RICHARD
(Hint of hysteria; incipience)

They're new!?

JENNY
(Calm)

Yes, and they're crystal, and I suppose they . . . well, I think they were about four-fifty each . . .

RICHARD
(After a pained look at JENNY; *to* ROGER, *shaking his head and sneering)*
Four-fifty each. You broke a god-damn glass and they cost four . . .

ROGER
(Digs into his pocket)
Well, here. Take it out of this.

RICHARD
(Unpleasant joy)
Give it to your mother.

JENNY
(Laughing, covering)
Don't be silly, darling. No, Roger, no.

ROGER
(Hand out of pocket again)
Anything to keep peace in the house.

RICHARD
Don't be fresh!

JENNY
(Mollifying; to ROGER*)*
Darling, go upstairs and change. People *will* be here soon, and I'll want you to help.

ROGER
Do I have to put on a tie?

RICHARD
(Furious)
Yes!

JENNY
(All on ROGER's *side)*
I'm afraid so, darling. Run along upstairs now.

ROGER
Tie?

RICHARD
Yes; *and* a shirt, *and* trousers, *and* socks, *and* shoes . . .

ROGER
(Going, shaking his head)
Wow.

RICHARD
And don't hang out the window watching the tennis.
Change.

ROGER
(Sloppy salute)
Yes, sir! *(Exits)*

RICHARD
And don't salute!

JENNY
(After a tiny pause; reasonable, calm)
It was only a glass.

RICHARD
(Turns on her; quiet wrath)
What have you been doing: buying things behind my back?
Crystal? Gold goblets? Clothes?

JENNY
Just a little.

RICHARD

Just a little what!

JENNY
(Sighs)

A few clothes; those glasses; nicer sheets. Didn't you notice?

RICHARD
(Still furious)

Notice what!

JENNY
(Quietly happy)

The nice sheets. I thought they'd . . .

RICHARD

No! I didn't notice the nicer sheets, and by God I won't sleep on them! I won't sleep in the same room with you!

JENNY
(Cool)

And where are you going to sleep?

RICHARD

What?

JENNY

I said, where are you going to sleep? Roger's home, there's no mattress in the guestroom . . .

RICHARD

Why not! Where is it!

JENNY

You threw it out. When you had the hepatitis and you slept in there you said it was awful—the mattress—so we threw it out.

RICHARD
Well, why didn't we get another one!

JENNY
(Shrugs, starts arranging things)
Oh . . . money, or something.

RICHARD
WELL, WE CAN DAMN WELL AFFORD ONE NOW!

JENNY
(Quiet, precise)
I don't see the need. You've told me to get out.

RICHARD
(This stops him for the briefest instant only)
WELL, WHEN ARE YOU GOING!?

JENNY
(Stops what she is doing)
Right now. Right this very minute.

RICHARD
You've got a party! You've got people coming over!

JENNY
(Pretending this complicates things)
Oh. Yes. Well then, I'll leave right after the party, right after everybody goes.

RICHARD
Fine.

JENNY
(Quietly withering)
Or shall I stay and clean up first?

RICHARD
(Can think of nothing for a moment, finally)
Tramp.

JENNY
There's no need for that now.

RICHARD
I can't hold my head up in front of those people; I won't be able to look any of them in the eye. I might scream, or cry, or something.

JENNY
You'll hold your head up. In fact, I should think you might be *able* to look Chuck and Perry and Gil straight in the eye, maybe for the first time.

RICHARD
Why! Because my wife is a whore?

JENNY
(Sort of cajoling)
No . . . well, because for once you won't be the poor relative, so to speak; you can talk about the new car you're going to get, and why don't we raise the dues at the club to keep the riffraff out, and Jenny and I were thinking about Antigua this winter—all those things.

RICHARD
(Some disgust)
You're hopelessly immoral.

JENNY
Not at all! I'm talking about money—that thing that keeps us at each other's throats; that standard of judgment; that measure of a man's worth!

RICHARD

There are other standards!

JENNY

Well, not in the circles *we* move in! Not in *our* environment.

RICHARD

There are *kinds* of money!

JENNY

Yes! Three! Too little, too much, and just enough!

RICHARD

Corrupt!

JENNY

Too much money corrupts; too little corrupts. Just enough?
Never.

RICHARD

It's how! *How!*

JENNY

Oh, don't tell me about how! Perry and that real estate he
sells? Ten thousand for an acre out near, uh, near the track,
and he doesn't even tell the god-damn fools there isn't any
city water? Gilbert and his fancy publishing house? What's
his advertising budget on trash? Thousands! How much does
he spend on a halfway decent book . . . nothing!

RICHARD

All right, all right . . .

JENNY

And you in your research laboratory. All those government
contracts? A little work on germ gas maybe?

RICHARD

I told you that in . . . I told you not to say a word about anything I told you . . .

JENNY

You told me in confidence? Well, I'm telling you *back* in confidence! You all stink, you're all killers and whores.

RICHARD
(Nods several times rapidly)
That's quite a performance.

JENNY

You're damned right.

RICHARD
(Great sarcasm)

Bra-*vo!*

JENNY

At least! Come on! More!

RICHARD

With your theories on money, you should have married Jack.

JENNY
(Self-mocking rue)
Unh-hunh; you may be right.

RICHARD

Though I don't necessarily think he'd take any better to having a whore for a wife than I do.

JENNY
(Comforting)
Well, if I'd married Jack none of it would have happened.

RICHARD
(As ROGER *re-enters; starts to go for her)*
Why, you . . .

ROGER
I'm dressed.
(They both pause, for ROGER's *tone has a curious impersonal disapproval to it)*

JENNY
(Recovering)
And in good time, too. They'll start coming any second. My,
don't you look nice and grown-up.

ROGER
You've seen me in a tie before. *(To* RICHARD) Were you
going to hit her?

RICHARD
Mind your own business.

ROGER
(Mildly puzzled)
I thought it was.

RICHARD
Well, it's not. I don't suppose you washed.

ROGER
Well, I didn't have time for a sit-down bath, if that's what
you mean. Why *isn't* it my business?

RICHARD
Because it isn't! Are your fingernails clean?

ROGER
(To JENNY, *the same mildly disapproving curiosity)*
Was he going to hit you? *(Looks at his nails)* Relatively.

JENNY

Don't be silly, darling; your father doesn't hit people bigger than he is. Come help me with things, now. Those glasses over there . . .

ROGER
(Grumbling, sort of)

People always hit each other when other people are out of the room.

JENNY
(Decidedly offended)

Roger!

RICHARD
(Snarl)

Little monster.

ROGER

I wasn't complaining; I was just stating a fact.

RICHARD

Keep your facts to yourself.

JENNY

Nobody hits anybody around here.

RICHARD

Anyway, not above the belt.

JENNY
("Not in front of Roger.")

Richard!

RICHARD
(Subsiding)

Sorry! Very sorry. Sorry about everything. Every single thing.

ROGER
(An aside, to JENNY)
What's the matter with Dad?

JENNY
(RICHARD *can hear them both, of course)*
Oh, nothing; parties upset your father, that's all.

ROGER
(Goes to RICHARD: *genuine)*
I'll help.

RICHARD
(Looks at him for a moment, then, with a head-shaking laugh that could be confused with mockery, but isn't)
Oh, boy! Thanks!

ROGER
(Withdraws a little; stung)
I'm sorry.

RICHARD
(Quite furious)
Roger! I mean it! Thank you!

ROGER
(A little bewildered)
O.K.

(Doorbell rings)

JENNY
(Sighs, girds herself)
Well. Here we go.

RICHARD
(Little boy)
I'm going to hate this.

ROGER

Hey, what shall I drink?

RICHARD

Ginger ale.

ROGER

Awww.

JENNY
(Exiting)

I'll go.

RICHARD

Roger, do me a favor.

ROGER

Sure. What?

RICHARD

Grow up right.
           (Sounds of greeting from hallway)

ROGER
(Offhand)

O.K. Got any ideas?

RICHARD

Just . . . be good.

ROGER

As the twig is bent, as they say.
           (JENNY *re-enters with* CHUCK *and* BERYL)

BERYL
(To JENNY, *as they enter)*

No, it's been lovely, but I would love some rain. Our lawn
is all brown and splotchy.

JENNY

Oh? Well, we manage ours.

BERYL

Green thumb, my darling.

CHUCK

Won't be any rain till we take off for . . . *Hello*, Richard!

RICHARD
(Shy)

Hi, Chuck; Beryl?

BERYL

Are we too early? I told Chuck we'd be first here.

JENNY

Don't be silly.

CHUCK

And I said, so what? First to come, last to leave; no breeding.
Roger!

ROGER

Hello.

BERYL
(To ROGER; *some wonder)*

Do you grow each time I see you?

ROGER

Probably; I don't see you very much.

JENNY

He grows fresher each time you see him, I can tell you *that*.

CHUCK
(Formality)

How's school, Roger?

ROGER

Fine.

CHUCK

Back for vacation? Now, that's a silly question. Got any silly answers?

ROGER

I keep those for exams.
                    (Some laughter)

RICHARD

How true. Hey! How about a drink? Champagne or proper stuff?

CHUCK
(Hearty)

Champagne!

BERYL
(To CHUCK*)*
You know what it does. *(To* JENNY*)* Keeps him up all night; bent double. Gas?

CHUCK
(To RICHARD; *ruefully)*
I guess I better have some scotch.

RICHARD

Right. Beryl? *(Goes to her)*

ROGER

Can I help?

BERYL
(Examining caviar; to JENNY*)*
Fresh, how nice. Do you get yours in the city?

JENNY
No, Blaustein's has the fresh.

BERYL
(*To* RICHARD)
Gin, darling, and a little ice. (*Back to* JENNY) Well, fresh
caviar can't keep, and I don't trust Blaustein's.

JENNY
(*A tiny bit of pique*)
Oh, it's perfectly fresh.

BERYL
(*Slight laugh*)
I'm sure it is. I just think Blaustein's cheats a little . . .
keeps it on ice a day or two more than they . . .

JENNY
Would you like some caviar, Chuck?

CHUCK
Sure would. (*Goes to it*) Toast?
Toast?

JENNY
No; crackers.

BERYL
(*Moving away from caviar, looks at garden, expansive*)
How do you keep it!? How do you battle the weeds, and
prune and dust . . . ?

JENNY
(*Proud*)
Green *thumb*.

CHUCK

Cheers!

THE OTHERS
(Nearly simultaneously)

Cheers!

BERYL

While I've got you now, I need you for the blood bank.

JENNY

Richard can't.

BERYL

Why?

JENNY

Hepatitis. And Roger shouldn't, either; he needs all he's got.

ROGER

I don't mind giving blood.

JENNY
(Light, but firm)

I don't think you *should*, Roger.

BERYL

Well, Jenny, then you'll have to give for the whole family.

RICHARD

I don't think she should.

BERYL

Why ever not?

JENNY

Yes. Why not?

RICHARD
(Dogmatic)
I just don't think you should.

JENNY
(A little annoyed)
Well, do you have a reason? Or are you just hoarding everybody's blood.

RICHARD
(Too much attempt at a joke; only JENNY *will see
what he means)*
Well, no; you . . . you might have some awful disease for all *you* know.

BERYL
(As CHUCK *laughs)*
Oh, Richard! Really!
(Doorbell)

ROGER
Shall I go?

JENNY
(Exiting; a quick look at RICHARD*)*
I'll go. Help yourselves to the . . . (*Leaves it unfinished;
exits*)

RICHARD
(The tiniest mockery)
How's high finance, Chuck? How's the old market?

CHUCK
Oh, just like marriage . . . up and down, up and down.
*(*BERYL *and* RICHARD *laugh flimsily)*

ROGER
What does *that* mean?

RICHARD

Nothing.

ROGER

Then why did he say it?

RICHARD
(*Annoyed*)

You know perfectly well what it means, so why did you ask?

ROGER
(*Shrugs*)

I thought it was polite. You told me to help.
(JENNY *re-enters, with* GILBERT *and* LOUISE)

JENNY

Richard! It's Gilbert and Louise!

RICHARD

Well! Come on in! You know Beryl and Ch . . .

LOUISE

Yes, I think we've met at the club.

GILBERT

Yes, of course we have.

BERYL

How nice to see you both again.

CHUCK

Drinks are over here. There's champagne *and* the real stuff.

LOUISE

How nice you were to ask us. Oh, will you look at your garden! And the lawn! *How* do you do it?

BERYL

I was commenting before. I *don't* know how they do it.

GILBERT

Who's your gardener? Shropie?

RICHARD

Who?

GILBERT

Shropshire; he has a whole team, and . . .

JENNY

No, we've been doing it ourselves.

LOUISE

We have Shropshire, and they send two men, but we have six
acres, too, so that makes a difference.

GILBERT

Charge an arm and a leg.

BERYL

But are they *good*. Chuck and I were thinking of using them,
and . . .

CHUCK

Not going to get me mowing weekends . . .

JENNY

It sort of spoils the fun to farm it out—the work . . .

RICHARD
(A *little tentative*)
We, we could have someone in, though.

JENNY
(Secret smile)
Oh? Well, why don't we?

RICHARD
(Bitter at being caught)
Spoils the fun.

JENNY
(To the others)
We thought we might put a greenhouse in, though.

RICHARD
Did we!

LOUISE
Oh, you must. We're so glad *we* did.

JENNY
I've always wanted one.

CHUCK
You must be in the chips, Richard old boy: greenhouse, champagne, caviar . . .

RICHARD
(Laughs lightly)
No; just . . . *(Shrugs, leaves it unfinished)*

JENNY
No, just not scrimping.

BERYL
(Her eyes narrowing slightly)
Oh, I'm glad.

ROGER
(*Weary of asking*)
Can I help?

LOUISE
Roger, *dear!* I didn't even say hello to you. Gilbert! Roger's
here.

GILBERT
Roger, my boy. Home from school?

ROGER
(*False heartiness*)
Yes, Sir!

GILBERT
Doing O.K.?

ROGER
Holding my own, as they say.

GILBERT
Good boy; good boy. Hey, Rich; this is good caviar. Where'd
you get it?

RICHARD
Jenny got it; it's Jenny's.

JENNY
I got it at Blaustein's, just as fresh as if you'd gone into
town and . . .

GILBERT
Damn smart little kike, that Blaustein, putting in caviar
and . . .

ROGER

We don't use words like that around here.
  *(Everybody looks at him, not quite sure of what he
  means)*
At least, not in the family.
          (Doorbell again)

JENNY
(Glad of the chance)

I'll get it! *(Exits)*

BERYL   LOUISE
(Both just to say something)

I still say if you get it in town   The first year we had *our*
it's bound to be fresher.   greenhouse, I was amazed.

RICHARD

Drinks now! Come on, kids; the bar's open.

GILBERT
(To RICHARD *as they approach the bar)*

What did I say?

RICHARD   CHUCK

Nothing, nothing.   Your kid's sort of a wiseacre,
                            hunh?

GILBERT
(Hurt)

What did I say?

          (Simultaneous)

RICHARD   BERYL

Nothing; forget it.   But aren't they a terrible
                            chore?

CHUCK

I don't get the champagne.
What for? What gives?

LOUISE

Well, no; not if you remember things, like water, and air,
and heat, and . . .

(Simultaneous)

RICHARD

What gives? Nothing.

BERYL
(Laughs)

Ah, just a few things like
that!

CHUCK

Looks pretty festive to me.

LOUISE

It takes getting used to,
that's all.

ROGER
(If anyone cares)

I apologize.

(JENNY re-enters, with CYNTHIA and PERRY)

JENNY

The stragglers. Cynthia and Perry Straggler.

PERRY

Hi, folks.

ROGER
(To himself)

Folk.

GILBERT

Well, if it isn't old Perry! Hi, Cyn!

CYNTHIA
(Generally)

Hello there!

RICHARD

Bar's here, kids.

CYNTHIA

Well, will you look at all that!

CHUCK

Is it true what I heard, Perr?

PERRY

Probably. What?

CHUCK

You been selling lots to the black folk twice the going price?
(Some laughter, for this is a joke)

PERRY

Not a word of it! Three times the going price, and at that
I don't let 'em have clear title.
(More laughter)

ROGER

There are two Negro boys at school, on scholarship.

GILBERT

(None too pleasant)

Oh yeah? *(To* RICHARD*)* You ought to send your boy to
Choate, Dick. That's a *good* school.

ROGER

There are Negro boys there, too.

GILBERT

You're kidding.

ROGER

Why not? I mean, why am I kidding?

BERYL
(Not snobbish)
It *is* getting to be a problem.

CYNTHIA
I *know*.

LOUISE
(Very serious)
Well . . . it's a time of change.

JENNY
It's time for a drink, that's what it's time for! Cynthia?
Louise?

ROGER
Actually, there won't be any solution to the color problem—
whatever *that* is—until we're all coffee-colored.

BERYL
Roger!

JENNY
Darling!

GILBERT
Where'd you pick up *that* theory?

ROGER
A book.

PERRY
A little knowledge is a dangerous thing, Roger.

CHUCK
Theories that come out of books ought to stay in books.

RICHARD
(To ROGER*)*

Why don't you pass the caviar? I thought you wanted to help.

ROGER

I've been *ask*ing! I've been standing around on my two hind feet asking if I could be any help and everybody's been ignoring me!

RICHARD
(Put out)

You've been standing around on your two hind feet insulting everybody, that's what you've been standing around doing.

ROGER
(Something of a pout)

That was after.

CYNTHIA

Oh, let him alone, for heaven sake! He's a sweet boy. How old are you, Roger, dear?

ROGER

I'm twelve.

JENNY

You're fourteen!

RICHARD

He *is* not; he's fifteen.

JENNY

I ought to know how old my own son **is.**

RICHARD

You ought; yes.

CHUCK

Where you going to put the greenhouse, Dick?

RICHARD

Hm? Oh . . . out there. *(Gestures vaguely)*

JENNY
(Rather pointed)

Show them *where*, darling.

RICHARD
(Trapped)

Hm?

LOUISE

Oh, I'd love to see! Show us!

CYNTHIA

Yes! And I want to look at Jenny's roses.
(CYNTHIA *and* LOUISE *start out through french doors;*
PERRY *automatically follows)*

CHUCK

Well, into the garden we go. Somebody bring a bottle of
champagne.

GILBERT
(Following CHUCK)

Nobody's *drinking* champagne.

CHUCK

Well . . . bring a bottle of scotch.
(The two men laugh, follow the others out)

JENNY
(To RICHARD)

Well . . . ?

RICHARD
(Getting it straight)
Show them where we're going to put the greenhouse.

JENNY
(Dazzling if mirthless smile)
Yes.
(Doorbell rings: JENNY starts)
Who's that? We didn't ask anyone else.

RICHARD
(Exiting to garden)
It's your party; you figure it out.

JENNY
(To BERYL)
I can't imagine who it is. Roger, darling . . . go see.
(ROGER exits through archway)
Unless it's Jack Foster. He always drops in, and . . .

BERYL
(Starts exiting to garden)
Well, if it is, I'll leave the two of you alone.

JENNY
(Annoyance showing through)
And what is that meant to mean!

BERYL
(Throaty laugh, as she exits)
Nothing, darling; nothing at all.
(We will probably see one or more of the people out in the garden while they admire it and while RICHARD improvises where the greenhouse will be, but their backs will be to us, and they will not see inside until they return.)

ROGER
(Re-entering)

It's a woman to see you.

(MRS. TOOTHE *enters;* JENNY *stares at her, open-mouthed)*

MRS. TOOTHE

Good evening, my dear.

(JENNY *just stares)*

I said, good evening, my dear.

JENNY
(Still staring at her)

Roger, go in the garden.

ROGER
(Bland)

Why?

JENNY
(Turns, snaps)

I said go in the garden!

ROGER
(Some disgust, turns on his heel, goes)

Good God!

JENNY
(Appalled)

What do you want?

MRS. TOOTHE

I want to talk. *(Sits)* Ah! That feels good. I do so hate to walk.

JENNY

You can't *come* here; you *mustn't.*

MRS. TOOTHE

I know, my dear, it's very indiscreet, but most important.

JENNY

(*Anger, and panic underneath*)

I'm having a party! Guests!

MRS. TOOTHE

Yes, I see; fine, I'm one of them.

JENNY

No! I'm sorry; no!

MRS. TOOTHE

Why not?

JENNY

They're friends; Richard thinks you're on the hospital committee, and . . .

MRS. TOOTHE

Fine, I'm on the hospital committee.

JENNY

But these are local people, and Beryl is on the hospital committee, and . . .

MRS. TOOTHE

Beryl?

JENNY

Yes, and Louise is too . . . and, and . . .

MRS. TOOTHE

Well, you'll just have to make up something: I'm not from *here*, I'm from . . .

JENNY

Please! Leave!

MRS. TOOTHE
(Firm, coldly polite)
I told you, my dear, it's a matter of considerable importance.
Does your husband know?

JENNY

Yes, I told him today. Oh, my God, if he sees you and knows
who you are, I don't know what he'll . . .

MRS. TOOTHE

Well, he will have to make the best of it. *(Pause, smile)* Will
he not?

JENNY
(The final supplication of her life)
Please! *Please* leave!
(BERYL *and* CHUCK *have started back in*)

MRS. TOOTHE

Your guests are coming back.
(JENNY *wheels*)

BERYL
(Not noticing MRS. TOOTHE *yet)*
Jenny, my dear, Chuck and I agree: your husband is an angel;
the greenhouse will be absolutely perfect; you'll . . .

JENNY
(Cutting in)
Beryl, Chuck, this is Mrs. Toothe; Richard and I met her
down in St. Thomas last year, and she's come by to say . . .

MRS. TOOTHE
(Quiet smile)
Hello, Beryl, my dear; I have a bone to pick with you.

CHUCK
(As JENNY *watches, openmouthed)*
My God, what's she doing here?

BERYL
(Cool, calm)
Oh? You have?

MRS. TOOTHE
Yes; indeed I have.

JENNY
(Finally, to BERYL, *flabbergasted)*
You!?

BERYL
(As MRS. TOOTHE *chuckles some, quite calm, with a
tiny smile)*
Yes; and you, too, it would seem.

JENNY
(Awe)
My God.
(The others are coming in now, LOUISE, CYNTHIA,
PERRY, GILBERT *and* RICHARD; ROGER *is still outdoors)*

LOUISE
. . . and it seems to me that if you want the afternoon sun,
well, then you'll have to make allowance for it, and . . .
(Sees MRS. TOOTHE)

RICHARD
(All have seen MRS. TOOTHE *save* RICHARD; *all are
staring at her save him)*
It *could* be swung about, I suppose, though we'd have to dig
up someth—*(He sees her, sees the silence; to* MRS. TOOTHE)
Hello; I've seen you before, haven't I?

MRS. TOOTHE
(Very nice)
Yes, but we didn't really meet; I'm Mrs. Toothe. Hello,
Cynthia; Louise, my dear.
(They nod)

RICHARD
(Not getting it yet)
Well, then, you all know each other, and . . .

MRS. TOOTHE
Where were you on Thursday, Beryl dear?

BERYL
I had, I had a headache, and . . .

MRS. TOOTHE
Well, that will cost you a hundred dollars. Someone was
disappointed.

RICHARD
(Not quite dawn yet)
You, you all know each other?

MRS. TOOTHE
Well, yes, I know all these ladies, and I've met their husbands, but I've known them, well, how shall I say . . . I
don't think we've all known before that we all know each
other.

JENNY
(Lame and unhappy)
This is . . . Mrs. Toothe, darling.

GILBERT
(Rather pleased)
Perry, you never told me.

LOUISE

Cynthia, dear, I'm surprised we haven't run into each other in town.

RICHARD
(Piecing it together)

Look, now, does this mean . . .

PERRY
(He, too, rather pleased)

Well, my God.

MRS. TOOTHE
(To RICHARD*)*

And isn't it charming that all my suburban ladies should be under one roof.

RICHARD

All your ladies, and . . . *(To the women) All of you? (To the men)* And *you've* known about it?

GILBERT
(Not quite pleasant)

Well, of course.

PERRY
(Slightly condescending)

Yes; naturally.

BERYL

But how absolutely marvelous none of us has known about the other.

CYNTHIA
(To LOUISE*: mock chiding)*

You and your shopping trips.

LOUISE
(Giggles a little; to BERYL*)*
And all that museum-going.

MRS. TOOTHE
(Businesslike)
Well. Here we all are.

RICHARD
(Backing off a little; quietly, as if facing a wall of strange shapes)
I don't believe it, I . . . I don't believe it, I . . .

JENNY
(Quietly pleading)
. . . Richard . . .

CHUCK
(Shakes his head, chuckles)
Oh, boy! Oh, Jesus Christ! *(Full laughter)*

RICHARD
(To PERRY*)*
You've . . . you've known? All the time?

GILBERT
(Slightly patronizing)
What did you do, just find out?

RICHARD
(Tiny pause, a real scream)
YES!!!!

(Pause)

CHUCK
(Calm, fairly stern)
Get yourself a drink, boy. Quiet down.
*(*CHUCK *pats* RICHARD *on the shoulder, makes for the bar)*

RICHARD
(Softer; great loss in it now)

Yes!

GILBERT
(Matter-of-fact)
Well, now you know; and now we all know.
(ROGER enters)

ROGER
Hi! You know, Venus is up already? The sun isn't even down
yet, and . . .

JENNY
Roger; go get something.

ROGER
M-m'am?

JENNY
Richard? *Do* something?

PERRY
(Digs into his pocket)
Roger, be a good fellow and run over to the club and get me
some pipe tobacco, will you?

ROGER
(Senses the silence)
Well . . . sure.

PERRY
And get yourself a Coke, or something.

JENNY
That's a good boy.

ROGER
(Puzzled, slightly reluctant)

O.K. . . . what, what kind?

PERRY

What?

ROGER

What kind of *pipe* tobacco?

PERRY

Ben at the desk; Ben knows; tell him it's for me.

ROGER
(Suspicion, confusion over, bounds out)

O.K. Be back!

RICHARD

Please, all of you, get out.

MRS. TOOTHE

As I said, I'm sorry I've had to come, but there's been trouble.

BERYL

What kind of trouble?

MRS. TOOTHE

So that I daren't use the phone; daren't call you.

PERRY

Police?

MRS. TOOTHE

Yes.

JENNY
(Quiet panic)

Oh, my God.

MRS. TOOTHE

A man named Lurie; detective, I think.

CHUCK

Can't you buy him off?

MRS. TOOTHE

Won't be had.

GILBERT

That's damned odd.

MRS. TOOTHE

Yes; well; nonetheless, he won't.
(RICHARD *watches all of this from a distance; maybe sits*)

PERRY

Asking questions?

MRS. TOOTHE

No . . . telling me to clear out.

LOUISE

He didn't ask for *names*.

MRS. TOOTHE

It wasn't a *raid*. Besides, he wouldn't get them.

BERYL
(*Sighs with relief*)

Well.

GILBERT

Yes; there is *that*.

MRS. TOOTHE
(Brightly)
I don't believe I've been asked what I would like to drink.
(Pause) Have I?

JENNY
(Quite preoccupied, mostly with what RICHARD *is
thinking)*
Oh, no; I don't guess you have.

MRS. TOOTHE
(To RICHARD)
Unless you have an objection to my . . . wetting my lips
in your house.

RICHARD
(Almost a monotone; a stunned quality)
No, you go right ahead; have what you like; there's cham-
pagne, and . . .

MRS. TOOTHE
(A little laugh)
Oh, heavens, no, I don't think so. *(To* CHUCK, *who is still near
the bar)* Is there whiskey?

CHUCK
Sure. Neat?

MRS. TOOTHE
Very, and one cube.

CHUCK
No sooner said. *(To* RICHARD; *an afterthought)* O.K. if I . . .
do the honors?

RICHARD
(As above)
No, you go right ahead.

CYNTHIA

I think I'd like one, too. Perry?

PERRY

Right.
(Some general movement to refill, hand drinks, etc.)

GILBERT
(To MRS. TOOTHE; *asking more than just his question)*
I . . . I suppose you'll have to . . . move out.

MRS. TOOTHE

I'm gone! I've left already. There'll be a psychiatrist moving in.

BERYL
(Giggles)
That'll be a surprise for the regulars.

CYNTHIA
(Laughing, too)
Oh, Beryl! Really!

PERRY
(Stretching, breathing out)
Well, I guess you'd better hold off on that greenhouse, Dick.

CYNTHIA

Yes, and put away the caviar.

LOUISE

What a shame. *(Afterthought)* What a shame for all of us!

RICHARD
(Barely registering)
Hm?

GILBERT
(Fairly sententious)
Yes . . . things are going to be a little harder for *all* of us.

MRS. TOOTHE
(Sipping her drink)
Why? *(Good spirits)* This sort of thing happens. It's never
the end.

BERYL
It's rather different for you: you're used to it.

MRS. TOOTHE
(Speculative)
Ohhhh, one can get used to anything . . . I should say. *(To*
RICHARD*)* Wouldn't you say?

RICHARD
Oh, God.

LOUISE
Yes, but one can't get used to the idea of jail, not to mention the newspapers and . . .

CHUCK
Cops are on to you.

PERRY
Where will you go?

MRS. TOOTHE
(Tiniest pause)
Why not . . . out here?

SEVERAL
(Tones of shock, disbelief)
Out here!

MRS. TOOTHE

Why not?

LOUISE
(Quite grand)
Surely you're not serious.

MRS. TOOTHE
V*ery* good train service; respectable . . . countryside . . .

CHUCK
(Not sure)
Yes, there's very good train service, but . . .

MRS. TOOTHE
If one could find some suitable property. *(Looks at* PERRY*)* Do
you think?

PERRY
No, no, this wouldn't do at all . . .

GILBERT
Absolutely not.

MRS. TOOTHE
(Makes as if to get up and go; very businesslike)
Well, then; I shall just have to find a more congenial city;
somewhere where the police are fast asleep or . . . amenable.
I shall miss you ladies, though.

BERYL
(Tentative)
Of course . . . *(Stops)*

PERRY, CYNTHIA, GILBERT
(More or less simultaneously)
Yes?

BERYL
(A little embarrassed, and pleased by the attention)
Well, I was going to say . . . it . . . it couldn't be right
here: I mean right *here*: it could be . . . nearby.

JENNY
(She hasn't spoken for quite a while)
Well, *yes*; it would be . . . *(Leaves it unfinished)*

RICHARD
(As if hearing through fog)
What did you say, Jenny?

BERYL
*(Naked and embarrassed, but if you're in a nudist
colony . . .)*
I was going to say . . .

RICHARD
Yes. Go on.

JENNY
(If JENNY can physically blush, yet be resolute, fine)
I was going to say that if it could be out here then . . .
then it would be handy.

RICHARD
What was that last word?

JENNY
(Tiniest pause)
Handy . . . it would he handy.

RICHARD
(Nods, chuckles)
Um-hum. Oh, yes. *(Chuckles some more)* Oh, God, yes.
(A few defeated tears in the words) Especially with Roger

home: you could make it back and do the jelly sandwiches
—now that he's not going to camp, 'cause we want him here,
not 'cause we can't afford it.

MRS. TOOTHE

I think we'd best keep this to a business discussion. Don't
you think?

PERRY

Yes; I think.

CHUCK

Good idea.

MRS. TOOTHE

Something to be talked about amongst us men. Jenny, why
don't you go out and show the girls your roses?

JENNY
(Occupied with observing RICHARD*)*

Hm?

MRS. TOOTHE

Show the girls your roses.

BERYL
(Leading the way)

Yes, why don't we see the garden again? There's so much
there; so very much to see.

CYNTHIA

Yes; coming, Louise?

LOUISE
(Gravely approving the proposition)

Of course.

MRS. TOOTHE
Jenny?

JENNY
(Loath to leave RICHARD, *but going)*
Well, all right . . . I . . . all right. *(Exits)*
(The men are left now, with MRS. TOOTHE*)*

RICHARD
(From where he sits; little emotion)
You're a little high-handed, aren't you?

MRS. TOOTHE
(Cheerfully soothing)
It's so much easier without them.

RICHARD
This *is* my house.

GILBERT
Oh, come off it, Richard.

CHUCK
We're lucky we're not all in jail.

MRS. TOOTHE
No, it won't come to that. Who will give me another drink?

PERRY
(Takes her glass)
Whiskey and ice?

MRS. TOOTHE
Yes. *Thank* you. *One* cube.

GILBERT
(To CHUCK*)*
How much do you stand to lose?

CHUCK
(Rueful laugh)
Too *much*; damn *far* too much.

GILBERT
(Mulling)
Yeeesss. Tax-free? Be able to retire early if you wanted to? If it kept up? Louise and I talked it over.

RICHARD
(Coming in, now; a neophyte)
You did? You talked it over? Just . . . talked it over?

GILBERT
Of course. Oh, I know how you *feel*; I felt that way . . . for a little.

CHUCK
Wanted to break the *place* up.

PERRY
(Returning with MRS. TOOTHE's *drink)*
I *did* break the place up. Gave us an excuse to redecorate.

CHUCK
(Settling)
Funny how quickly you get used to the idea.

PERRY
Yes.

CHUCK
And, there *is* the money.

GILBERT
It's going to be a little tough to manage without it . . . *now.*

PERRY

I can't take Martin away from his school at *this* stage . . .

GILBERT

Same with Jeremy; and there's Jennifer's pony. I'm paying
through the nose to keep it at that damn stable, but I can't
sell it . . . she'd *kill* me.

CHUCK
(Fairly grim)

Anybody want to buy a nearly paid-for Aston-Martin?

PERRY

That's the trouble: we're all involved in things. We can't
. . . just stop.

GILBERT

And just between us, I don't mind admitting Louise and I
get along together much better these days.

PERRY

So do Cyn and I. Most of our arguments were over money.

CHUCK

Yes.

MRS. TOOTHE
(To RICHARD)

Do you begin to understand better now?

RICHARD
(Still rather numb)

Oh yes; I understand.

MRS. TOOTHE
(Hears the women talking in the garden)

Listen to them. The girls chattering away.

PERRY
(Smiles)

Yes.

MRS. TOOTHE

Shall we talk business?

GILBERT

Right! Richard? Will you be chairman?

RICHARD
(A haze)

Will I what?

GILBERT

Be chairman. We want a proper business meeting.

CHUCK
(Moving in)

Here you are. Besides, it's your chair.

GILBERT

Who will propose him?

CHUCK

I.

PERRY

Seconded.

GILBERT

Carried.

CHUCK

Call the meeting to order, Richard.

RICHARD
(Brief hesitation, then)

Meeting come to order. *(Pause)* Well?

PERRY

Mr. Chairman, there *is* a property in our office that might
suit Mrs. Toothe's needs, and ours, very well indeed.

GILBERT

Not *here.*

PERRY

No; two stops up. Big house, pretty cheap, too: it's only a
couple of minutes' walk from the station.

MRS. TOOTHE

Sounds very good. How many rooms?

RICHARD

How many bedrooms, you mean, don't you?

MRS. TOOTHE

Will you be quiet! *(Back to normal tone)* If the price is reasonable . . .

PERRY

Thirty-six.

MRS. TOOTHE

Twenty-eight. Yes, that will be all right. I shall look at it
tomorrow. I don't want there to be too much of a gap in
. . . *(Smiles)* our services.
                    (RICHARD *snorts*)
Look here: I've spent time, and money, and energy building
up this enterprise, with a first-class clientele and . . .

RICHARD
(Mumbled)
All right, all right, all right . . .

MRS. TOOTHE

Well, are there any questions?

CHUCK
(*Satisfied*)

Fine.

GILBERT

Seems good.

MRS. TOOTHE
(*To* RICHARD; *none too pleasant*)

You?

RICHARD
(*Again, an attempt at sarcasm*)

Oh, a couple.

MRS. TOOTHE
(*Impatient, but not hurried*)

Well, let us have them.

CHUCK
(*Chiding*)

Oh, Dick . . .

RICHARD

Doesn't it seem to bother any of you . . . Christ, everybody's
going to know! Inside of two weeks it'll be all over the . . .
doesn't that *disturb* any of you?

MRS. TOOTHE

We don't advertise in the local paper.

RICHARD

There's a thing called word-of-mouth.

MRS. TOOTHE

Your wives will know if there is any danger. Believe me . . .
I know what I'm doing.

RICHARD

There's such a thing as messing on your own doorstep, isn't
there?

GILBERT

That's a pretty rotten thing to say.

RICHARD

True.

GILBERT

Any other business?

CHUCK
(Guesses)

No . . .

PERRY

No . . .

RICHARD
(Heavy sarcasm)

Well, in that case, I declare the meeting closed.

MRS. TOOTHE

There is one other thing . . .

GILBERT

Mm?

PERRY

What is *that*?

MRS. TOOTHE

It's important that you carry on normally. You shouldn't talk
about all this any more. I mean, even among yourselves.

GILBERT

We should forget it, you mean.

PERRY

Yes. We should forget it.

CHUCK

Quite right.

RICHARD
(A *little quivering laugh*—*rage in this*)
I don't quite see how we can . . . just forget it.

MRS. TOOTHE
(*Wise counsel*)
Oh, yes you can. One can forget. If something isn't good to
live with, or convenient, one can forget. After all, there are
things you *have* to forget if you want to live at all.

RICHARD

Yes, but . . .

MRS. TOOTHE

But you all know this. You're men of family and education.
You're not fools.

CHUCK

No; of course we're not.

PERRY

Quite right.

MRS. TOOTHE
(*Rises, moves toward garden*)
I think I'll go collect my ladies. (*Stops; to* RICHARD) One
other thing for you to remember—one thing which might
help you forget; two things: we do nobody any harm . . .

RICHARD

And the other?

MRS. TOOTHE

There's very little chance your wife will ever take a lover behind your back. *(She exits)*

GILBERT
(After a small pause)

Well, then; it's all set.

CHUCK
(Going to the bar)

Shall we drink on it?

PERRY
(Raises his glass)

Yes; here's to us.

GILBERT

To us. *(Notices* RICHARD *is just looking at his glass)* Richard? To us? To all of us?

RICHARD
(Pause, self-deprecating little laugh; raises glass)

Sure; to us.

GILBERT
(Older brother)

You'll be all *right*, old man; you will be.

CHUCK AND PERRY
(Softly)

Cheers.

RICHARD
(Little boy; something lost)

Cheers.

(The ladies start coming back in)

BERYL

I find it quite hopeless to try to grow azaleas here, and I don't
know why.

JENNY

It's the lime in the soil, I think, but you can take care of that.

BERYL

Ah, well; your thumb.

MRS. TOOTHE

Who will tend my garden? Are there local people?

CHUCK

Yes, good ones . . . but expensive.

MRS. TOOTHE

Ah, well, there will be enough . . . if everything works out.
Jenny, dear, may I use your telephone?

JENNY

Of course; let me show you.
             (JENNY *and* MRS. TOOTHE *exit*)

BERYL

Well, let us ladies all have another drink, and then we must
go. It's all arranged, I understand.

CHUCK
(Moving to the bar)
I'll do the honors. Yes; all fixed.

PERRY

Perfect set-up.

LOUISE

Fine.

CYNTHIA

I couldn't be happier.

BERYL

Richard, no one is drinking your champagne, what a shame;
but I *will* have some of your caviar, crackers and all.

RICHARD
(Sarcasm intended)

The champagne will keep; perhaps we can use it to christen
Mrs. Toothe's new house.
(General laughter as response; sarcasm not seen)

CYNTHIA
(Giggling)

Oh, Richard; really!

(JENNY returns)

JENNY

What did I miss?

LOUISE
(Her laughter dying)
Oh, nothing; Richard said something funny.

JENNY
(Relieved)
Oh. How very nice.
*(ROGER and JACK appear in the doorway to the
garden; JACK is quite drunk, but, even so, he is exag-
gerating it)*

JACK

Hullo! Hullo! The gate-crasher is here; say hullo to the gate-
crasher. Say hullo to the gate-crasher. Say hullo!
*(They all turn, look at JACK; complete silence from
them)*

ROGER
(*Giving tobacco to* PERRY)
Here's your tobacco; I hope it's right.

JACK
Young Roger found me by the club; well, *at* it, actually; *at*
the club, and *at* the bar.

BERYL
(*Cool*)
That's rather evident.

JACK
Ooohhh, *honestly,* Beryl! (*Generally again*) Annnddd so,
I said to old Roger, how's the party, an' he told me, but I
thought I'd come anyway. And here I am, and all my old
friends, and isn't it wonderful.

JENNY
(*Uncomfortable*)
I . . . I thought you had a game, or something.

JACK
Backgammon with old Digby . . . well, old Digby died; yes
he did. Farnum was kneading away at him on the old mas-
sage table, finished up, slapped him gently on the ass and
said, "All done, Mr. Digby, sir," and he just lay there. Died
horizontal on a metal board, which is as splendid a way as
any. Got the good vod out, Richard? Got it hidden?

PERRY
(*As* JACK *makes for the bar*)
Go easy on the vodka, Jack.

JACK
(*A dare*)
Your house? Your vodka?

PERRY

No; but, still . . .

JACK

Tell you what I'll do, Perr, old thing: next time you give a
garden-type party, and I come unasked—which is the only
way I'll make it, if old Cyn has anything to say about it, eh,
kid?—*then* . . . I will go easy on the vod. O.K.?

LOUISE

Do you, uh . . . do you bring any *other* charming news
from the club with you, dear Jack?

JACK

Anything other than poor old Digby? Weeellll . . . Oh!
Yeah! They got rid of Harry Burns.

GILBERT

Got rid of him? How?

JACK

Dug back—someone did; found out it was short for Bernstein; asked him to go.

CHUCK
(Disbelief, but not offended)

Oh, come *on*.

JACK

True; true.

LOUISE
(*To* BERYL)

Is Monica Burns *Jewish?*

BERYL

Well; I *suppose*.

LOUISE
(Some wonder)

I never would have *thought*.

CYNTHIA

She never let *on*.

LOUISE

Can you *imagine*.

JACK

For God's sake, you'd think she was a common prostitute, or something.
(Small silence)

BERYL
(Cold)

A what?

JACK
(Wagging his head)

A prostitootsie.
(Another small silence)

CYNTHIA

I can't say that Harry and Monica look . . .

LOUISE

No, no, they don't . . .

BERYL

Funny how you can sort of know, though . . .

JACK

After the fact, you mean.

PERRY
(Wincing a little)

Threw him out of the club?

ROGER

Some people say we're *all* Jews.

JENNY
(Not offended; startled)

What?

ROGER

The ten lost tribes.

GILBERT

Some people will say anything.

ROGER

And quite a lot of us are circumcised.
(Silence, save JACK, *who laughs softly)*

RICHARD
(Short, cold)

Go to your room.

ROGER

What?

RICHARD

Go to your room!

ROGER

Why!?

JENNY

He didn't mean to say anything.

ROGER

What did I say?

RICHARD

I told you to go to your room!

ROGER
(Standing his ground)
I want to know what I said wrong!

RICHARD
(Feeling foolish; this, though, merely pushes him further)
Don't you stand there and defy *me!!*

ROGER
It's not fair! You say much worse things!

RICHARD
I am your father and I tell you to go to your room. You're not fit to associate with decent people.

JACK
(Laughing, but serious)
Oh, come on, Richard!

RICHARD
(To JACK)
SHUT YOUR MOUTH! This is my house and my son! I tell him what to do! *(To ROGER) Go on!*

ROGER
(Supplication to the rest of the group)
But it comes up all the time in the Bible.

RICHARD
So do the Ten Commandments. Do you know the Ten Commandments?

ROGER
Yes.

RICHARD
Say them.

ROGER

Now?

JENNY

Darling . . .

RICHARD
(Wheeling on her)
Leave me something! (To ROGER) Now!

ROGER

Thou shalt not kill.

RICHARD

That's one. Go on.

ROGER
(Looks to JENNY for help, but there is none there)
Thou shalt not . . . (Falters)

RICHARD
(To them all)
There; and a liar as well. Go up to your room.
(ROGER pauses, gives up, turns, begins going, shaking
his head)

JACK

The poor bastard didn't say anything.

RICHARD
(Following ROGER)
Are you going to go to your room, or am I going to have to
take you UP there?

JENNY
(To RICHARD)
Darling, let him . . . let him go out, or something. Let him

go to the club. Just . . . (*Between her teeth*) . . . get him *out* of here.

RICHARD
(*Sighs*)

Oh . . . all right. (*Exiting, calling after* ROGER) Roger? Roger?

BERYL

They do need discipline.

GILBERT

A few licks with a belt from his father never did a boy any harm.

PERRY

Mine kept a riding crop.

GILBERT

And you never resented it, did you?

PERRY
(*Can't recall*)

I . . . I guess not.

JACK

How savage you all are today. Savage . . . and strange. All embarrassed, and snapping. Have I caught you at something?

BERYL

What do you mean!

JACK
(*To audience*)

Is there something going on here?

CHUCK

Have another drink, Jack.

JENNY

Yes! Let's everybody! Perry?
             (General agreement and movement)

JACK

(Grabbing JENNY *by the arm as she moves by him)*
Jenny, my darling! Why do you all hate me? Why are you
all trying to get me drunk?

JENNY
(Artificial little laugh)

Jack!

JACK

What's going on, Jenny?

JENNY
(Transparently lying)
Nothing, Jack. Nothing at all.

JACK

Do you still love me, Jenny?

JENNY
(Soothing the little boy)
Yes, Jack; of course.
             *(*RICHARD *re-enters)*

JACK

Ah! Thank God! *(Rises)* Kiss and make up. *(He kisses her)*

RICHARD

I sent him out for a . . . What do you think you're doing!

JACK

I am kissing your beautiful wife.

RICHARD

Then stop it!

JACK

I *have* stopped.

RICHARD

I don't care for that sort of behavior.

JACK

Oh, come on, Richard. It might have been anyone. Hasn't Jenny been kissed before?

RICHARD

You are not to kiss her!!

JACK

What is the *matter* with all of you this evening?

BERYL

There is *nothing* the matter with us.

JACK

There is something . . . very wrong.
(MRS. TOOTHE *re-enters*)

MRS. TOOTHE

Well, my dear children, my flock, I have made the necessary calls, and I think we . . . *(Sees* JACK*)* Ah. *(Her eyes move from one person to another quickly)* I, uh . . . I do believe we've met before.

JENNY
(Jumping in)

Jack, you *do* remember Mrs. Toothe; you met her . . . oh, six-seven months ago, and . . .

JACK
(Staring at MRS. TOOTHE*)*
Yes; your fairy godmother.

MRS. TOOTHE
(To JACK; *very naturally)*
How nice to see you again.

JACK
How nice to see you. *(Turns away, thinking)*

MRS. TOOTHE
(To the others)
I *do* think I should be off now. It was so nice meeting you
all . . .

JACK
(Suddenly remembering)
Yes! *(Turns around, a smile of fascination)* You're English,
aren't you?

MRS. TOOTHE
(Playing it cool and natural)
British, yes.

JACK
And you lived in London . . . some, some time ago.

MRS. TOOTHE
(Hedging)
Yes, I . . . well, I *have* lived in London, but . . .

JACK
(Very pleased)
I *do* remember you, dear lady. By God, if I were *sober,* I
doubt I would. *(Laughs greatly)* Oh yes! Do I remember you!

MRS. TOOTHE
(Playing it through)
You must be mistaken. I never forget faces, and . . .

JACK
Oh, lady; I remember you well, I remember your . . . *(Another fit of laughing)* . . . your ladies, I . . . *(Looks about the room, sees the trapped and embarrassed faces, breaks into more laughter)* Oh no! No! Tell me it's not true! It is! It is true! *(More laughter)*

BERYL
I don't know what you're thinking, Jack, but I suspect that you may have had a little too much to drink, and . . .

JACK
Has Madam found herself another group of ladies? *(Laughter as he talks)* Are we operating in the suburbs now? *(Mock commiseration, laughter)* Oh, my poor Beryl! Dear Cynthia! Proud Louise! *(Sees JENNY; his tone now is a cross to disappointment and wonder at the future possibilities)* And oh my darling Jenny!

RICHARD
Stay away from her.

JACK
And all that . . . and all that money lying on the . . . *(Breaks into more laughter)* . . . "Someone sent it to us in the mail?" *(Laughter)* Gentlemen . . . I don't know who arranged all this; but if you guys did, you're better businessmen than I ever thought you were. *(Laughs, starts for french doors)*

MRS. TOOTHE
(Eyes narrowing)
Stop him.

PERRY

Where do you think you're going?

JACK
(Still laughing)

Hm?

PERRY

I said where do you think you're going?

JACK

Why, I thought I'd go back to the cl— (Breaks down in laughter again)

MRS. TOOTHE

He'll talk. (This was a command)

JENNY

Yes. He will.

MRS. TOOTHE
(Even more clear than before)

He'll talk.

(PERRY grabs JACK by the arm; CHUCK steps in front of him, barring his way)

PERRY

Hold on, old friend.

CHUCK

Easy now.

JACK
(Panic and anger rising)

Let . . . Let me go. God damn it, let me . . .
(He begins to struggle; RICHARD and GILBERT come to the aid of PERRY and CHUCK)

GILBERT

Get him!
> (*They are on him, just restraining at first, but the more* JACK *struggles, the more they are on him*)

JACK

Let me . . . Get your hands off me . . . Let! Me! God damn it! Let! Me!
> (*They have him down, are on top of him*)

PERRY

Hold him! Hold him down!

JACK
> (*Really shouting*)

STOP IT! STOP IT!

MRS. TOOTHE
> (*On her feet, but not in a rush; a commander*)

He's drunk; he'll talk. You must make him be quiet.
> (JACK *continues to struggle, bites* CHUCK's *hand*)

CHUCK
> (*In rage and reflex, strikes* JACK *across the face with the back of his hand*)

God damn you!

JACK

STOP! IT!

MRS. TOOTHE

Keep him quiet!
> (RICHARD *grabs a pillow from the sofa and, together, two or three of them press it over* JACK's *face. His shouts become muffled as they hold the pillow on his face, stiff-armed. Finally there is silence. The men relax a little, slowly get off their knees, unwind*)

some, look at JACK's *prone, still form; they move*
about a little)

GILBERT

He's out.

RICHARD
(Grim laugh)

For a while.

MRS. TOOTHE
(Goes over, bends over JACK, *examines him for a*
moment, straightens up)
No. Not for a while. *(Begins to walk back to her chair)*

JENNY
(Pitiful; moves toward JACK*)*

Jack?

MRS. TOOTHE
(Cruelly casual, but serious)
Don't bother. He's dead.

GILBERT
(Offended)
What do you mean he's dead!

MRS. TOOTHE
Look for your*self*. He's *dead*.

GILBERT
(Looks for himself)
Yes. He is. He's dead.
*(*JENNY *and* CYNTHIA *begin to weep, quietly;* LOUISE
turns away; the men look at one another)

BERYL
(Final; catatonic)

Well.

CHUCK

I, I don't think we did that, he . . . We didn't do that.

GILBERT

No, we were just . . .

PERRY

He must have had a heart attack.

JENNY
(Going to him)

Oh, my poor, darling Jack . . .

RICHARD

Stay away from him, Jenny.

CHUCK

What . . . what shall we do?

LOUISE
(Ordering it)

He *can't* be dead; it doesn't happen.

CYNTHIA

He would have talked! It would have been all over town.

JENNY
(Defending JACK*)*

Who says!?

BERYL

You said, for one.

JENNY
(Furious, and near tears)

I did not! I said . . .

MRS. TOOTHE
(Calm)

You said he would talk. You agreed he would.

GILBERT

No one meant to kill him . . .

PERRY

No, it was . . .

RICHARD
(Grim)

I think I'd better call the police, hunh?

CHUCK
(Nodding)

Yeah, yeah.

GILBERT

Yes; you'd better.

MRS. TOOTHE
(Calm, forceful)

Do you think so?

RICHARD
(Sort of disgusted)

What?

MRS. TOOTHE

Do you think you had better call the police?

RICHARD

There's a *dead* man there!

MRS. TOOTHE

I know; I can see. But what will you tell them? The police.

RICHARD

I'll, I'll tell them . . . we were having a party, and, and Jack
came in, and he was drunk, and . . .

MRS. TOOTHE

And so you all smothered him?

RICHARD
(Furious)

No! That he was drunk!

BERYL

. . . he kept on drinking . . .

GILBERT

. . . and he had a heart attack.
(Pause, they look to MRS. TOOTHE*)*

CHUCK

No?

MRS. TOOTHE

You may call the police, if you want to. *Do* let me leave first,
though. I wouldn't want to be listed among those present
when the autopsy is done and they find the marks on him
and the hemorrhage in the lungs. That happens when people
are killed that way, you know; the lungs rupture.
(Silence)

GILBERT

Oh.
(Silence)

PERRY

I see.
(Silence)

BERYL

Well. We can't take *that* chance, can we.
(*Silence.* JENNY *weeps quietly*)

LOUISE
(*Slowly*)

No. We can't.

RICHARD
(*Quietly loathing*)

What do you suggest we do, then?
(*They all look to* MRS. TOOTHE, *save* JENNY)

MRS. TOOTHE
(*To* RICHARD)

I know you think I'm a monster, so . . . if I ask you a question, it won't matter much.

RICHARD
(*Waiting*)

Yes?

MRS. TOOTHE

What . . . what is the purpose of that deep trench you've dug near your brick wall?
(*Silence*)

RICHARD
(*Calm response; much underneath*)

I've been looking for the cesspool line.

MRS. TOOTHE

Have you found it?

RICHARD
(*Still staring at her*)

No.

MRS. TOOTHE
(After a pause)
Well, then. Bury him.
*(Silence. The guests look at each other, calmly,
speculatively)*

RICHARD
(Slowly)
You can't mean that.

MRS. TOOTHE
(To all the men)
Go on; bury him.

RICHARD
(Smiling a little)
No.

MRS. TOOTHE
All right, then. Call the police.
*(Silence; the men look at one another, slowly, stead-
ily. Then, as if it had all been organized, they slowly
move to work. They go to* JACK, *take him by the
legs, arms, under the head, and take him out into
the garden, disappear from our sight)*

JENNY
(After they have gone; rises, starts after them)
Jack! Richard!

MRS. TOOTHE
Jenny! Come here!
*(*BERYL *and* LOUISE *go to* JENNY, *who is helplessly,
quietly crying now, and gently bring her back to the
group. They all sit)*

JENNY
You . . . they just can't . . . do that.

MRS. TOOTHE

Hush, my dear. Hush.
(This is a wake and the ladies have sorrow on their faces)

LOUISE
(Sincere; helpless)

Poor Jack.

BERYL

Yes; poor Jack.

LOUISE

At least it wasn't . . . one of us. I mean, someone, well . . .
with a family, someone . . . regular.
(JENNY is quietly hysterical)

MRS. TOOTHE

You haven't put up with death, have you, Jenny?
(JENNY shakes her head)
I'm sorry to say you get used to it!

JENNY

N-never!

MRS. TOOTHE

You should have been in London in the war. You would have
learned about death . . . and violence . . . All those nights
in the shelters, with the death going on. Death and dying.
Always take the former if you can.

LOUISE
(Nodding at the sad truth)

Yes.

MRS. TOOTHE

You must help your husbands. You'll have to, I think . . .
for a while. They may wake up at night; sweat; they may . . .
lose heart. You'll have to be the strong ones . . . as usual.

BERYL
Yes.

MRS. TOOTHE
I wouldn't try to make them go on as if nothing has happened. For something *has* happened . . . very much so. One of the things that *does* happen . . . one of the accommodations that have to be made. Do you see, Jenny?

JENNY
I don't know.

MRS. TOOTHE
(Sweet; gentle)
You can't go *back*. You have to make do with what is. And what is leads to what will be. You make the best as you go on. Like our looks, when we age, as we are doing, or will. Some of us have our faces lifted, I suppose, and we convince . . . some people—not as many as we'd like to—but we don't believe it ourselves, do we, Jenny?

JENNY
(A little girl at lessons)
I shouldn't think so. No.

MRS. TOOTHE
No. We do what will help, which is all we can.

JENNY
(Instructed)
Yes.
> *(The men come back in, subdued, clothes a little awry, hands dirty)*

GILBERT
All done.

PERRY

Finished.

CHUCK

You'd never know.

RICHARD

. . . unless you had a mind.

CHUCK

Unless you knew.

RICHARD

Yes.
(*Goes to* JENNY; *in fact, all the men gravitate to their wives*)

CYNTHIA
(*Kindly*)

Would any of you like a drink? Darling?

PERRY

No; no thanks.

LOUISE

Darling?

GILBERT

Yes. A quick one.

RICHARD
(*To* JENNY; *comforting*)

You O.K.?

JENNY
(*Brave smile*)

Sure. You?

RICHARD
(Empty)

Considering.

MRS. TOOTHE

Well; you've all done very well. I think it's time I should be getting on.

BERYL

Yes; well, we all should.

GILBERT

Yes. What time are Don and Betty coming over?

LOUISE

Oh, my God! Eight o'clock. You're right, we've got . . .

CHUCK

Your husband is hungry.

BERYL

Well, all right then, I'll feed you.

MRS. TOOTHE
(To PERRY*)*

I'll call you tomorrow and come to see the house?

PERRY

Yes; fine.

RICHARD

You're all just . . . leaving?

CHUCK
(What else?)

Yes; I think we should.

PERRY

There's nothing we can do, is there?

RICHARD
(Quiet, intense)

There's a body out there; Jack.

GILBERT

It's all *right*, Richard.

PERRY

Really, Richard; it's O.K.

BERYL

Yes, it *is*.

MRS. TOOTHE

Go home, children, it's all right.

CHUCK

Yes, well, I don't know what more we can do.

LOUISE

Yes, we do have Don and Betty coming over.

CYNTHIA

Do you mean Don and Betty Grainger?

LOUISE

Yes.

PERRY

I still can't get over Harry Burns.

GILBERT

Harry Bernstein, you mean.
(The guests have gone)

MRS. TOOTHE
(*To* JENNY *and* RICHARD)

The grass will grow over; the earth will be rich, and soon—
eventually—everything in the garden . . . will be as it was.
You'll see.

(MRS. TOOTHE *exits, followed by* RICHARD *and* JENNY
*seeing her out almost by reflex. Bare stage for a mo-
ment*)

(JACK *comes in from the garden, his clothes dirty,
sod in his hair*)

JACK
(*He will speak only to the audience from now on,
even when* RICHARD *and* JENNY *return; nor will they
notice him, of course*)

Oh, don't get any ideas, now. I'm dead, believe me. I'm
dead. It's amazing how dying sobers you up. Well, I certainly never thought it would be *this* way—like this; I'd
imagined sliding gently from the bar stool at the club, or
crashing into a truck on a curve some night, but never this.
Shows you can't tell. God! Would you believe it? Mrs.
Toothe, and Beryl and Cynthia and Louise? And poor Jenny?
I wouldn't have; but, then, I'm rather selfish—self-concerned.
Was. I must get *used* to that; past tense. Poor Jenny and
Richard. They're the only ones I feel badly about—the guilt,
and all the rest. That old Madam can take care of herself,
and the others . . . who cares? But Jenny and Richard . . .
that's a different matter. I *worry* for them.

(JENNY *and* RICHARD *re-enter, move about slowly.*
JACK *puts a finger to his lips, to shush the audience,
whether necessary or not*)

JENNY
(*Timid*)

Well.

RICHARD
(*Emptied*)

Yes.

JENNY
(Trying to be conversational)
Where did you send Roger?

RICHARD
To the club. To swim.

JENNY
(Genuine)
That was nice of you.

RICHARD
Stupid taking it out on him.

JENNY
Yes. *(Pause)* I think we'd better clean up—all the glasses
and everything.

RICHARD
All right.

JACK
(Watches them for a moment; back to the audi-
ence)
Here's the *awful* irony of it.

JENNY
(Remembering)
We're to say . . . nothing.

RICHARD
What will happen? He'll have just . . . disappeared?

JENNY
Yes; I guess so.

RICHARD
Roger *brought* him here.

JENNY

Yes, but we'll say Jack just stayed for a little, and then went
on.

RICHARD

They'll ask?

JENNY

Someone will; someone's bound to—insurance people, some·
body.

RICHARD

We must make a story.

JENNY

Yes. I'll talk to the others.

RICHARD

All right.

JENNY
(So sincere; explaining so much)

Darling . . . I do *love* you.

RICHARD
(Timid)

Yes; and I love you.

JACK

The irony; I was going to tell you the irony. Remember I
said I'd made my will over, left it all to Richard and Jenny?
Well, it was true; I wasn't kidding. Three and a half million;
every penny, and my house here, *and* in Nassau. It's all theirs.

JENNY

Let's put the glasses on the tray here.

JACK

Problem now is, they'll have to wait. If I've just . . . van-
ished . . . disappeared from the face of the earth, it'll be
seven years until I can be declared officially dead. And
there'll *be* an investigation; you can be sure of that. I hope
they make it stick—the story they tell. I imagine they will.

RICHARD

What shall I do with the caviar?

JENNY

Give it here; I'll cover it and put it in the fridge.

JACK

But seven years; that's a very long time. So much can happen. With all they're doing, in seven years their lives can be
ruined. They have so much to live with. (*To* RICHARD *and*
JENNY) You've got to be strong! You've got to hold on!

JENNY

Darling?

RICHARD

Mmm?

JENNY

I was thinking . . . that house Mrs. Toothe is taking.

RICHARD

What about it?

JENNY

I think it ought to be planted nicely, flowers and shrubs and
all. Make it look like it's really lived in. It mustn't look like
it's been let go. It might draw suspicion. You notice things
like that.

RICHARD

Yes; you do.

JENNY

Gardens that have been let go. If people let them go, you know there's something wrong in the house.

RICHARD

Yes.

JENNY

I think it should be well planted and taken care of; kept up. I think it should look like all the others. Don't you think so?

RICHARD
(Straight)

Yes; I think you're right.

JACK

Well . . . I think they'll make it.

CURTAIN

MALCOLM

ADAPTED BY

EDWARD ALBEE

FROM THE NOVEL BY

JAMES PURDY

FOR JAMES PURDY

WITH EVER-GROWING ADMIRATION

January 11, 1966, New York City, Shubert Theatre

MALCOLM	MATTHEW COWLES
COX	HENDERSON FORSYTHE
LAUREEN	ESTELLE PARSONS
KERMIT	JOHN HEFFERNAN
A YOUNG MAN	VICTOR ARNOLD
MADAME GIRARD	RUTH WHITE
GIRARD GIRARD	WYMAN PENDLETON
A STREETWALKER	ESTELLE PARSONS
ELOISA BRACE	ALICE DRUMMOND
JEROME BRACE	DONALD HOTTON
GUS	ALAN YORKE
JOCKO	ROBERT VIHARO
MELBA	JENNIFER WEST
MILES	HENDERSON FORSYTHE
MADAME ROSITA	ESTELLE PARSONS
HELIODORO	VICTOR ARNOLD
A MAN	WILLIAM CALLAN
A WASHROOM ATTENDANT	HENDERSON FORSYTHE
A DOCTOR	HENDERSON FORSYTHE
VARIOUS PEOPLE	VICKI BLANKENSHIP
	JOSEPH CALI
	WILLIAM CALLAN
	ROBERT VIHARO

Directed by ALAN SCHNEIDER

Designed by WILLIAM RITMAN
Costumes by WILLA KIM
Lighting by THARON MUSSER
Music by WILLIAM FLANAGAN

ACT ONE

SCENE ONE

(A golden bench; MALCOLM seated on it; no expression save patient waiting. COX enters, behind MALCOLM, grimaces, stands for a moment, hands on hips, tapping his foot, finally advances)

COX

(Rather petulantly) You seem to be wedded to this bench. (MALCOLM smiles, does not look at COX, but, rather, down at the bench) You!

MALCOLM

(Looks up; a sweet smile) Oh, I'm here all the time. (Tiny pause) My name is Malcolm.

COX

(A trifle edgy) Good morning; my name is Cox. (MALCOLM smiles, nothing more; COX pauses a moment, then) I suppose, of course, you are waiting for somebody; your sister, perhaps.

MALCOLM

(His attention slipping away) No. (Then back) I'm waiting for nobody at all.

COX

(Impatient; suspicious) You have such a waiting look; you've been here forever. For months and months.

MALCOLM

(Surprise) You've seen me?

COX

Of course I've seen you; this is my . . . I, I walk by here
every day.

MALCOLM

Oh. Well, in that case, I suppose I *am* waiting for somebody.

COX

(Helpful; after MALCOLM *says no more)* Yes?

MALCOLM

(Statement of fact) My father has disappeared.

COX

Well, don't tell me you've been waiting for *him* all this time.

MALCOLM

(Thinks for a moment; then) Yes; perhaps I may be waiting
for *him.* *(Then he laughs, openly, agreeably)*

COX

(Snorts) Waiting for your father!

MALCOLM

I'm afraid I have nothing better to do.

COX

Ridiculous! I've taken special notice of you, because nobody
has ever sat on this bench before. I don't think anybody
should sit on it, for that matter.

MALCOLM

(Firmly; clearly enunciated) Poppycock.

COX

(Dogmatic) I am speaking of the regulations. This bench was
set out here in front of the hotel as decoration, to . . . to

set things off, and I don't . . .

MALCOLM
(No apology) Well, I am a guest in the hotel and I sit where I please.

COX
(Miffed) I see! *(Tiny pause)* It's clear you've not heard of me. *(Clears his throat)* I am an astrologer.

MALCOLM
(Innocent delight) People still study the . . . stars . . . for, for . . . ?

COX
(Snort of disgust) People!

MALCOLM
(Gentle apology) I'm sorry.

COX
(Regarding MALCOLM *carefully, appraisingly)* Do you have no one, then?

MALCOLM
(As if the question were odd, unfamiliar) No one?

COX
No one.

MALCOLM
(Clearly dropping the above) I'd invite you to sit down, sir, but you quite clearly don't think it should be done, and I wouldn't want to ask you if you didn't want to do it.

COX
(Intentional bored tone) Your way of refusing to give information?

MALCOLM

Things are, well, a bit too much for me, you see: I'm quite
young, I guess. So I sit here all the time . . . I suppose.

COX

Guess!? Suppose!? You *know!*

MALCOLM

(*A sweet smile*) Well, sir; yes; I know.

COX

(*Broods*) Hmmmmmmmmm.

MALCOLM

(*A fact*) I suppose, though . . . that if someone would tell
me what to do, I would do it.

COX

(*Regards him; chooses his words carefully*) Would that be
wise, though? For someone so young?

MALCOLM

(*Finally touching the bench with his hand, to emphasize a
point*) If I could leave the bench . . . if I saw some purpose
. . . I would risk it.

COX

(*Relieved, energized; takes a notebook and pencil from his
pocket*) Good. When were you born, Malcolm? The date of
your birth. (MALCOLM *is silent*) Don't tell me you don't know!

MALCOLM

(*Quite simple about it*) I'm afraid you're right: I don't.

COX

Then I don't see how you expect me to help you.

MALCOLM

(Quietly confused) Help . . . sir?

COX

(To himself) I don't think I've ever met anybody who didn't
know when he was born.

MALCOLM

But since he—my father—disappeared, I've had nobody to
remind me of dates.

COX

How *old* are you? Do you know *that? Vaguely?*

MALCOLM

(Sweet smile) I'm . . . I'm afraid not, sir.

COX

(Regarding MALCOLM *closely)* You look really quite young.
Well, are you . . . have you . . . do you, uh, have . . .
hair?

MALCOLM

Sir?

COX

(Embarrassed) Hair. Do you have hair, uh, under your arms,
and, uh. . . .

MALCOLM

(A winning smile; laughs) Oh. Yes. Recently.

COX

Ah, well, then, you are probably . . . Did your father never
talk to you about plans? Plans for when you were grown up?

MALCOLM

(Hesitant) Grown . . . up?

COX

(Gloomily) Grown up.

MALCOLM

(A little sadly) No. *(Rather tentative, then growing in pleasure)* My father . . . my father seemed to feel I was always going to stay just the way I was, and that he and I would always be doing just about what we were doing *then*. We were both satisfied. You have no idea, Mr. Cox, sir. *(A faint frown)* We were very happy together, my father and I.

COX

Well, for God's sake, Malcolm, you're not happy now!

MALCOLM

(Quite level) No, sir; I'm not.

COX

Well, you've got to do something about it!

MALCOLM

Do?

COX

Yes; *do*.

MALCOLM

(A quiet appeal) But, what is there to do?

COX

You must . . . give yourself up to things.

MALCOLM

(Rises, a little apprehensive) Give myself up to . . . things?

COX

Of course, my dear boy. You must begin your education.

MALCOLM

But, my father taught me . . .

COX

Your education to *life*, Malcolm!

MALCOLM

Sir?

COX

Since you are going out into the world—leaving your bench,
so to speak—you must prepare yourself. You have the look of
innocence, Malcolm . . . and that will never do!

MALCOLM

No, sir?

COX

Innocence has the appearance of stupidity, my boy.

MALCOLM

It does, sir?

COX

Yes, the two are easily confused, and people will take the easy
road, Malcolm, and find you stupid. Innocence must go!
(Softer) And I can help you; I can give you people, if you
think it's people you're looking for . . . addresses.

MALCOLM

(Confused) Addresses, sir?

COX

Addresses. That is, if you want to give yourself to things—to
life, as an older era said.

MALCOLM

Well, I have no choice, have I. But . . . addresses?

COX

(Hands MALCOLM *a calling card; uses his lecturer's voice)*
Here is the first. I want you to take this card, and you are to
call on the people whose names are written on it, *today,* at
five o'clock.

MALCOLM

(After folding his arms, and a long pause) I will *not!* I will do
no such thing. *(Then, suddenly he takes the card and studies
it, then reacts with consternation. Intense displeasure)* Kermit
and Laureen Raphaelson indeed! *(Throws the card on the
ground)* I'll have nothing to do with such an absurd introduc-
tion. You must be . . . out of your mind.

COX

Pick up that card at once! What would your father think of
you!

MALCOLM

Kermit and Laureen Raphaelson indeed!

COX

If you do not obey me . . . I will never speak to you again!
(Scoffs) Sitting there, day after day, moping over your father,
who probably died a long time ago . . .

MALCOLM

Disap*peared,* sir.

COX

(Pushing on) Yes, and when help for you arrives in the shape
of an address, what do you want to do! Nothing! You prefer to
stay on that bench. You prefer that to . . . *beginning.* . . .

MALCOLM

(Reconsiders) Well, I will do as you say in this one case.

COX

You will do as you're told, since you don't know what to do at all.

MALCOLM

(*A gentle smile*) Very well, sir.

COX

And remember the exact hour: five.

MALCOLM

Yes, sir.

COX

(*As he leaves*) Remember, Malcolm . . . you must *begin*.

MALCOLM

(*Looking at the card*) Yes, sir . . . begin.

COX

You'll rather enjoy Kermit and Laureen, I think . . . they're children—like yourself.

MALCOLM

(*Disappointed*) Oh? Yes?

COX

Grown-up children. (*As he exits*) Remember, Malcolm. . . . You must *begin*.

ENTRE-SCENE

(MALCOLM *leaves the bench scene, which changes in darkness.*
He comes forward, broods some, then speaks to his father,
rather as if they were standing together)

MALCOLM

Dear father . . . I am to begin. Begin what? I don't know,
but . . . something. My education, I believe. Oh, father; I
miss you so very much, and I don't understand . . . at all:
why you've left me, where you have gone, if you *are*, as they
say, dead or if you will ever return. I miss you so. But I am to
begin now, it would appear, and I will try to be all you have
taught me . . . polite; honest; and . . . what is the rest of
it, father? That you have taught me? (*Looks at card*) Do you
know . . . do you know Kermit and Laureen Raphaelson,
father? By chance, do you know them? Grown-up children,
father?

SCENE TWO

(The lights come up on the set of the Raphaelsons' house.
LAUREEN *is in it. She calls to* MALCOLM)

LAUREEN

Malcolm? Hurry up, now. Over here.

MALCOLM

(Moving tentatively into the set) Uh . . . yes. You're . . .
uh, Laureen Raphaelson?

LAUREEN

Oh, *am* I. And you! You *are* Malcolm; you *are* from Professor
Cox.

MALCOLM

Uh . . . yes, I suppose.

LAUREEN

Kermit is not with us at the moment, as you can see.

MALCOLM

Well, no . . . , I . . .

LAUREEN

As a matter of fact, he's in the pantry finishing his supper. He
eats in there alone now quite often, just to spite me, I think.
I'm afraid Professor Cox may be right . . . that we're headed
for the divorce courts. What do you think of that?

MALCOLM

Divorce courts are entirely out of my range of experience. But

I'm sorry you're headed for them.

LAUREEN
(*Thinking it over*) I haven't said divorce is actually imminent, mind you.

MALCOLM
No?

LAUREEN
Though it probably is. My God, you're young, aren't you? (KERMIT *enters;* LAUREEN *sees him*) There he is, Malcolm. It's Kermit! There's Kermit. (*To* KERMIT, *very eager to please*) You have a caller, Dolly.

MALCOLM
(*Observing* KERMIT, *open-mouthed, as he advances*) Why, who are *you*?

KERMIT
(*Rather amused, but slightly imperious*) Who am I? You heard her. I am Kermit. *Her* husband. Oh, I can't tell you how glad I am to see somebody nice for a change, and stop looking so surprised, Malcolm, you are Malcolm, right?

MALCOLM
Why . . . uh, yes. . . .

KERMIT
Why don't you just ignore Laureen there, and pay proper attention to *me*? After all, I'm the lonely one.

LAUREEN
Good God alive, it's beginning already. I beg you, Kermit: don't bring on a scene in front of this child.

KERMIT
(*Settling into a chair*) So . . . you are the boy who is infatuated with his father.

MALCOLM
I? Infatuated?

LAUREEN
Professor Cox has already told us all about you.

MALCOLM
But there's nothing to tell . . . yet.

KERMIT
(*Gravely*) There is always a great deal to tell, Malcolm, as I have learned.

MALCOLM
(*To break a stared-at feeling*) And you really *are* married.

KERMIT
She proposed.

LAUREEN
I warn you, I will not tolerate your telling secrets about our marriage to a third party again. Ever!

KERMIT
(*To* MALCOLM; *proudly*) I am the oldest man in the world.

LAUREEN
(*Familiar argument*) You are not!

KERMIT
I most certainly am!

LAUREEN
You most certainly are not!

KERMIT
(*To* MALCOLM) I am one hundred and ninety-two years old.

LAUREEN

You are no such thing!

KERMIT

(*To* LAUREEN) I am one hundred and ninety-two years old.

LAUREEN

You're ninety-seven years old . . . (*Mutters*) for God's sake. (*Louder*) You're not even one hundred.

KERMIT

I'm much too old to argue with you. (*Back to* MALCOLM) Why did you decide to come to see us, Malcolm?

LAUREEN

(*To herself*) One hundred and ninety-two years old indeed! (*To* MALCOLM; *something of a challenge*) Yes, why did you come?

MALCOLM

Why did I come to see you? Why, Mr. Cox ordered me to.

LAUREEN

Professor Cox has ruined Kermit here with his ideas. Kermit and I were *so* happy before we met that awful man.

KERMIT

(*Laughs derisively*) Laureen, sweetheart, if you're going to start a sermon, I'll have to ask you to leave the front room and go out and sit in the back parlor with the cats.

LAUREEN

(*Rather steely for all-suffering*) You should tell Malcolm how many cats you have out there so he can have a picture of where you're ordering me to go. (KERMIT *makes a little face;* MALCOLM *stifles giggles*) We have fifteen cats! Malcolm, am I getting across to you?

KERMIT

(In confidence, to MALCOLM*)* Professor Cox has a rather low opinion of Laureen at the moment.

LAUREEN

He has a low opinion of everybody, I would suspect. *(Turns to* MALCOLM*)* Malcolm, sweetie, do you know what Professor Cox suggested to me, only last week? *(*MALCOLM *shakes his head)* But you're too young to hear it! Oh, God! So terribly young, and unaware.

KERMIT

Nonsense! No one's too young to hear anything about people! And where's my hot tea, by the way? I asked you for my tea nearly an hour ago.

LAUREEN

(Hastening to the tea table) Dolly, didn't I bring you your tea? I won't have it said I've neglected my duties by you, no matter what may happen later on. Malcolm, honey, will you join Kermit in a cup of tea?

MALCOLM

(Very little boy) Yes, please.

KERMIT

(As LAUREEN *brings the tea)* Just what *did* Professor Cox command you, Laureen? Why don't you regale us with it?

LAUREEN

(Giving MALCOLM *his tea, kissing him on the cheek, ignoring* KERMIT's *last remark)* Here, precious.

MALCOLM

Thank you, Laureen. Yes, what did Mr. Cox command you?

KERMIT

I'll tell you what Mr. Cox commanded her.

LAUREEN

(Put upon) Let me tell it, Kermit; I want the boy to hear it without your embellishments.

KERMIT

Will you allow me to entertain *my* guest in *my* fashion? I am one hundred and ninety-two years old.

LAUREEN

You are not.

KERMIT

(To MALCOLM*)* We are poor people. *(To* LAUREEN*)* Quiet! *(Back to* MALCOLM*)* And knowing my wife's *propensities,* a long history we need not go into here, Professor Cox merely and sensibly proposed that Laureen go out with certain gentlemen who would pay her for her compliance with their wishes, since she was not entirely unknown for her favors before her sudden proposal of marriage to me. *(To* LAUREEN*)* Silence! *(Back to* MALCOLM*)* Laureen had promised when she proposed marriage to me and I had agreed to be her husband that my days of struggle and difficulty would be over. *(To* LAUREEN, *as if she were threatening to speak)* YES? *(Back to* MALCOLM*)* The exact opposite, alas, has been true. Since the prolonged weekend of our honeymoon in Pittsburgh, there has not been a day . . .

LAUREEN

(Quite the tragedienne) When one's husband no longer respects one, when he can tell the most intimate secrets of a marriage in front of a third party, there is, indeed, nothing left for one but the streets. Malcolm, baby, do I look like a streetwalker? *(Goes right up to him, towers over him)* Answer me, dear boy, for you're not yet corrupt. *(*MALCOLM *does not answer)* Do I . . . or don't I?

MALCOLM

(Quite confused) But aren't you . . . already one, dear Lau-

reen? I . . . I thought your husband said you . . .

KERMIT

(*Laughs uproariously*) Go back there and talk to the cats; I want to be with Malcolm. Go on! I certainly deserve to see somebody else in the evening besides your own horrible blonde self.

LAUREEN

(*Disdainfully, at* KERMIT) A true pupil of Professor Cox. (*Kisses* MALCOLM *benevolently, retires without looking at Kermit again.*)

KERMIT

(*Shouting after her*) Back with the other alley cats! (*Laughs pleasantly*)

MALCOLM

Are there really cats back there?

KERMIT

As Laureen said: there are fifteen.

MALCOLM

What an extraordinary number of cats.

KERMIT

Well, I've been collecting them for a while. After all, I'm one hundred and ninety-two years old.

MALCOLM

How . . . how odd that Laureen should be a . . . a . . .

KERMIT

(*Quite conversationally*) Odd she's a whore? Well, it's the only thing she ever wanted to be, and why she thought marriage would straighten her out, especially marriage with *me*, God only knows.

MALCOLM

I don't seem to recognize women like that when I meet them.

KERMIT

You *do* have beautiful clothes.

MALCOLM

Do I? (*Looks down at himself*) They're all suits my father picked out years in advance of my being this size. He's picked out suits for me all the way up to the age of eighteen. I think he had a presentiment he'd be called away, and he left me plenty of clothes.

KERMIT

(*More polite than anything*) Your father was quite extraordinary.

MALCOLM

(A *little whine in the voice*) That's what I tried to tell Mr. Cox, but he wouldn't believe me. I'm . . . I'm glad you think my father was extraordinary. (*Surprisingly near tears*) You see, he's all I've got . . . and now I don't have him. (A *few brief, genuine sobs*)

KERMIT

(*After a decent interval*) You have *me*, Malcolm; I'll be your friend.

MALCOLM

(*Recovering; a sweet smile*) Thank . . . thank you, Kermit.

KERMIT

I'll be your friend.

MALCOLM

You . . . you have beautiful clothes, too.

KERMIT

(Modest) Oh, well, they're . . . they set me off.

MALCOLM

I've . . . I've never met anybody as old as you are, before.

KERMIT

Well, you haven't met many people, have you, Malcolm?

MALCOLM

No. There's one thing, though, I must get straight. Are . . .
are you really as old as you say you are?

KERMIT

(Tossing it off with a little laugh) Well, of course.

MALCOLM

But you can't be!

KERMIT

(Quite petulant) Why not?

MALCOLM

Well . . . nobody *could* be!

KERMIT

(Straight curiosity) Do you want me to tell you about the
Boston Tea Party?

MALCOLM

Uh . . . no. (KERMIT *sticks his tongue out at* MALCOLM)
Golly, you look awful when you do that.

KERMIT

(Offhand) I *am* awful sometimes.

MALCOLM

I think I like you, though; you're not usual.

KERMIT

Well, I could say the same thing of you, Malcolm, but I won't. Not that I don't like you; I do—but that you're unusual. You're not bright, I gather, but you have your own charm, an air of . . . innocuous fellowship.

MALCOLM

(Solemnity and awe) Aren't you . . . afraid? I mean . . . well . . . being so old and all . . . aren't you afraid of . . . dying?

KERMIT

(After a mouth-open pause, quite casually calls) Uh, Laureen? Laureen?

MALCOLM

I'm, Im sorry if I . . .

KERMIT

Laureen?

LAUREEN

(Enters, examining her hand) One of your damn cats bit me. I think it was Peter. Honestly, Kermit, I wish you'd do something about . . .

KERMIT

Laureen, Malcolm just said the oddest thing.

MALCOLM

I'm sorry, Kermit, really I am.

LAUREEN

(Still with her hand, barely interested) Yeah? What did you say, Malcolm?

KERMIT

(As if it were funny) Malcolm asked me if I wasn't afraid of dying.

LAUREEN

(Only the mildest, matter-of-fact criticism, offhand) Oh, you shouldn't say anything like that, Malcolm.

KERMIT

(Just a hint of self-reassurance) When I was your age, Malcolm, the idea of death occurred to me, and I was very frightened.

LAUREEN

I mean, that isn't a nice thing to say at all.

KERMIT

And I lived with it all through my forties and fifties and everything, and by the time I was a hundred or so . . .

LAUREEN

You're ninety-seven. I don't see why we can't get rid of those damn cats.

KERMIT

. . . by the time I was a hundred or so . . . I'd resigned myself to it.

LAUREEN

It just isn't a nice thing to say to anybody, Malcolm.

KERMIT

But on my one hundred and forty-fifth birthday the idea suddenly hit me that there wasn't any death. So when I was a hundred and eighty-five I married Laureen here . . .

LAUREEN

I mean, when you're dealing with a person who's over ninety and all, I . . . I just don't see why you want to scare me like that.

KERMIT

. . . and we have each other, and the cats, and everything. . . .

LAUREEN

I don't think you know how to behave around grownups,
boy.

KERMIT

Malcolm doesn't know what life is, Laureen; he just doesn't
know, that's all.

MALCOLM

Well, no, I . . . I suppose I don't.

LAUREEN

You come back and see us, Malcolm, some other time. *(Beginning to stroke* KERMIT*)* We wanna be alone for a little
now. You'll understand when you're married. We got our
own problems, Kermit, being ninety-seven and all. . . .

KERMIT

One hundred and ninety-two.

LAUREEN

But you call us. Call us now, you hear?

MALCOLM

Yes, well . . . thank you both for the evening. Thank you
for . . .

KERMIT

(Enjoying being fondled etc.) Come back and see us, Malcolm. Come back and see *me*. *I'm* the lonely one.

MALCOLM

Yes, I . . . good, goodnight to both of you.

LAUREEN

Goodnight, baby.

KERMIT

I'm your friend, Malcolm, no matter what you think of me. Who knows, I may be your only friend in the world. You can cry here any time.

LAUREEN

Oh, Dolly, you're wonderful, you really are. So wonderful.

(As this set fades, as MALCOLM *moves away)*

KERMIT

(Cheerfully) I'm one hundred and ninety-two years old.

LAUREEN

(Teasing him) You are not.

KERMIT

(A tone creeping in) I am one hundred and ninety-two years old!!

LAUREEN

Dolly, you are *not* a hundred and ninety-two years old.

ENTRE-SCENE

(MALCOLM *backs away from the Raphaelsons' as it fades to*
blackness. MALCOLM *is alone*)

MALCOLM
Love . . . Love is . . . *Marriage* is . . . Married love is the
strangest thing of all. *(More or less to his father)* Of everything I have seen, married love is the strangest thing of all.
(COX *enters, unseen by* MALCOLM)

COX
What are you doing, Malcolm?

MALCOLM
(A smile, self-assurance) Thinking aloud.

COX
Thinking what?

MALCOLM
(A recitation) That married love is the strangest thing of all.

COX
(Stern) Not true!

MALCOLM
(Quiet smile) Ah, well.

COX
I was talking with my wife only last night.

MALCOLM

(Astonishment) You mean there is a *Mrs.* Cox?

COX

(Rather sniffy) Of course! Everybody is married, Malcolm . . . everybody that counts.

MALCOLM

(Dubiously) I don't understand why Laureen won't admit that Kermit is one hundred and ninety-two years old.

COX

(Hedging) Well, she has a certain personal right to deny it, if she wishes to. Besides, maybe he isn't.

MALCOLM

Well, Kermit was very firm about it.

COX

That is so like Kermit!! The day will come . . . the day will come when Laureen will have to admit that Kermit is one hundred and ninety-two years old, or Kermit will have to admit that he isn't.

MALCOLM

You mean they can't both go on believing what they want?

COX

(A flicker of kindness) Well, not if they're the only ones who believe it.

MALCOLM

(Sad glimmer of knowledge) Aaaahhh.

COX

(All business again; takes card from his wallet) Well, here

is your second address, Malcolm. Society, great wealth, position, sadness.

MALCOLM

(*Rather sadly*) So soon.

COX

(*Brandishing, presenting a card as if on a platter*) The Girards. Madame Girard, and her husband. You must hurry,
though. The Girards are very wealthy people, and while the
very wealthy have no sense of time, their interests do . . .
shift, the portals close, the beautifully groomed backs . . .
turn . . . no loss . . . but yours.

MALCOLM

(*Looking at the card*) Mr. and Mrs. Girard . . . "The Mansion."

COX

(*Moving off*) Hurry to them; hurry now.

MALCOLM

(*To the retreating* COX) Maybe . . . maybe they've met . . .
maybe they'll know where my father is!

COX

(*Exiting*) Ah, well . . . if your father exists, or has ever
existed . . . perhaps they will. (*Exits*)

SCENE THREE

MALCOLM

(Alone for a moment; the Girard set will light directly. Great bewildered wonder; to himself) If he exists . . . or has existed! If he exists! (To his father, now) Do you know them, father? . . . Mr. and Mrs. Girard, who live in the mansion? Are very wealthy, have great position, and have . . . beautifully groomed backs—and fronts, I would venture? *(Laughs, joyously)* Is that where you are, father? Will you be waiting for me there?

(A YOUNG MAN *appears)*

YOUNG MAN

Are you Malcolm?

MALCOLM

Oh! Uh, yes, sir, I am.

YOUNG MAN

I thought you were; you look like you should be. Come along now. Madame Girard is demanding a settlement from her husband; you're just in time for the evening performance.

MALCOLM

A settlement? Of what sort?

YOUNG MAN

Money, of course! Divorce. What are settlements for? *(Shrugs)* Peace at the end of wars, settlements, money, what else? Come now.

(They enter the Girard set. MADAME GIRARD *is*

seated on a throne of sorts. GIRARD GIRARD *stands
near her, another* YOUNG MAN *to the other side of
her.* MADAME GIRARD'S *make-up is smeared all over
her face; she is drinking; is drunk)*

MADAME GIRARD

(As the YOUNG MAN *ushers* MALCOLM *into her presence)*
Who admitted this child? *(Takes a drink)*

GIRARD GIRARD

Why, Professor Cox called up, my dear, and asked if this
young man could not be received. *(Goes to* MALCOLM, *hand
out)* Good evening, Malcolm.

MALCOLM

*(After difficulty getting his hands out of his pockets, shakes
hands with* GIRARD GIRARD) Good, good evening, sir.

MADAME GIRARD

(To her husband) And who gave you leave, sir, to accept
invitations by proxy for me? I have a great mind to take
proceedings against you, to in*crease* the settlement, proceedings with reference to the matter we discussed earlier in the
evening.

GIRARD GIRARD

(Sotto voce) Please try to be more hospitable, Doddy.

MADAME GIRARD

Don't use pet names for me in front of strangers! *(Points to*
MALCOLM) You! Come here. (MALCOLM *advances,* MADAME
GIRARD *looks him over carefully)*

MALCOLM

Is my . . . my tie straight?

MADAME GIRARD

(Wonder and sadness) Heavens! You can't be more than six

years old. (*To* GIRARD GIRARD, *peremptorily*) Get him a drink.
(GIRARD GIRARD *moves to do so*)

MALCOLM

(*To* MADAME GIRARD) Are . . . are all of you friends of Mr.
Cox? (*The four* YOUNG MEN *laugh and exchange knowing
glances*)

MADAME GIRARD

(*Glowering at her husband*) Why is it you're not entering
into the spirit of the party? Do you want me to begin proceedings against you at once? (*The* YOUNG MEN *giggle*)
Well!?

GIRARD GIRARD

(*Giving* MALCOLM *his drink*) Now, Doddy.

MALCOLM

(*To* GIRARD GIRARD) I had no idea it was going to be like this.

MADAME GIRARD

What is *it*?

MALCOLM

(*With some distaste*) Your party, or . . . gathering, or whatever you call it.

MADAME GIRARD

(*Drinking again*) We are here . . . for the sole purpose of
taking proceedings against my husband—boor and lecher—
seducer of chambermaids and car hops. . . .

GIRARD GIRARD

(*So patiently*) Now, Doddy . . .

MADAME GIRARD

(*To* MALCOLM, *still*) And I think I can arrange this settle-

ment quite properly without comments from the newly arrived and half-invited.

MALCOLM

(*Rather loud and self-assertive*) Perhaps *Mr.* Girard may
want a divorce first!
(*The* YOUNG MEN *laugh*, GIRARD GIRARD *smiles quietly*)

MADAME GIRARD

Newly arrived and *un*-invited!

MALCOLM

(*Is he a little drunk himself? Still rather loud. Genuine concern*) You must drink a *great* deal, Madame Girard.
(*Again, guffaws from the* YOUNG MEN)

MADAME GIRARD

(*Crafty, eyes narrowing*) What was it you said, young man?

MALCOLM

I think you are intoxicated, Madame.
(*Great laughter*)

MADAME GIRARD

(*Drunk dignity*) Do you realize in whose mansion you are?

MALCOLM

Why, Mr. Girard's mansion.

MADAME GIRARD

Clearly you do not.

MALCOLM

(*To the others*) This is only the second place I've visited at
Mr. Cox's request, but I can't say it's the more pleasant or
comfortable of the two.

MADAME GIRARD

Hear him!? He's not a guest—he's a critic! Not only a critic,
but a spy! Throw him out! THROW him OUT!!

GIRARD GIRARD

Doddy; *dear.*

MADAME GIRARD

A filthy spy for that vicious old pederast!

GIRARD GIRARD

Doddy, not in front of a child.

MALCOLM

(*Fascinated*) Old what? Ped . . . what? What did she call
him?

GIRARD GIRARD

Doddy, please. (*To* MALCOLM) I believe I've heard mention
of your father.

MALCOLM

(*To* GIRARD GIRARD, *with wonder and hope*) You really knew
my father!

GIRARD GIRARD

Ah, no; I said, I believe I've heard mention of him.

MADAME GIRARD

(*An announcement*) I . . . do not think your father exists.
(*Takes a great gulp*) I have *never* thought he did. (MALCOLM
swallows, stares at her open-mouthed) And what is more . . .
(*Takes another drink*) . . . *nobody* thinks he exists . . . or
ever *did* exist.

MALCOLM

That's . . . that's . . . blasphemy . . . or, a thing above

it! (MADAME GIRARD *laughs, echoed by the* YOUNG MEN) *And*
. . . (*Quite angry now*) . . . this is the first time where I
have ever attended a . . . a . . . *meeting* . . . a meeting
where the person in charge was *drunk!* (*A strained tiny silence*)

MADAME GIRARD

Oh, my young beauties, see how I'm suffering. (*Stretches out
her hands to the* YOUNG MEN, *who take them*) Come and
comfort me, beauties.

MALCOLM

(*An aside to* GIRARD GIRARD) What a pretty face she must
have under all that melted make-up.

MADAME GIRARD

Oh, dear God, I've been through so much; nobody knows
what I've suffered. (*Whimpering*) And now with this spy
here from Mr. Cox; he'll go directly back to that old pederast and tell him *everything* about this evening. . . .

MALCOLM

Old *what?* Pederast?

MADAME GIRARD

How I was *not* at the top of my form, and Cox will call his
clients and tell *them* I was not at the top of my form, and
they in turn will call . . .

GIRARD GIRARD

(*Solicitously*) Would champagne help?

MADAME GIRARD

(*Weeping a little*) Yes; it would help a little; a lot might
help a little. (GIRARD GIRARD *motions to one of the* YOUNG
MEN, *who fetches champagne*) It's so hard to bear one's bur-
dens sometimes, and we don't *need* MALCOLM, do we? (*Re-

fers to the YOUNG MEN) And haven't I my young beauties
around me already. Aren't they enough? Do we need a paid
informer? A paid informer in the shape of this brainless,
mindless . . . (*Suddenly as if seeing* MALCOLM *for the first
time*) . . . this *very* beautiful young boy?

MALCOLM

(*Sort of drunk; flattered, childishly "with it"*) Perhaps we
should all drink to Madame Girard.

MADAME GIRARD

My dear, dear young friend. Oh, thank you. Leave Mr. Cox,
dearest Malcolm; be mine; be my own Malcolm, not his.

MALCOLM

Let's all drink to Madame Girard!

MADAME GIRARD

(*Approaching him, putting her hands on him, kissing his
cheek, etc.*) Do you know, my young, my very young dear
friend, the company you've been keeping? Do you know
what Mr. Cox *is?*

MALCOLM

(*Raising his glass, in a gleeful toast*) A pederast!

ALL THE OTHERS IN UNISON

WHAT!?

MADAME GIRARD

(*A bemused smile*) What word did I hear? What word, Malcolm? Did you say something?

MALCOLM

(*Draining his glass*) I don't intend to repeat myself. My
father never did. Hurrah!

MADAME GIRARD

Champagne! Champagne for everyone; a prince has come
among us! Royalty!

GIRARD GIRARD

Champagne! Champagne!
*(The scene will start fading now . . . swinging off,
whatever. Everybody is talking at once. But above
it all we hear . . .)*

MADAME GIRARD

Royalty! Real royalty! A prince has come among us! A true
prince!

SCENE FOUR

(Kermit's. KERMIT *alone in his set.)*

MALCOLM

(Enters) Kermit—Kermit, I've been to the Girards'.

KERMIT

Poor Kermit; poor little man; poor poor little man.

MALCOLM

(Nodding, embarrassedly) And . . . and they've accepted me and . . .

KERMIT

I knew you wouldn't fail me . . . as much as one can know anything. Laureen has left me . . . the bitch has up and taken off.

MALCOLM

(Sympathizing) Left *you.*

KERMIT

(Bitterly) Oh, what's so surprising about that? *(Grabbing* MALCOLM's *hand, weeping freely)* She left me all alone, Malcolm.

MALCOLM

I . . . I . . . *(Shrugs sadly)*

KERMIT

Oh, I'll grant I hadn't really *loved* Laureen in . . . months; she'd lost her sparkle, and there were times when she almost disgusted me, but I'd got so *used* to her, her waiting on me, her . . . her being *around.* I'm . . . all alone now.

MALCOLM

Did she . . . did she run off with somebody?

KERMIT

(Anger coming back) How else would she go!? Like a decent human being? Alone? Of course not! She ran off with a Japanese wrestler!

MALCOLM

(Terribly puzzled) But . . . how did she find one?

KERMIT

I don't know!

MALCOLM

(Softly, to solace) Was he—the Japanese wrestler—also very old?

KERMIT

He was the . . . usual age for a man.

MALCOLM

It's pretty scary, isn't it, being alone?

KERMIT

We're both alone, you and I. Aren't we lucky Professor Cox brought us together? We're both in an impossible situation.

MALCOLM

Certainly *I* am.

KERMIT

(Quite put out; after a tiny pause) Why you more than I?

MALCOLM

Well, you *have* something; your marriage, which means you know *women*. I have . . . nothing; there's nothing I can *do*. All I have is the memory of my father. My father . . .

KERMIT

(Quivering with rage) SHIT ON YOUR FATHER!! *(Total silence.* MALCOLM *slowly rises.* KERMIT *slowly comes over to him, tugs at his sleeve)* Malcolm! Forget I ever said that. *(MAL- COLM moves away a few feet)* You just listen to me, and for- give me. You must let me apologize, dear, dear Malcolm.

MALCOLM

(Removed, sort of lost) How can I ever listen to you *again?* And how can I forgive you? To have said *that* about my father! This is the very last straw of what can happen to me. I'm going to pack up and leave the city today!

KERMIT

You have no right to desert me or, for that matter, desert your father. He . . . he may come back for you. Malcolm, my entire world has gotten out of bed and walked away from me. I'm depending on you so! I have no one else to depend on.

MALCOLM

A likely story coming from a man who insults the dead . . . the *disappeared*.

KERMIT

Forgive me, Malcolm, I only meant irritation. There you were, talking on and on about your father, and I wanted to talk about *my*self, and about the whore of a wife . . . *(Begins sniffing)* . . . who I miss so much. . . .

MALCOLM

(Rather kingly) Very well, then, Kermit, you're forgiven for this once.

KERMIT

Laureen, Laureen, Laureen . . .

MALCOLM

(*Shyly*) Kermit? Why did Laureen really leave you?

KERMIT

(*Sighs*) It was so strange. At exactly the same minute I decided to tell her I was only ninety-seven, to make it easier for her, she walked into the room, looking sort of funny, saying she'd decided to live with the fact that I was a hundred and ninety-two. And so we argued about it for a while, me insisting I was only ninety-seven, and she telling me that I was older than hell itself, and then she said she couldn't take it any more, and . . .

MALCOLM

How . . . how old are you? Really?

KERMIT

Hm? Oh . . . well, I don't remember any more. I'm up there, though . . . two . . . two hundred and something.

MALCOLM

I . . . I like you, Kermit. I like you very much.

KERMIT

Yes? Well, come and see me soon, Malcolm. I'm really very lonely now.

ENTRE-SCENE

(MALCOLM, *between sets, alone, stands, shakes his head a little, sadly, suddenly sees, leaning against the proscenium, a* STREETWALKER *who looks like Laureen, is played by the actress who plays Laureen, false wig, too much make-up, ridiculous dress.* MALCOLM *walks toward her, slowly, mouth open)*

MALCOLM

Why . . . why, Laureen. *(The* STREETWALKER *pretends not to notice him; he speaks now somewhat as if he were punishing a naughty child)* Laureen! You go home at once! Shame on you, leaving Kermit like that.

STREETWALKER

(Bored, tough, not a parody, though) What do *you* want, kid?

MALCOLM

Laureen, it's Malcolm.

STREETWALKER

Laureen!? My name's Ethel.

MALCOLM

Why, it is not! Your name is Laureen Raphaelson, and you're married to Kermit Raphaelson, who is a terribly old man, at least one hundred and ninety-two years old and maybe two hundred and something . . .

STREETWALKER

(Nodding her head as if MALCOLM *were insane)* My name is

Laureen Raphaelson, and I am married to a terribly old man at least one hundred and ninety-two years old and maybe even two hundred and something.

MALCOLM

Yes, and you've left him and you've run off with a Japanese wrestler, and I think you ought to go home right this minute.

STREETWALKER

(*Nodding her head even more*) My name is Laureen Raphaelson, and I am married to a terribly old man who is at least one hundred and ninety-two years old or maybe even two hundred or something except that I've left him and run off with a Japanese wrestler.

MALCOLM

(*Quite stern, oblivious of her incredulity*) Yes, and I think you ought to go home right this minute.

STREETWALKER

(*Ponders this a little*) And where is this Japanese wrestler right now?

MALCOLM

(*Flustered for a moment*) Why . . . why, wrestling, I'd imagine.

STREETWALKER

Uh huh. I think you better go home yourself, kid.

MALCOLM

No! I think you had. (*Whines*) Laureen . . . please.

STREETWALKER

(*Shakes her head*) Amazing. I thought my name was Ethel, and I thought I was not married, save once, a long time ago, for a couple of weeks to a nice kid turned out was a fag and is now shacking up with a cop picked him up one night in a bus depot, very happy I believe, stays home, cleans the gun, cooks . . .

MALCOLM

(*Whining*) Laureeeeeeeeeeeeen!

STREETWALKER

You got a family, kid?

MALCOLM

(*Struck by her question*) A what? A family?

STREETWALKER

Mommy? Daddy?

MALCOLM

I . . . I *had* a father, but he . . .

STREETWALKER

(*Soberly, not unkindly*) Died?

MALCOLM

(*Nods, solemnly*) Uh . . . yes, it would seem.

STREETWALKER

Gee, I thought your name was maybe something like Donald or Malcolm, and you lived in a big hotel, except your money was going, and your father wasn't dead, but had only . . . disappeared. Not dead . . . gone away.

MALCOLM

Yes! That's *right*. Disap*peared*.

STREETWALKER

(*Walking slowly toward off*) You better get home, kid;

Mommy and Daddy spank they find you out late, talking to
. . . grownups.

MALCOLM

My father isn't dead! He only disap*peared!*

STREETWALKER

Good for you, baby, better go home to Daddy . . . *(Exits)*

MALCOLM

Laur . . . ! *(Pause; softly; alone)* Not dead . . . only gone
away. I didn't mean to say that you were dead, father, but
you've been . . . disappeared so long, and everybody says
. . . I'm sorry, father, but please come back . . . so it won't
be true.

*(Begins to move toward the set of his bedroom in
the hotel, which begins to light)*

SCENE FIVE

(Malcolm's hotel bedroom; old, stately furniture. GIRARD GIRARD *is there, his back to the audience.* MALCOLM *enters, not from a door, but right onto the set)*

MALCOLM

(Deep in thought, takes off coat, does not see GIRARD GIRARD *at first, then)* Why . . . *(*GIRARD GIRARD *turns around)* . . . why, Girard Girard! What are *you* doing here?

GIRARD GIRARD

My dear Malcolm, my dear boy, I hope you'll forgive me waiting for you in your own bedroom, but I had to see you, and . . .

MALCOLM

(Rather put off) But how did you get in here?

GIRARD GIRARD

(Kindly) Getting here was no problem, Malcolm; I own the hotel, and as for *why* I am here . . .

MALCOLM

(Sniffing) Well, if you own the hotel, I should think you'd do something about the water pipes: there's rust and it takes ages for the hot water to come.

GIRARD GIRARD

It's an old place, Malcolm, a great one, but old. Besides, when I told you I owned the hotel I didn't mean to suggest that I managed it as well. It is a . . . property, a . . . something that's passing through my portfolio.

MALCOLM
(*Quite formal*) So much for the how, sir; but what of the
why? *Why* . . . are you here?

GIRARD GIRARD
If I've disturbed you, I'm deeply sorry, but my coming is
dictated by an emergency.

MALCOLM
(*Concerned*) Nothing serious? Madame Girard hasn't taken
ill, or died?

GIRARD GIRARD
Madame Girard is at home, sleeping in her private wing of
the mansion.

MALCOLM
(*Quiet wonder*) Private wings. Indeed, that *is* an extension
of separate rooms, is it not?

GIRARD GIRARD
It is indeed. I've come here to make a very unusual suggestion to you, and I hope you'll hear me out. And I want to
make it very clear to you that I've come here on my own
volition, despite the fact that Madame Girard herself ordered me to come. Madame Girard has taken such an im-
mediate and violent fancy to you that we wondered—and
please don't think us too outrageous—we wondered if you'd
care to come with us to our chateau for the summer.

MALCOLM
(*Pacing for a moment*) Why, I'm speechless with surprise at
your generosity. It's . . . overwhelming.

GIRARD GIRARD
You have no idea how . . . pleased Madame Girard would
be, Malcolm.

MALCOLM

No, sir; of course I haven't.

GIRARD GIRARD

And since you will make both me and my wife very happy
if you will come with us to our chateau for the summer, we
may expect you?

MALCOLM

. . . No, sir.

GIRARD GIRARD

But, Malcolm!!

MALCOLM

(*Ponders it, then*) You see, I'm terribly afraid of leaving here
where I'm always alone, and waiting, and going to where
people may demand me at all hours . . .

GIRARD GIRARD

(*A little less patiently than before*) No one will demand anything of you that you don't want to give.

MALCOLM

. . . and then there is the bench.

GIRARD GIRARD

The bench, Malcolm?

MALCOLM

It is where I receive my addresses, sir! Where I have made
contact . . . with *people*, sir. And there is Kermit, sir . . .

GIRARD GIRARD

Kermit? Kermit?

MALCOLM

(*Slow and very serious*) My very best friend in the world, I think; one person whom I could never leave.

GIRARD GIRARD
(*Sigh of relief*) Well, then bring him with you—bring your
Kermit with you.

MALCOLM
(*Almost thinking aloud*) Perhaps . . . if Kermit were to
come . . . perhaps, then, I could accept.

GIRARD GIRARD
(*Last lollipop*) You could have one of the gatehouses, if you
liked . . . anything!

MALCOLM
(*Very sincere*) I will try very hard, sir.

GIRARD GIRARD
(*So gentle*) That is all we ask. Come spend the summer with
us; be our son.

MALCOLM
Be *like* your son, sir.

GIRARD GIRARD
(*As he prepares to leave the set; wistfully*) Between simile
and metaphor lies all the sadness in the world, Malcolm.

MALCOLM
(*As* GIRARD GIRARD *turns, starts to leave*) It does, sir?

GIRARD GIRARD
Do let us know; come with us; be ours.

MALCOLM
(*Nods; not an acquiescence, but a pondering*) Yours.

GIRARD GIRARD

(Leaving) Goodnight, Malcolm.

MALCOLM

(GIRARD GIRARD *has left*) Good—goodnight, Mr. Girard . . . sir. (COX *enters from left*—KERMIT *enters from right on his chair on treadmill*) Kermit, we are going to the chateau for the summer. We are going with the Girards.

KERMIT

The Girards . . . the chateau . . .

COX

(To himself) Oh, I wouldn't count on that, buddy, if I were you. I wouldn't be so sure about that at all.

MALCOLM

We're on our way, Kermit.

COX

I wouldn't count on anything in this whole damn world.

MALCOLM

We're on our way, Kermit. We're on our way. *(Exits)*

SCENE SIX

(Kermit's sitting room, but rearranged, this time, so that when Kermit is facing his front door, his back will be to the audience. cox standing, kermit sitting, his knees together, his hands clasped on them)

COX

I suppose you think you're going to go. *(No answer from kermit)* I said: I suppose you think you're going to go. *(kermit looks up, but does not speak; his eyes are near tears)* Is there to be a long parade? . . . of all of you? . . . all my students, all whom I've raised from nothing, you, Malcolm, God knows who else? . . . streaming after that pied piper of a Girard woman . . . like rats?

KERMIT

(A weak whisper) Mice?

COX

(Intimidating, loud) hm? what?

KERMIT

(Clears his throat; a tiny voice) Mice. Pied piper: mice. *(A little malice now)* Rats leave a sinking ship.

COX

(Choosing to ignore it) All of you, whom I've educated beyond your state, risen up so that you can look at life, if not in the eye, at least at the belt buckle? All of you, running off? No thank you, sir! *(kermit says nothing)* Hm? hm?!

KERMIT

(Still cowed) I have been asked . . .

COX

SPEAK UP!!

KERMIT

I have been asked.

COX

(*Fuming, to himself*) It is the fate of sages and saints, I suppose, to serve, teach . . . *give*, if you will, of their substance . . . and be abandoned in the end, left desolate on the crag, like our beloved Francis, while the mice, the *rats*, scurry off . . . playing in the great gardens, nibbling at the pâté, the mousse . . . garnering.

KERMIT

(*So timid, apologetic*) I have . . . been asked.

COX

(*Looks at* KERMIT *carefully, changes his tack a little*) Well, yes, of course you have, my fine fellow . . . asked.

KERMIT

Yes!

COX

(*Comforting a child*) Of course! And you want to go.

KERMIT

(*The wonder is too much for him*) The . . . Girards . . .

COX

The Girards? Yes?

KERMIT

(*Blurting it out*) The Girards have invited me to the chateau and it would be wonderful. I'd see nice people . . . and everything might be all right there.

COX

(A vicious confidence) Now look here, I don't mind playing
games, but the time comes we gotta get serious, right?

KERMIT

Right.

COX

You're very special, a very special person; you're fragile, Kermit, and your eyes aren't strong; you couldn't stand the . . .
grandeur. . . . You'd be blinded by the splendor, Kermit.

KERMIT

(Breathes the word with loss and awe) The . . . splendor.

COX

It'd knock your eyes out, kid; you couldn't take it.

KERMIT

Then I . . . I can't go?

COX

Unh-unh.

KERMIT

I can't go with Malcolm to . . . to the chateau, with Madame Girard and . . .

COX

Unh-unh.

KERMIT

(Knowing it's all up) But I'd be so happy there.

COX

You couldn't take the splendor, kid; I'm sorry.

KERMIT

(As cox *starts to leave, but not by the front door; off to one side)* I would have been so happy there, with Malcolm, and . . .

[MALCOLM, GIRARD GIRARD *and* MADAME GIRARD *will come on-stage and move to Kermit's front door*]

COX

(Exiting) Whatever happens, Kermit, don't let them in. Remember, the splendor. *(Exits)*

MALCOLM

(To the GIRARDS, *as* KERMIT *huddles within)* . . . and he told me on the phone he washed the walls with ammonia and scented it all with patchouli oil and rosewater, which are your favorites for a dwelling, are they not, Madame Girard?

MADAME GIRARD

They are essential for a habitation. *(Squints)* What a charming little building; you must buy it for me, Girard.

GIRARD GIRARD

All right, Doddy.

MADAME GIRARD

I smell cats!

GIRARD GIRARD

(Some wonder) Do you, Doddy?

MALCOLM

(Eager glee) There are fifteen!

KERMIT

(Huddled in a corner; whispers to himself) Go away, oh, do go away.

MALCOLM
(*At the front door*) Kermit? Hello?

KERMIT
(*Not heard by the others*) Go away . . . *please.*

MALCOLM
(*Knocks*) Ker-mit. (*No answer; tries the doorknob*) He . . .
he doesn't answer.

MADAME GIRARD
Nonsense! (*She tries it, too*) Why doesn't he answer? Is he
expecting us?

MALCOLM
Of course! Kermit? Don't play games with me.

GIRARD GIRARD
Perhaps your friend is indisposed.

MADAME GIRARD
When *we* are visiting? Don't be absurd. (MADAME GIRARD
enters imperiously, followed by MALCOLM *and* GIRARD GIRARD)
Do you hear me, my good man? It is I, Madame Girard! I am
issuing a command! You are coming with us to the country.

KERMIT
(*Shaking his head, sobbing*) I can't; I . . . cannot.

GIRARD GIRARD
Here, let me try.

MADAME GIRARD
(*Motioning him away*) *You* can't do anything; *I* have the
splendor here.

MALCOLM
Kermit! Please! We're going to the chateau! Don't be a

coward; come with me; I can't go without you!

KERMIT

(*A trapped animal, very loud*) Go away! I . . . can't bear
the splendor!

MALCOLM

(*Whining a little*) Kermit!

MADAME GIRARD

What is it you can't bear?

KERMIT

(*Shouting*) I can't stand the splendor of your presence!

MADAME GIRARD

(*Awe and joy*) The *splendor* of our presence!

MALCOLM

(*As above*) Kermit, please!

KERMIT

(*Moans*)

MADAME GIRARD

Why, the creature is moaning! (*At which* KERMIT *moans
louder*) He is moaning . . . over *us!*

MALCOLM

(*Loss*) Kermit? . . . Please?

KERMIT

(*Weeping to himself*) I . . . I can't. I cannot.

MALCOLM

(*Intensity*) Kermit! (*The three wait for a little, in silence, the
only sound being* KERMIT's *sobbing as he and his chair slide
off*)

MADAME GIRARD

(Finally, softly) Well, then, we shall have to go without him.
Girard?

GIRARD GIRARD

It would seem so, Doddy. I'm sorry, Malcolm, you shall have
to come with us without your friend.

MALCOLM

(Soft, loss) Kermit!

MADAME GIRARD

(As they all begin to move away from Kermit's door) Kermit
has rejected me.

MALCOLM

It's *me* he has rejected.

MADAME GIRARD

(Patiently) He has rejected *all* of us. I must have a drink.

MALCOLM

(Rather severe) What of?

MADAME GIRARD

(Sweetly, patiently explaining) Dark rum.

GIRARD GIRARD

Completely out of the question.

MADAME GIRARD

Explain the meaning of that last remark.

GIRARD GIRARD

Your drinking days are over. At any rate, with me around.

MADAME GIRARD
You pronounce my doom with the sang-froid of an ape! You are an ape!

GIRARD GIRARD
I warn you, Madame Girard, I'm at the end of my tether. We must leave for the country at once; my lungs demand the air. Malcolm? You shall have to come with us . . . alone.

MALCOLM
I can't, Mr. Girard, sir; I can't abandon Kermit now.

GIRARD GIRARD
(*Sad shrug*) Alas.

MALCOLM
(*Rueful agreement*) Yes; alas.

MADAME GIRARD
(*Bravura cheerfulness*) We have tried and failed. (*Puts her hand out*) Lead me, Girard.

GIRARD GIRARD
Goodbye, Malcolm?

MALCOLM
Goodbye, Mr. Girard, sir; goodbye, Madame Girard.

MADAME GIRARD
(*Being led off by* GIRARD GIRARD) Goodbye, dear child, dear ungrateful child. (*They both exit*)

MALCOLM
(*Rather petulant*) Well, you've made rather a hash of things, I must say, Kermit. A whole summer, two people who loved me, or so they said, a man like Mr. Girard who said he would

be like my father—all of it, everything, for *both* of us, and you won't do it! *(Tapping his foot, rather impatient)* Well? What's to become of me now? I hope you've got plans for me. I've given up everything for you! *(But* MALCOLM *is alone. Frightened little boy)* What's to become of me?

ENTRE-SCENE

(COX *comes on, sees* MALCOLM *alone*)

COX
(*Feigning surprise*) What? You still here? Lucky boy, aren't you off with the tycoon and his lady, and where is your friend Kermit?

MALCOLM
(*Surly*) You study astrology and things, don't you?

COX
(*Shakes his head*) Tch-tch-tch-tch-tch; up the ladder too quick, down they plunge to the bottom rung, as the saying goes. Arrogant, weren't you, crowing over your triumph and all?

MALCOLM
(*A front*) It's . . . it's just a matter of a day or two, until I get things settled here, and then I'm off.

COX
Good thing, too, I must say, since your room is gone, your bags out in front of the hotel. Checked out, have you?

MALCOLM
Of course! I . . . (*Bursts into tears*) What am I to do? It was all arranged, and then Kermit lost his courage and said he wouldn't go, and . . .

COX
Tears? What would your father, or whoever it is, or was, say? Hm?

MALCOLM

(*Trying to stop crying*) And where has Kermit gone, and what's *wrong* with him?

COX

(*Quite casual*) Kermit, I'm sorry to say, is probably going to have a nearly complete collapse.

MALCOLM

(*Wonder with the stopping tears*) A nearly complete collapse?

COX

Yes, poor little man; the presence of the unattainable often brings one on.

MALCOLM

(*Great wonder*) Poor Kermit.

COX

Yes, but poor Malcolm, too, poor of pocket as well as other resources.

MALCOLM

My bags . . . you say . . . were . . .

COX

(*Jolly*) Out on the curb. Empty, though.

MALCOLM

But my clothes! My shells! My . . .

COX

(*Jollier*) Sold, whisked off, taken in payment, gone.

MALCOLM

(*Great awe*) And what am I to do!?

COX

(Bringing out another card) Start lower, I think; ascend again. Oh, you should count yourself lucky I bother with you at all.

MALCOLM

(Some spunk left) Should I! Well, let me tell you, everyone in and out of the Girards' speaks slightingly of you.

COX

(Coolly) Those in possession of the truth are hardly ever thought well of.

MALCOLM

(Some awe) You are in . . . possession of the . . . truth?

COX

(Calm, with a small smile) I thought you knew I had it.

MALCOLM

Then, you *are*, as people say, a magician as *well* as an astrologer.

COX

(Tossing it off) I merely try to help—sometimes I fail, as in your case, child. You are very difficult to educate. *(Handing* MALCOLM *a card)* Here. Take it.

MALCOLM

(Some enthusiasm) Another address, sir?

COX

Not so much enthusiasm, Malcolm. What did your father— such as he was or was not—teach you?

MALCOLM

(Ingenuous) To be polite, sir, and honest.

COX

(*A little sour*) Your father spoke in contradictions, then.

MALCOLM

Sir?

COX

These people . . . be cautious.

MALCOLM

(*Genuine alarm*) But why are you sending me to them, Mr.
Cox, sir!?

COX

(*A great shrug*) What is left for you, Malcolm? Maybe you're
on the way down, for good; maybe not. 'S'up to you. Besides,
it's the only card I happen to have with me. (*Starts to go*)
Goodnight, kiddie.

MALCOLM

(*Looks above, sees it has gone dark*) Why . . . it *is* night.

COX

Yes, gets dark pretty quick around here, don't it?

MALCOLM

(*Still amazed*) Yes; very. (*Sees that* cox *is leaving*) Mr. Cox!

COX

Hm?

MALCOLM

(*Real anger*) I don't understand your world, Mr. Cox, sir! Not
one bit!

COX

You will, sonny, you will. (*Walks offstage, leaving* MALCOLM
alone)

SCENE SEVEN

(*Eloisa Brace's studio begins to light.* ELOISA *is in it, in the growing light. There is distant jazz music going on*)

MALCOLM

(*Half calling after* COX, *half talking to himself*) Not a bit of your . . . world, Mr. Cox, sir, not one little bit. Caution? How do I do that?

ELOISA

(*Having listened to* MALCOLM) O.K., kid; all right, O.K. All right?

MALCOLM

(*Startled to see her*) Oh! My goodness.

ELOISA

You the new kid, hunh? Malcolm? Is it you? (MALCOLM *nods*) Practicing caution?

MALCOLM

Is that what I'm doing? Are you . . . ?

ELOISA

O.K., then, either come in or go out. You can't just stand there, O.K., you know? I'm giving a concert.

MALCOLM

(*Enthusiasm*) Are you!

ELOISA

I'm Eloisa Brace, O.K.?

MALCOLM
How do you do? Mr. Cox . . .

ELOISA
(*Irritable*) Yeah, yeah, O.K.

MALCOLM
(*Entering the set*) You're awfully cross tonight, aren't you?

ELOISA
Look, buddy, if you had a bunch of musicians lying around
the house . . .

MALCOLM
I'm sorry!

ELOISA
Yeah? O.K. Hey! I'm gonna paint your portrait. (MALCOLM
only smiles a little) I said: I'm gonna do a picture of you.
Paint. O.K.?

MALCOLM
Are . . . are you a painter?

ELOISA
(*A little suspicious*) I don't know where we're gonna put you
while you're living here, every bed in the damn place is full
of musicians and all, but you look pretty small, we'll find part
of a bed for you. O.K.? My God, I hate kids how old are you!

MALCOLM
Well, I think I must be fifteen by . . .

ELOISA
O.K.! There's that face of yours, I'm gonna paint. (*Rather
mysterious*) It's like a commission: I mean, I think I can sell
it right away I got it done. O.K.?

MALCOLM

O-O.K.

JEROME

(Entering) Is that the new boy? *(Sees* MALCOLM*)* Ooh, yes, it does look to be.

ELOISA

Will you please take over from here, O.K.? You know I can't stand kids, and I got all these musicians waiting.

JEROME

(Rather sweet, urging her out) O.K., baby.

ELOISA

(To MALCOLM, *as she exits)* I gonna paint the hell out of you, kid. O.K.?

MALCOLM

(As she goes) Y-yes . . . certainly.

JEROME

(Taking MALCOLM *by the arm, walking him further into the set)* My wife is a bit nervous when we have these concerts.

MALCOLM

(Astonished) Eloisa Brace is *your* wife?

JEROME

(Nods) Oh, yes. *(Leads* MALCOLM *further)* But do come clear into the room, why don't you—where I can see you.

MALCOLM

(Uncertainly) Sure.

JEROME

(Looking at MALCOLM *carefully)* Yup, you're just as Mr. Cox

described you. Yup. *(Nods several times)* Would you like some wine, Malcolm?

MALCOLM
(As a glass is being poured for him) I usually don't drink.

JEROME
(Hands MALCOLM *a glass, takes one himself)* Do have some.

MALCOLM
You're so . . . very polite.

JEROME
(Returning the compliment) You're much nicer than I even thought you would be for a boy of your class. My name, by the way, is Jerome. *(They shake hands. Hope and enthusiasm in his voice now)* I don't suppose you've heard of me. I'm an ex-con, a burglar. You're not drinking up. *(Pours* MALCOLM *more wine)*

MALCOLM
(Rather drunk, vague) But you see . . . I don't drink. Jerome, what *is* an ex-con?

JEROME
A man who's been in prison. An ex-convict.

MALCOLM
Ah; I see!

JEROME
I wrote a book about it.

MALCOLM
How *difficult* that must have been!

JEROME
(Going to get a copy) Would you like to read my book?

MALCOLM

Well, I . . . I don't know; I've . . . I've never read a complete book—all the way through.

JEROME

(*Leering some*) You'll read this one. (*Hands it to* MALCOLM) It's called *They Could Have Me Back.*

MALCOLM

(*Looking the book over*) What a nice title. Is that you naked on the cover? (JEROME *smiles, touches* MALCOLM *lightly on the ear*) I . . . I don't read very much.

JEROME

(*Touches* MALCOLM *gently on the ear again*) Do you dig that music, kid?

MALCOLM

(*Touching his ear where* JEROME *had touched it*) What did you do that for?

JEROME

(*Pouring* MALCOLM *more wine*) Look, Malcolm, I know you make a point of being dumb, but you're not *that* dumb. (JEROME *sits at* MALCOLM's *feet, his arm around his leg, his head against his knee*) I *do* want you to read my book; I want you to, well, because, because I guess you don't seem to have any pre-judgments about anything. Your eyes are completely open. (MALCOLM *jumps a little as* JEROME *starts stroking his thigh*) Look, Malcolm, I'm not a queer or anything, so don't jump like that.

MALCOLM

(*Drunk, vague*) I see.

JEROME

Will you be a good friend, then?

MALCOLM
(*From far away*) Of course, Jerome.

JEROME
Thank you, Malcolm. It's going to be a wonderful friendship.
(*Strokes some more*) But I think you better give up Girard
Girard and Mr. Cox and all those people, because they don't
believe in what you and I believe in. . . .

MALCOLM
(*Very dizzy*) But what do we believe in, Jerome?

JEROME
What do we believe in, Malc? What a lovely question, and
you said we; I'll appreciate that for one hell of a long time.
One hell of a long time from now I'll think of that question
of yours, Malc: What do *we* believe in? You carry me right
back to something. . . .

MALCOLM
(*The jazz music is louder,* MALCOLM's *head spins*) But you
see, I don't know what I believe in, or any . . .

JEROME
Don't spoil it, Malc! Don't say another word!

MALCOLM
(*A tiny voice; he is about to pass out*) Jerome . . .

JEROME
Don't say a word, now. Shhhh . . . (*At this moment the
glass falls out of* MALCOLM's *hand, and he topples from the
chair, head first, across* JEROME's *lap*) Jesus Christ! Malc?
(*Shakes* MALCOLM, *but he has passed out*) MALC?

(*Lights fade on the tableau*)

SCENE EIGHT

(*Eloisa Brace's studio again.* ELOISA *and* COX *swing on, with portrait, etc.*)

ELOISA

Well, whatta ya think of the portrait, hunh?

COX

It's . . . it's . . . very interesting.

ELOISA

(*Put out*) Oh? Really?

COX

I mean . . . it's beautiful.

ELOISA

I thought that's what you meant.

COX

It's lovely, my dear.

ELOISA

It has a certain . . . *him* about it, don't you think?

COX

Well, that depends on what you mean, Eloisa. It doesn't look exactly like *him*—or he doesn't look exactly like *it*. . . . Maybe it's a picture of what he used to be . . . or what he's becoming.

ELOISA

(*Her leg is being pulled*) Ooohhh . . . you astrologers, you're something.

COX
(*Down to business*) I happened—just in passing, you under-
stand—to mention the portrait of Malcolm to Madame
Girard.

ELOISA
(*Going along with it*) Just in passing.

COX
Yes, and she seemed—well, how shall I put it?—she seemed
beside herself.

ELOISA
(*Feigned lack of interest*) Oh? Yes?

COX
Ah. How we dissemble.

ELOISA
I can't imagine what you're talking about.

COX
Madame Girard finds herself in the curious dilemma of, on
the one hand, feeling that Malcolm is the most ungrateful
child who ever lived, and, on the other hand, retaining for
the boy—or, to put it most accurately, for the fact of him—a
possessiveness that borders on mania.

ELOISA
(*More openly interested*) Oh, really?

COX
Yes; and when I mentioned to her that you were painting his
portrait, her eyes flashed with the singular fire that's the ex-
clusive property of the obsessed.

ELOISA
(*Tiny pause*) Meaning?

COX

Meaning simply that Madame Girard will stop at nothing to have Malcolm's portrait. That I think you've got a big sale coming.

ELOISA

(Knowingly) Yeah? And?

COX

And that I hope you'll not forget my commission.

ELOISA

(Airily) Oh, Professor Cox, you'll have your ten percent.

COX

(Clears his throat) Uh, twenty.

ELOISA

(Steely) Fifteen.

COX

Agreed.

MADAME GIRARD'S VOICE *(offstage)*

Eloisa Brace? Eloisa Brace?

COX

Aha! You see? I think I'll go out this way, if you don't mind.

MADAME GIRARD'S VOICE

Eloisa Brace?

COX

And leave you two ladies to your business.

ELOISA

(Fact, but no judgment) You're a terrible man, Professor Cox.

COX

(Exiting) Yes? Well, do keep in the back of your mind that the role of a post-Christian martyr is not an easy one.

ELOISA

(As cox *exits)* A post-Christian martyr!

MADAME GIRARD

(Entering) Eloisa Brace? It is I!

ELOISA

(Feigned surprise) Why, Madame Girard!

MADAME GIRARD

I'm lonely, my dear.

ELOISA

Well, sure you're lonely, but . . .

MADAME GIRARD

You have a young man named Malcolm here, and don't pretend you've not.

ELOISA

Why, yes! I'm painting his portrait.

MADAME GIRARD

Oh? Then I must buy it at once! I've not been so taken with a person in years.

ELOISA

(Drinking, or pouring brandy) But, lady, I haven't finished it yet, and . . .

MADAME GIRARD

What are you doing?

ELOISA

I'm sipping brandy.

MADAME GIRARD

At nine-thirty in the morning?

ELOISA

You upset me so, Madame Girard, as you well know, and sometimes a finger of brandy helps me get through.

MADAME GIRARD

I know nothing of your anxieties. All I know is Malcolm is here and you are painting his portrait. *I* discovered *him,* and *I* claim *it.*

ELOISA

Madame Girard! Listen to reason!

MADAME GIRARD

I am claiming my own is all. If that is decent brandy, I might just have a taste.

ELOISA

Oh, please! You know we buy only a cheap domestic.

MADAME GIRARD

(Sniffs with displeasure) Well, naturally, what can one expect?

ELOISA

Why don't you just toot along, Madame Girard? Your wealth and position don't entitle you to come into a private house and . . .

MADAME GIRARD

(Snorts) A public house, from what I've heard! The things you've done to that sweet, though ungrateful child.

ELOISA

Like what!

MADAME GIRARD

(*Momentarily stopped*) Well, you have *done* something to
him, haven't you?

ELOISA

Well, it's a little crowded around here—what with musicians
coming and going at all hours—and there aren't enough
beds, so Malcolm gets shifted around sometimes, in the
middle of the night—you know, from bed to bed and all,
and sometimes we gotta put *three* people in one bed. . . .

MADAME GIRARD

Three! People!

ELOISA

(*Puzzling it through*) Yeah; Malcolm said it was like traveling in Czechoslovakia during a war. Though how Malcolm
could know that, I can't imagine.

MADAME GIRARD

I'm glad for his own sake that Malcolm's father, or whatever he was, died or whatever he did.

ELOISA

There you go: your middle-class prejudices coming out. Everybody's gotta begin sometime. (*Exits*)

MADAME GIRARD

Eloisa! Eloisa Brace!

(MALCOLM *enters, sees* MADAME GIRARD)

MALCOLM

Madame Girard!

MADAME GIRARD

Are you all right, dear child? Loss? What have they done to you?

MALCOLM

Not . . . not much.

MADAME GIRARD

Have you kept your innocence! Oh, Malcolm, have they *used* you?

MALCOLM

Well, it *is* a little crowded when it comes to bedtime, and I suppose I've . . .

MADAME GIRARD

(*Envelops him*) Oh, my dear child!

GIRARD GIRARD

(*Entering*) *Monstre!* Take your hands off Malcolm at once!

MALCOLM

Mr. Girard!

MADAME GIRARD

Is that you, Girard Girard?

GIRARD GIRARD

It is I, Madame Girard.

MALCOLM

How . . . how wonderful.

MADAME GIRARD

(*Still sweet*) Why aren't you in the midst of one of your adulteries, Girard Girard?

GIRARD GIRARD

I have been in Idaho, Madame Girard, making six million dollars.

MADAME GIRARD

You said you would be in Iowa, making four.

GIRARD GIRARD

You misheard me, then, when I told you where I was going and to what end.

MADAME GIRARD

All I can believe is what the detectives say is so.

GIRARD GIRARD

And all I can believe, Madame Girard, is what my wits tell me is so.

MADAME GIRARD

(So sweet) Then I have the better of it, Girard Girard.

GIRARD GIRARD

This once, my dear, I think it is I.

MADAME GIRARD

(After a tiny pause) Oooooooohhhh?

MALCOLM

(To GIRARD GIRARD) I'm so glad to see you!

GIRARD GIRARD

(Not too unpleasantly) Be quiet, Malcolm.

MADAME GIRARD

Why are you here, Girard Girard?

GIRARD GIRARD

I have come for something of great value.

MADAME GIRARD

Yes? As have I! And you shall not have it, sir!

GIRARD GIRARD

I am in the habit of finding my desires satisfied, Madame Girard.

MADAME GIRARD

Oooohhhh, are you ever!

GIRARD GIRARD

But since I find you here, let me speak of a related matter. Do you remember, Madame Girard, that night, so long ago, when we sat in the dark woods, near the lagoon, by the Javanese temples . . . ?

MADAME GIRARD

When I gave you your victory, Girard Girard? The night I surrendered myself to your blandishments and agreed to become your wife?

GIRARD GIRARD

That very night.

MADAME GIRARD

I recall it. I gave up . . . everything, my life, in return for but one thing, which now I cherish: my name—Madame Girard.

GIRARD GIRARD

It is that which I propose to take from you now.

MADAME GIRARD

(*After a pause*) I do not think . . . I hear you well.

GIRARD GIRARD

I have decided, my dear, upon reflection, to give you the

separation which you have demanded without cease since the melancholy day of our marriage.

MADAME GIRARD

Certainly, sir, you will let me determine the relationship between what I wish and what I say I wish.

GIRARD GIRARD

(Doom-ridden) No longer! I am divorcing you, Madame Girard.

MADAME GIRARD

(Haughty) You will do no such thing, sir.

MALCOLM

Please.

GIRARD GIRARD

Listen carefully to what I say: I am divorcing you, Madame Girard; I am marrying Laureen Raphaelson.

MALCOLM

Laureen Raphaelson!

MADAME GIRARD

That slattern.

GIRARD GIRARD

I am taking your name from you, the name I gave you many years ago.

MADAME GIRARD

You have taken many things from me, Girard Girard: my youth, my job, my self-respect, but there is one thing you may never take from me—my name.

GIRARD GIRARD

You may have the mansion and the chateau, and wealth

enough to satisfy your every whim. I will take but two
things: myself and your name.

MADAME GIRARD

Never, sir!

GIRARD GIRARD

You are history, Madame Girard; you no longer exist.

MADAME GIRARD

(*After reflection*) I will die, Girard Girard; I shall take my
life.

GIRARD GIRARD

I think not, madame.

MADAME GIRARD

(*Very genteel*) But what will become of me? (*Loud*) YOU PIG!

GIRARD GIRARD

(A *little weary, a little sad*) You will move from the mansion
to the chateau, and from the chateau back. You will sur-
round yourself with your young beauties, and hide your
liquor where you will. You will . . . go on, my dear.

MADAME GIRARD

Girard Girard!! The name!! The name is mine!!

GIRARD GIRARD

No longer, my dear. You are history. And now I think I
shall obtain what I came here for.

MADAME GIRARD

Never, sir!! You may not have everything!!

GIRARD GIRARD

Is that a rule, madame? (*Calls, begins moving off*) Eloisa

and Jerome Brace? Are you there? It is I, Girard Girard.

MADAME GIRARD

(*Moving off in the opposite direction, taking Malcolm's portrait with her*) Eloisa! Eloisa!

GIRARD GIRARD

It is I, Girard Girard. (*Exits*)

MADAME GIRARD

Eloisa? Eloisa Brace? (*Exits, leaving* MALCOLM *alone onstage*)

MALCOLM

Girard Girard, sir! Madame Gi . . . everything . . . everything I touch is . . . each place I go, the . . . the, THE WHOLE WORLD IS FLYING APART!! The . . . the whole world is . . . Have . . . have I done this? Is . . . is this because of me? I've . . . I've been polite, and honest, and . . . I've *tried.* I don't understand the world. No, I don't understand it at all. I feel that thing, father . . . Loss. Loss . . . father?

SCENE NINE

(Still Eloisa Brace's studio, immediately following. ELOISA
precedes JEROME onstage)

ELOISA
(Shrugs) O.K. (Calls) Uh, Malcolm, baby!

JEROME
How's the old Malc!?

MALCOLM
(Patient, but confused) I'm fine, Jerome.

JEROME
(False heartiness) Well, good, kid!

ELOISA
(Hating to start) Uh . . . Malcolm . . .

JEROME
(Coming to her aid) Malc, we think it's time you were
moving on, boy.

MALCOLM
Moving? On?

JEROME
(False heartiness) Sure, you don't wanna spend your life in
a place like this, buncha jazz musicians, concerts going on,
lotta drinking and all, you wanna . . . you wanna go be
with your own type, Malc.

MALCOLM

But . . . don't you like me here? *(Looks from one to the other)* I mean, where would I go?

JEROME

Oh, that's all set, kid. . . .

ELOISA

Malcolm, Jerome and I have come into quite a bit of money . . . and we're gonna close up shop for a couple 'a months, an' . . . take a little trip. You know? O.K.?

JEROME

(As MALCOLM *is silent)* Fact is, Malc, Madame Girard got what she came for . . .

ELOISA

. . . your portrait, sweetheart . . .

MALCOLM

(Confused) She . . . she really wanted the picture?

JEROME

Well, she must of, kid; I mean, that lady right next to you there is happy possessor of the check for the sale of one portrait of someone looks very much like you.

ELOISA

(Patting her bodice) Ten thousand dollars, Malcolm. I am, next to Madame Girard, probably the happiest woman on God's green earth.

MALCOLM

(Amazed) Ten . . . thousand . . . dollars?

ELOISA

(Blushing) Yup!

MALCOLM

(Doubt on his face, and confusion) For . . . that *painting?*

ELOISA

(Ire rising) Well, some people think my brushwork is worth a great deal more than others, it would appear.

MALCOLM

(Lying nicely) I didn't mean *that*, Eloisa; it's a . . . it was a lovely painting.

JEROME

Ten thousand bucks lovely, Malc.

MALCOLM

(Thinks a moment, then) Wow.

ELOISA

And Jerome's come into a little money, too, himself.

JEROME

(Blushing) Aw, you don't have to mention that, baby. . . .

MALCOLM

Do . . . do you paint, too, Jerome?

JEROME

(Explaining away something a little shady) Well, no kid, not that, I . . . well, you see, Malc . . .

ELOISA

You see, Malcolm, with Madame Girard getting the painting and all, Girard Girard wondered if he couldn't have you. And we told him, naturally, that you were happy here, with us, and our friends, and all, and that we didn't see any reason why *he* should have you when we were all so happy *together*. I mean with Madame Girard coming along and practically stealing your portrait right from under our collective nose—for a song!—and now all we have left *is* you . . .

JEROME

. . . and why would he want to take *that* away from us, too . . .

ELOISA

. . . exactly.

MALCOLM

(*After a short pause; rather unhappy*) Did you *sell* me to him, Jerome? Did you sell me to Mr. Girard?

JEROME

(*Whining*) Aw, now, Malc . . .

ELOISA

(*Rather put out*) I wouldn't put it *that* way, Malcolm. . . .

MALCOLM

How much did you *get* for me, Jerome? (*Jerome fidgets, doesn't answer*) How much did I fetch?

ELOISA

(*To fill an awkward silence*) I'm afraid you didn't do quite as well as your picture, sweetheart. . . .

MALCOLM

(*Sad, but steely*) How much did you sell me for, Jerome?

JEROME

Thirty-five hundred dollars.

MALCOLM

(*Sad, nodding*) I see.

JEROME

You'll be happy with Mr. Girard, Malc.

ELOISA

Oh, you *will*, sweetie!

MALCOLM

(Tiny voice) Where am I to go? *(Clears his throat)* I say, where am I to go?

JEROME

He's waiting for you . . .

ELOISA

(Enthusiastically) . . . at the entrance to the botanical gardens.

JEROME

(Soft) Right now!

ELOISA

Unh-hunh.

MALCOLM

(Confused, lost) Well . . . well, I think I'll say goodbye, then.

JEROME

Not goodbye, Malc; au revoir!

ELOISA

You come see us when we get back . . . if we go.

MALCOLM

(As things fly apart, as the BRACES *vanish)* Yes, well . . . Goodbye, Jerome the burglar, goodbye, Eloisa Brace. Goodbye. Goodbye. *(Alone)* Sold? Sold to Mr. Girard? Like a

. . . a white slave or something? Well, why not? I mean, I suppose it's as natural as anything in the world. But really! You'd think I could stick . . . somewhere! Sold? SOLD? The . . . THE WHOLE WORLD IS FLYING APART! And . . . what's to become of me? WHAT'S TO BECOME OF ME NOW!!??

ACT TWO

SCENE ONE

(The entrance to the botanical gardens. Daylight. MALCOLM
asleep. GUS *enters: tall, brawny, got up in motorcycle uniform;
regards* MALCOLM *briefly, kicks him gently)*

GUS
Hey, buddy; hey; hey, you, there.

MALCOLM
(Waking up, sort of beside himself) Hm? Hm? Girard
Girard, is that . . . ? Oh; excuse me; I'm sorry.

GUS
(Not unfriendly; just all business) You a contemporary?

MALCOLM
(Looking around for GIRARD GIRARD*)* Have you seen . . . you
haven't seen Mr. Girard Girard nearby, have you?

GUS
Don't kid around, buddy.

MALCOLM
(Very sincere) Oh, I'm not kidding around. I assure you, I'm
quite serious. He was supposed to be here last night, and he
and I . . .

GUS
Unh-hunh. I said: you a contemporary?

MALCOLM
(Ponders it) A contemporary of *what?*

GUS

(Not understanding) What?

MALCOLM

Of what?

GUS

(A little edge to his tone) I don't know what you talkin'
about, mister.

MALCOLM

(Rubbing his eyes) Well, I'm afraid I don't know what
you're talking about, either.

GUS

(Shrugs) Don't matter. If you one of the contemporaries, we
go right on over to Melba's. If you ain't, it don't matter too
awful much anyhow, on account of you are the type.

MALCOLM

(Rather abstracted) You don't seem to understand. I came
here yesterday afternoon, at the—I suppose I should say
invitation—of Mr. Girard Girard—I'm sure you've heard of
him—the magnate?

GUS

(Shaking his head) Unh-unh.

MALCOLM

Well; I would have thought everybody had.

GUS

Let's go.

MALCOLM

(Rather panicky) Go! I can't go anywhere, I've been too far

already. You don't know what's happened to me, sir!

GUS

(Firm, but not ugly) Stow it, buddy! Now, come on.

MALCOLM

No! I won't! *I can't!*

GUS

You really waiting for anybody?

MALCOLM

(Small, lost) I . . . thought I was.

GUS

Unh-hunh. Figgered. Come on, boy.

MALCOLM

(Being dragged) Who is . . . who is . . . Melba?

GUS

Melba? You don't know who Melba is?

MALCOLM

I've heard of who Melba was, but this can't possibly be the same lady.

GUS

Where you been living, boy?

MALCOLM

Oh, lots of places.

GUS

An' you never heard of Melba. Well, buddy, you got a pleasure comin'. Melba is a *singer.* And she ain't just any

singer, she is . . . man, she got solid gold records stacked up
like they was dishes.

MALCOLM

(Quite pleased) Really?

GUS

You ain't never heard her records? . . . *Hot in the Rocker?*

MALCOLM

N . . . nooo.

GUS

Or, *When You Said Goodbye, Dark Daddy?*

MALCOLM

(Uncertain) I . . . don't think so; no.

GUS

Boy! You ain't been anywhere. *(Sings)*
    "When you said goodbye, dark daddy,
    Did you know I'd not yet said hello?"

MALCOLM

(Somewhat dubious) That's . . . very catchy.

GUS

She sold eight million of that one.

MALCOLM

(Fascinated by the high figure, nothing else) Eight million!
Really!

GUS

Melba gonna like you. Boy, I *hope* she like you. She say to
me, Gus, you go out and find me a contemporary. *(Small
threat)* You better be a contemporary.

MALCOLM

(Noticing where they're coming to) Well, I'm bound to be, aren't I, of . . . something.

GUS

(Shaking his head) You better be, that's all I gotta say.

SCENE TWO

(*We have come to the backstage area of the club wherein* MELBA *is performing; we hear screaming from "onstage," and we hear* MELBA *singing, vaguely; what we hear mostly is applause and screaming*)

MALCOLM

Where *are* we?

GUS

You hear that? You hear them people?

MALCOLM

(*Rather put off*) Yes, what . . . what *is* all this?

GUS

(*Proud*) That's Melba. Listen to 'em yellin. Boy! She gets 'em. (*Shouting*) GO TO IT, MELBA, BABY!

MALCOLM

But, where are we?

GUS

Why'n't you sit yourself down wait a bit. GO TO IT, BABY. GIVE IT TO 'EM!

MALCOLM

(*Whining some*) I shouldn't be here; Mr. Girard won't know where to find me, and . . . or anything.

GUS

Melba be offstage soon, you just sit wait on her. (WAITER

enters) Hey, Jocko, give us a couple of drinks, now, I brought me a contemporary.

JOCKO

Usual, Gus?

GUS

Natcherly. What you wanna drink, boy?

MALCOLM

(To JOCKO, *sensing he looks familiar)* How do you do? *(To* GUS*)* I . . . I don't know; I don't drink very . . .

GUS

Two of the usual, Jocko-boy; two big ones. (JOCKO *nods, begins to exit)* She knockin'em out, hey?

JOCKO

Right out flat. Two big ones. *(Exits)*
(The song ends, great screaming, shouting. MELBA *backs onstage)*

MELBA

All right! All right! Jesus! God, they love me! Give me a drink. JOCKO!

JOCKO

Here you go, Melba: a big one, the usual.

MELBA

Oh, Jocko baby, you like chimes. *(To them all)* Listen to those bastards out there. Doesn't that warm the old cockles? Wow!

JOCKO

They love you, Melba.

MELBA
(About "them") Nudnicks.

MALCOLM
(To JOCKO) Th-thank you.

MELBA
(Shouting) ALL RIGHT! I'LL BE OUT! SHUT THE . . . *(Mutters)*
Bums. *(Notices* MALCOLM) What you got here, Gus?

JOCKO
(Exiting) Something mighty young, Melba.

GUS
Hey, Melba? You asked me to go find you a contemporary.
How's this? He contemporary enough?

MELBA
(Circles MALCOLM) Hmmmm. What's your name, baby?

MALCOLM
M-Malcolm . . . Melba.

GUS
(Proud) He a contemporary or not?

MELBA
(Still appraising) Unh-hunh. Yup, that's what it is.

GUS
(Proud) I knew I could do it.

MELBA
(Sitting next to Malcolm, putting her arm on him) I'm
Melba, honey . . . sweet little Malcolm.

MALCOLM
(Blushing) Aw, gee . . .

MELBA

(Stroking his cheek) You like me a little bit, Malcolm, baby?

MALCOLM

(About to say something else, does not, kisses MELBA's *hand)*
I've . . . I've had such a . . . long . . . short . . . life.

MELBA

(Raises her glass) To Malcolm, and his long short life. *(Leaning to him)* I could marry you, baby. (MALCOLM *kisses her hand again)*

GUS

You can't get married again, Melba; think of . . .

MELBA

(Threatening) That will do, Gus. *(To* MALCOLM, *now)* Gus was my first husband, old number one, as we sometimes call him.

GUS

I'm not ashamed of it, Melba.

MELBA

I'm so glad he found you, baby. *(Kisses* MALCOLM *on the mouth)* Do you think you could find happiness with me? Hunh?

MALCOLM

(Hesitates briefly, then in tearful, tired relief) Oh, yes I do, Melba; I really do.

MELBA

(To GUS) Isn't it wonderful? Us young people are so . . . are you sulking again? *(No answer; addresses* MALCOLM *again)* Would you marry me, Malcolm?

GUS

(Some anguish) It's too sudden. Wait till Thursday, or somethin'.

MELBA

(To MALCOLM*)* Do you really care for me? I mean, honest-really?

MALCOLM

(Slowly, seriously) I . . . I do, Melba. I've lost so much. *(Kisses her on the throat, impulsively)* I DO, MELBA: I DO!

MELBA

I have never been so quickly surprised, or so quickly happy. *(To* GUS; *rather ugly)* You begrudge me this happiness, don't you! You begrudge me this tiny, tiny bit of happiness in my life of pettiness and struggle. . . .

GUS

Melba, honey, happiness is the last thing I begrudge you, but I don't want you to rush into matrimony this here time; think of all the other times you done got stung. Think of the courts, Melba, honey.

MELBA

(To MALCOLM*)* He begrudges me. *(Snuggles)* God, we'll be happy—for a long, long time.

MALCOLM

(A gurgling sound, resembling a coo) Rrrooooooooo. *(Sits up, startled)*

MELBA

Isn't he beautiful, Gus? You notice the dimples when he smiles. *(Snuggles again)* Aw, *sweet*heart!

MALCOLM

Rrrrooooooo. But *you're* beautiful, Melba. You're the . . . beautiful one.

MELBA

And you really feel you want to marry me, dearest?

GUS

(A cry of pain) MELBA, SWEET JESUS!!

MELBA

(To MALCOLM*)* He's carrying a torch, sweetheart; don't pay
any attention to him.

MALCOLM

(Stammering) You're . . . my girl . . . Melba.

MELBA

(Sighing happily) I've simply got it is all; it's come like light-
ning, and . . . well, I've been got.

GUS

I may be carryin' a torch, Melba, honey, but SWEET JESUS,
HE AIN'T OLD ENOUGH!!

MELBA

(Stopping MALCOLM's *ears)* Don't listen to him; jealousy and
rage, that's all it is. Six weeks of marriage teaches you an
awful lot about a man. But *our* marriage, Malcolm, will last.
on, and on . . . precious.

MALCOLM

(About to swoon with joy) Oh, Melba!

MELBA

(Rising, more businesslike) Good boy. Now, I gotta go out
and sing some more, sing for our wedding supper, babyface.

MALCOLM

But . . . but, Melba!

MELBA

No buts, baby. Momma gotta work.

MALCOLM

Aw, Melba . . .

MELBA

(*Hand on hip*) Well, of course, I *could* quit my career, honey, and you could go out run telegrams or something.

MALCOLM

(*Little boy*) I . . . I understand, Melba.

MELBA

(*Effusive again*) Aw, give me a kiss, sweetheart. (*Engulfs* MALCOLM *again, kisses him lots*)

MALCOLM

Rrrrrroooooooo.

MELBA

You hear those bastards out there? They're my public, angel-face, those nogoods. You my private. See ya Thursday, hunh?

MALCOLM

(*Very serious*) Till . . . till Thursday . . . Melba.

MELBA

Bye, sweetpants. (*As the crowd sounds increase*) I'M COMING! YA BUMS! (*To* MALCOLM, *kissing him one last time*) Gus'll take real good care of you, baby. (*To* GUS) Gus, you take real good care of, uh, Malcolm here, ya hear? (*Waving at* MALCOLM, *blowing him a kiss. Sotto voce to* GUS, *taking money from her bodice, giving it to* GUS) Mature him up a little, you know? You know what I mean? Mature him up a little. (MELBA *exits, the crowd sounds swell.*)

ENTRE-SCENE

(GUS *and* MALCOLM *walking, the last scene having faded*)

GUS
(*Shaking his head*) I don't know; I just don't know.

MALCOLM
(*Lost little boy*) Gus? . . . What have I done?

GUS
(*Talking more or less to himself*) Mature him up a little bit, she says. Mature him up! How the hell I gonna do that, hunh?

MALCOLM
Gus? What have I done?

GUS
Hm?

MALCOLM
What have I done?

GUS
What have you done!? You have got yourself engaged to Melba baby, that what you done.

MALCOLM
I don't under*stand.*

GUS
(*Remembering*) She sure is a knockout, hunh?

MALCOLM

I mean, I've never *felt* like that before, and everything happened so quickly, and . . .

GUS

Bang! it hits! Unh? The old kazamm; pow!

MALCOLM

(Wonder) But I just met her, and . . .

GUS

Well, you get a chance to get to know her some.

MALCOLM

It's . . . it's being so close to her like that . . . when she . . . hugs and everything.

GUS

(Pained) Don't talk about it, boy.

MALCOLM

(Blushing) And . . . and when she kisses and all . . .

GUS

(Anguish) Just *don't!* Don't *stir* me.

MALCOLM

. . . and everything happens, and . . .

GUS

(Returning slowly to businesslike stature) An' . . . an' now we gotta mature you up some. *(Shows* MALCOLM *the money)* See this? This is money to mature you up, boy. Now, look, Malco-boy, I gotta ask you a plain question.

MALCOLM

(Nodding happily) Yes.

GUS

To put it delicate-like, boy, have you ever been completely and solidly joined to a woman? Have you ever been joined to a woman the way nature meant? Yes or no.

MALCOLM

(After a puzzled pause) Well, it's always been so very dark—where I was—and people were—shifting so . . .

GUS

I can see you ain't, and that's what Melba meant—what she sent us out for, to mature you up.

SCENE THREE

(Set comes on. Sign saying PRIVATE AND TURKISH BATHS. CABI-
NETS AND OVERNIGHT COTTAGES. $2.00)

GUS

You see that place over there? That's where I'm gonna take
you: Rosita's. Madame Rosita they used to call her. You
heard of her?

MALCOLM

(Shakes his head) No.

GUS

You ain't heard of anything! Well, that's what I'm here for.
(Mumbles) That what sweet Melba told me t'do—get you
ready. . . .

MALCOLM

(A little confused) You're . . . you're very kind, Gus.

GUS

(Gives MALCOLM *a funny look; calls)* Hey, Miles, Miles? *(A
seedy man comes out, green visor; played by the actor who
plays* COX) Miles? How you doin', boy?

MILES

Gus, is that really you? Well, I'll be damned. *(Looks at* MAL-
COLM, *who is staring at him, open-mouthed)* Where'd you get
him—the one with his mouth hangin' open?

MALCOLM

(Rather hurt) But, Mr. Cox!

MILES

(It is not cox, *of course)* Name is Miles, boy. Gus, how long's
it been?

GUS

(Bringing out the money) Need some work done, Miles; quick
and special.

MALCOLM

(Very hurt) Mr. Cox!

MILES

(Very straight) That ain't my name, boy. Work, Gus?

GUS

(Yawning) Yeah, house special for the boy.

MILES

(Looks at MALCOLM *dubiously)* I was just wonderin' if you'd
noticed this kid here is sorta young.

GUS

(Waves the money under MILES' *nose)* Oh, I don't know.

MILES

Yeah, well, looks is deceiving.

GUS

He gonna marry Melba.

MILES

Hunh! Who ain't!

MALCOLM

(Offended) Please!

GUS

(To MALCOLM*)* Now, upstairs is where you're gonna go, kiddie.
When you through, you come down here an' wake me up.
Which is my room, Miles?

MILES

(Counting the money) You pick one out; nobody here tonight
at all.

GUS

O.K., I take me old number twenty-two. *(To* MALCOLM*)* You
got that, boy? Twenty-two.

MALCOLM

(Shivering a little) R-right.
    *(Enters a woman of indeterminate age, a parody of
    a whore; to be played by the actress who plays*
    LAUREEN*)*

ROSITA

Gus! Baby! It's been years! *(Goes to embrace him)*

GUS

It's the boy this time, uh, sweetheart. I just gonna get me a
shower and a snooze; I ain't had no sleep in a week, if you
know what I mean.

ROSITA

Let me get this all down. You are sending *him* . . . upstairs
for *you.*

GUS

Break him in, for Christ's sake, will ya?

MALCOLM

(A little scared) I could swear I know you, madame.

GUS

(To MALCOLM; *weary)* You do like I told you now, back in the street. I want you to go through it all just like I told you nature meant.

ROSITA

(Gives GUS *a quiet raspberry; says to* MALCOLM*)* O.K., you come on with me, honey. *(Begins dragging* MALCOLM *off)*

GUS

(To MALCOLM *as he is exited)* An' don't you come back down without you had it, you hear?

MALCOLM

(Being exited) Had . . . had what!

ROSITA

Come on.

MILES

(Shakes his head; laughs) Jesus!

GUS

(Chuckling) Poor baby boy.

MILES

Gonna shack up with Melba, hunh?

GUS

Weddin' bells and all. *(Moving off, slowly, wearily)* Oh, I tell you, Miles, I am so weary, so sad. . . . I think I'll lie down, not wake up again. Wouldn't matter . . . 'cept for the kid, there.

MILES

(As they exit) How old *is* he?

GUS

Malco? I don't know: fourteen, fifteen, maybe. Don't matter:
Melba'll age him up a little.

(MILES *and* GUS *have exited*)

SCENE FOUR

(MALCOLM *and* ROSITA *come on,* MALCOLM *carrying the locket*)

ROSITA

Well, goodbye and God bless, kiddie. You're the real stuff.

MALCOLM

Gee, thanks, Rosita.

ROSITA

You've made an old woman very happy. *(She exits as soon as possible)*

MALCOLM

(Left alone, joyous) Melba? Melba? (MELBA *appears, way down right, say, with open arms*)

MELBA

Here I am, baby. Come to Momma!

MALCOLM

(Going to her, puppylike enthusiasm) I . . . I did it, Melba, all the way through . . . three times! Wow! It looks like I'll be a bridegroom after all.

MELBA

(Pleased) Yeah?

MALCOLM

Yes, and Madame Rosita paid me a compliment; she said I was the real stuff, and she gave me tea . . . in between . . . and when we were all done she gave me this locket, which has a real, little tiny American flag all rolled up inside.

MELBA

Yeah; that's great. Let's go to Chicago, baby!

MALCOLM

But . . . but why?

MELBA

You ever been married in Chicago?

MALCOLM

Well . . . no!

MELBA

Well, neither have I, baby! Let's go! *(They race off together)*

ENTRE-SCENE

(*Another no-set promenade.* MADAME GIRARD *comes on, followed by* KERMIT; *they stroll*)

MADAME GIRARD
(*Not looking at* KERMIT *as they walk;* KERMIT *keeps eyeing her, with a set mouth and mistrustful eyes*) I understand—though one is never sure of one's information in a world of gossips—that they were married in Chicago. Would you like a peppermint? No? That they were married in Chicago, by some defrocked justice of the peace—a scandal, if you care for my opinion—stop eyeing me—that they flew to the Caribbean for a honeymoon which was interrupted by their having to move from hotel to hotel, country to country, that they have returned here, where that loathsome brat of a chanteuse has resumed her career of caterwauling, and that Malcolm—that poor, dear child—walk with me, can you?—is virtually a prisoner in some den she keeps. (*Sobs*) I have written *letters*! I have *tele*phoned! My calls have been answered by a manservant who sounds Cuban at the least, and my letters! Stop staring at me! My letters have been returned to me, unopened, with semi-literate notes, scrawled by that girl Svengali, informing me that Malcolm—oh, dear God, child, come back to me!—is busy at being married, is too occupied and happy to be, as she puts it, dragged under by his past! If you will not walk like a proper companion, we shall both stand still. (*They stand still*) Too occupied! Too happy! Dear Lord, can people be that? (KERMIT *stands in front of her, rather like a bulldog about to spring*) Are you going to bite me? You?—you who ruined everything? You who cringed when we came to take you with us? You, but for whom we should all be together now, Malcolm with us? Malcolm's pic-

ture! His picture stares at me, and tells me, "It is not I, dear
Madame Girard, not I. Not I, dear Madame Girard, not I."
I can't look at it any more! It is *not* my Malcolm. Help me!
Help me, please! Get me my Malcolm back! (KERMIT *starts
walking off*) Wait! Help me! Dearest Kermit! Wait! (*She
exits after him*)

SCENE FIVE

(As MADAME GIRARD *exits, we hear* MALCOLM *and* MELBA
giggling, she shrieking a little, too. Lights come up on MAL-
COLM *in bed, naked to the waist, or wearing pajamas, depending on the build of the actor playing the part.* MELBA *in a
negligee, on the bed beside him.* MELBA *is tickling him)*

MALCOLM
(Very ticklish, speaks between giggles) Melba . . . honey
. . . please . . . Melba . . .

MELBA
How's my kitchy-koo? Kitchy-kitchy-kitchy? Hmmmm?

MALCOLM
(A cry-giggle) MMMM EEEEELLLLLBBBBB AAAAA.

MELBA
Kitchy-kitchy-kitchy? Aw, sweetheart. *(Kisses him all over)*
Aw, baby. Come to Melba.

MALCOLM
(Giggles subsiding some) Aw, honest, Melba, I love you; I do.

MELBA
(Seriously, sensuously; hand on his crotch) Oh, I do love you,
too, sweet pants. Yes, I do. . . . You have *got* it, baby; you
have got what Melba wants.

MALCOLM
We . . . do an awful lot of being married, don't we, Melba?

MELBA

(Eyes closed) Oooooh, you are good at marriage, sweetheart, yes, you are. Gimme that mouth of yours, tonguey-boy. Ummmmmmmm. *(Kisses him fervently)* Oh baby let's do marriage right this second sweetheart lover baby dollface, c'mon, c'MON!

MALCOLM

(Seeing that HELIODORO, *the Cuban valet, has entered with a tray of coffee)* Uh, Melba . . .

MELBA

C'mon, sweetpants, let's get some action goin'. . . .

MALCOLM

Uh . . . good—good morning, Heliodoro.

MELBA

Hunh? *(Sees* HELIODORO*)* What the hell do you want?

HELIODORO

(Who is played by one of the YOUNG MEN*)* Coffee; coffee time.

MELBA

Nuts! It's take the frigging coffee and get the hell out of the bedroom time; that's what time it is.

MALCOLM

I'd . . . *(timidly)* . . . I'd like some coffee, Melba, and . . . and maybe some breakfast? Breakfast, too?

MELBA

(Mock tough) Married six weeks, an' he's cold as a stone. Look at 'im. *(Cuddles)* Baby want breakfast?

MALCOLM

Just . . . just a little.

MELBA

(Gets up off the bed, stretches, shows off a little for HELIO-
DORO*)* O.K. Momma got to go to work anyway. But you stay
right there, sweetheart; you just lie there an' read a funny-
book, or somethin', so Momma know where you are when
she want you. O.K.?

MALCOLM

(So smitten) I'll . . . be right here where you want me,
Melba.

MELBA

Right on top, baby! That's where I want you. Hey, don't
forget, hotrocks, we're goin' out clubbin' tonight after I get
done work.

MALCOLM

(Small protest in this) We go . . . to a nightclub *every* night,
Melba. At least one.

MELBA

(To a child) Well, I'm proud of my baby. *(To* HELIODORO*)*
Fix him a Bloody Mary or somethin', will you?

HELIODORO

Maybe he shouldn't drink so . . .

MELBA

(Murderous) Fix him a goddam Bloody Mary! *(Blows* MAL-
COLM *a kiss)* See you, sweetheart. *(Exits)*

HELIODORO

You want coffee?

MALCOLM

Yes, please, and . . . I don't need a Bloody Mary, O.K.?
Some . . . eggs and toast and bacon, and . . .

HELIODORO

You gettin' thin.

MALCOLM

(*Sweet and innocent*) Melba says marriage is a thinning business.

HELIODORO

(*Shrugs*) I suppose she oughta know.

MALCOLM

Have you been married, Heliodoro?

HELIODORO

(*Laughs*) Me? No, I'm too young.

MALCOLM

How old *are* you?

HELIODORO

Twenty-two.

MALCOLM

(*Sad*) Yes, that's very young. (*Brightly*) I'm . . . fifteen, I think.

HELIODORO

(*Changing the subject*) That . . . that lady called again today.

MALCOLM

(*Some gloom*) I don't know why Melba won't let me see Madame Girard or . . . or anybody . . . any of my friends. I . . . well, I love Melba like all get out, and everything . . . but . . . I get lonely . . . just being here like this.

HELIODORO

(*A little embarrassed*) You . . . you want to start your Bloody Marys?

MALCOLM

(*Weary; head back on pillow*) I suppose so; I suppose I'd better if Melba thinks I should.

HELIODORO

I'll bring you a Bloody Mary.

MALCOLM

(*Weary*) I suppose you should: I've got a long, hard day ahead of me.

(FADE)

ENTRE-SCENE

(ELOISA *and* JEROME *come on, huffily, pursued by* GIRARD GIRARD. *No set needed; this* can *be in the nature of a promenade*)

ELOISA

I have never been so insulted; never, in my long and scrabby life—the life of an artist, always hurt, always wanting—have I been so insulted. Jerome? Don't talk to the man.

GIRARD GIRARD

But my dear Mrs. Brace . . .

ELOISA

Never.

GIRARD GIRARD

(*Both of the others are huffily silent. Reasoning*) I have come to you, beseeching, a humble man, casting about in the dark . . .

ELOISA

You have not! You came in here, you came upon us, near-*flagrante*, howling your insults. . . .

GIRARD GIRARD

I DID NO SUCH THING!

ELOISA

(*Snappish; for confirmation*) Jerome?

JEROME

Never, in all my years behind bars . . .

GIRARD GIRARD

(Anguish) Where is Malcolm? Please!

ELOISA

Hah! Accusing us again, are you?

GIRARD GIRARD

(Patient) I have accused you of nothing, my good woman. I merely explained that I had a business matter of some urgency to settle and when I arrived at the botanical gardens, some hours later than I had intended to . . .

ELOISA

He'd gone!

GIRARD GIRARD

Yes!

ELOISA

And that *we* had stolen him!

GIRARD GIRARD

No!

JEROME

(Sneering) We heard you.

GIRARD GIRARD

I suggested no such thing!

ELOISA

We may be poor . . .

JEROME

. . . and I may have a record a yard long, but . . .

GIRARD GIRARD

WHERE IS MALCOLM!?

ELOISA

(Sniffs. After a tiny pause) I'm sure we don't know.

JEROME

(Oily) It's out of our hands, buddy; we delivered the merchandise, free and clear, good condition; we don't take no responsibility for . . .

GIRARD GIRARD

Please! I must have him!

ELOISA

(Grand) It would seem to me that if you're careless enough to . . . abandon the child under some bushes somewhere while you go about your filthy moneymaking . . .

JEROME

. . . that it's hardly our affair.

ELOISA

We did not steal him.

GIRARD GIRARD

(Sad, defeated) I . . . I merely wondered.

ELOISA

Well, we . . . we have problems enough of our own, without running any sort of . . .

GIRARD GIRARD

If . . . if he returns to you . . .

ELOISA

There you go again.

JEROME

Prison was nothing! The unimaginable indignities of the

cell block were . . . were frolic next to . . . to your vile and tawdry suggestion, sir.

GIRARD GIRARD

Jerome, I merely . . .

ELOISA

Never! Tell me this, Girard Girard: do you think your wealth entitles you? Do you?

JEROME

The older prisoners, after lights out, making straight for the cells where the younger inmates cower, their rough blankets pulled over their heads . . .

GIRARD GIRARD

My dear friends . . .

ELOISA

La vie de Boheme, Girard Girard, may indeed seem loose and unprincipled to some, but . . .

JEROME

. . . or the entrapments in the shower room, two or three, coming at you . . . lathered bodies, all glistening, slow smiles . . .

ELOISA

(An aside) Control yourself, Jerome.

SCENE SIX

(*To one side of the stage, a nightclub table, with* MALCOLM *and* MELBA *at it, both noticeably drunk. Lots of noise in the background, music, chattering*)

MELBA

You like rum sours, baby?

MALCOLM

I would seem to, Melba-honey. This is number . . . what?

MELBA

Who cares? Drink up.

MALCOLM

(*Notices* MELBA *open a vial*) Melba, what *is* that stuff you're always putting in our drinks and all?

MELBA

(*Pouring some in their drinks*) Magic, sweetheart, magic; makes you feel all athletic when we get home, right?

MALCOLM

(*Giggles sillily*) Right, baby.

MELBA

And, of course, I *didn't* marry you for your mind.

MALCOLM

(*Drunken pondering*) I . . . . noticed that.

MELBA

You're gettin' awful thin, big boy. I *like* you thin, you understand, but I suppose I'd like you fat, too.

MALCOLM

(Puppydog) I . . . I like you, too, Melba-pussy.

MELBA

(Abrupt, faintly histrionic) Don't call me that; number three called me that; it's sacred.

MALCOLM

What is?

MELBA

(Embarrassed at the sacredness; almost whispers it) Melba-pussy.

MALCOLM

(Laughs) Well, what shall I call you? Melba-puppy? *(Laughs greatly, happily)* Melba-puppy?

MELBA

You're annoying, kiddie, you really are.

MALCOLM

(Having noticed a MAN *walk across the stage to a dark area)* That's HE . . . THAT'S MY FATHER! *(Rises)*

MELBA

Sit down, baby.

MALCOLM

(Moving to go after the MAN*)* THAT'S MY FATHER.

MELBA

(Sharp) Come back here, Malcolm!

MALCOLM

(Unrestrainable, moving to the other side of the stage) THAT'S
MY FATHER!

SCENE SEVEN

(The area on MELBA *blacks out, and the lights come up on the* MAN, *in a washroom, facing the audience, washing his hands at a basin)*

MALCOLM

(Stretching his arms out to the MAN, *weaving a little)* Father! Where did you go all this time? *(The* MAN *either touches his hair or his mustache, does not reply or take notice of* MALCOLM*)* Don't you *recognize* me? I'd . . . I'd recognize *you* anywhere. *(Still no response from the* MAN*)* Father! *(Goes up to him, puts his arm on his shoulder)* Please, father . . .

MAN

(Looks straight at MALCOLM, *no recognition; cold)* Would you allow me to pass?

MALCOLM

You're . . . you're pretending not to recognize me! Is it . . . is it because I married Melba, or because I left the bench, or because I . . .

MAN

(Making an effort to get by) Allow me to pass!

MALCOLM

(Starting to grapple with the MAN; *the struggle gets hotter)* Please, father! It's me! It's Malcolm!

MAN

Help! Help!

MALCOLM

(Grappling) Please, father! I've missed you so, and I've been so lonely, and . . .

MAN

(Struggling) Let go of me!

MALCOLM

(In tears now) Father! Father!

(The MAN seizes MALCOLM and throws him hard; MALCOLM either hits the washbasin or the floor, heavily. An ATTENDANT enters, played by the actor who plays COX)

MAN

(Pointing to the crumpled MALCOLM) Have that child arrested. He attacked me!

MALCOLM

(Weeping, from the floor) Father, I am Malcolm!

MAN

Indeed! *(Turns on his heel, walks into blackness)*

ATTENDANT

Well, now, what's going on? *(MALCOLM babbles a few thank yous as the attendant helps him to a sitting position)*

MALCOLM

Melba? Have you seen my wife, sir?

ATTENDANT

(Incredulous) You? Are married?

MALCOLM

(Cheerful through the pain) Yes, sir! Would you like to meet my wife?

ATTENDANT

(Examining MALCOLM's *head)* You're bleeding, boy.

MALCOLM

I . . . I am?

ATTENDANT

That's quite a cut.

MALCOLM

My father refused to recognize me.

ATTENDANT

Who?

MALCOLM

My . . . my father.

ATTENDANT

That couldn't have been your father, sonny.

MALCOLM

N-no?

ATTENDANT

That old pot's been coming here for years. He's nobody's father.

MALCOLM

I . . . I thought it was my father.

ATTENDANT

Better get you home, kid. You don't look so hot.

MALCOLM

Maybe . . . maybe my father . . . never existed.

ATTENDANT

Who knows, son? Better get you to a doctor before you
bleed to death, or something.

MALCOLM

Maybe he never existed at all!

SCENE EIGHT

(MADAME GIRARD *and* HELIODORO *walk on. They are moving toward the solarium*)

MADAME GIRARD
(*All camp is gone from here to the end of the play*) I apologize to you, young man, if I have bothered you with my calls, my constant ringing.

HELIODORO
That's O.K.

MADAME GIRARD
My search for the one decent thing in this entire world.

HELIODORO
It's O.K.

MADAME GIRARD
Where is my Malcolm? And where is that girl?

HELIODORO
She—an' you mean, I think, great Melba-baby—is with the doctor.

MADAME GIRARD
Why was I not told until now?

HELIODORO
You wanna come in the solarium?

MADAME GIRARD
Of course I want to come into the solarium. My God, what

a bright solarium! Where *is* she? Where is that filthy girl?

HELIODORO
(Embarrassed) You better watch who you talkin' about, buddy.

(MELBA *enters)*

MADAME GIRARD
Is that her?

HELIODORO
She call you filthy, baby.

MELBA
(Indifferent) Yeah? Go fix us a drink. *(As* HELIODORO *hangs back)* Well, go on, kiddo.

HELIODORO
I don't wanna leave you here with her, baby.

MELBA
Aw, go be a sweetheart and go get us a drink, hunh?

MADAME GIRARD
Keep your hands off the servants. You are a married woman, if you care to remember.

HELIODORO
See? *(Exits)*

MELBA
(Braying) Yeah? Well, look here, Madame Hotsy-Totsy, or whatever your name used to be . . .

MADAME GIRARD
IS!

MELBA

I been married a few times, you know? And I know how to act.

MADAME GIRARD

Have pity on us human beings, please!

MELBA

What do you want, a job or something? You looking for work?

MADAME GIRARD

I am looking for Malcolm!

MELBA

Yeah? Well, I got him, lady; move on.

MADAME GIRARD

I can have you arrested, you know that?

MELBA

Get the hell out of here, will . . .

MADAME GIRARD

THE CHILD IS FIFTEEN YEARS OLD!!!!

MELBA

GET OUT!!

MADAME GIRARD

I warn you, youngish woman, if there is so much as one hair of his precious head that I find damaged, you'll rue the day you ever took it on yourself to . . .

MELBA

(*Really beside herself*) GET OUT!!!!

MADAME GIRARD

(*While the* DOCTOR *is entering*) THERE ARE THINGS IN THIS LIFE

WHICH MAY NOT BE PERMITTED!! *(Sees him)* Are you the
doctor?

DOCTOR

I am.

MADAME GIRARD

How is my Malcolm!?

DOCTOR

Are you family?

MADAME GIRARD

I am more than family.

DOCTOR

(Picking his words carefully) He . . . is beyond human care.
(MADAME GIRARD *stifles a cry.)*

MELBA

(Dryly, after a moment) What do you mean, buddy?

DOCTOR

(Looking at neither of them) The child is dying.

MADAME GIRARD

DYING!!

MELBA

(Pause) Don't be stupid.

DOCTOR

There is nothing that can be done: give him rest, a bed to
himself, quiet. He is very near death.

MADAME GIRARD

You are a *quack!*

DOCTOR

I may have seen better days, lady, but I know dying when I look at it.

MELBA

(*Clears her throat*) Uh, what is my Malcolm-baby dying of?

MADAME GIRARD

(*Hoping to make it true*) This man doesn't know what he's talking about. People like Malcolm do not die: there isn't room for it.

MELBA

(*Rather harsh*) What's he dying of, hunh?

DOCTOR

(*Reticent*) The . . . young man . . . is dying of a combination of acute alcoholism and, uh, sexual hyperaesthesia, to put it simply.

MADAME GIRARD

(*A command*) NO!

MELBA

(*To the doctor; wincing a little*) I, uh, didn't get you, baby.

MADAME GIRARD

(*Turning full, loss and sickened wrath on* MELBA) You . . . ! you . . . WANTON! Malcolm? MALCOLM? (*Runs off into the blackness*)

DOCTOR

(*Repeating it, mumbling some*) Acute alcoholism and sexual hyperaesthesia: the combination of the two . . . well, one would be enough, but . . .

MELBA

(*Trying to avoid it, quite nervous*) Look, uh, what is this . . .

this sexual stuff, hunh? I mean, he's only been with me, and . . .

DOCTOR

Sexual hyperaesthesia?

MELBA

Uh, yeah; that.

DOCTOR

Sexual hperaesthesia is, or can be more easily described as, a violent protracted excess of sexual intercourse. (MELBA *just stares at him*) I can give you a prescription . . . for the child . . . useless, of course. . . . (*Sees the answer is "no," shrugs, exits*)

HELIODORO

(*Who is entering as the* DOCTOR *exits*) You O.K., baby? (MELBA *is just standing there, swaying a little*) Hey . . . Melba . . . you O.K.?

MELBA

(*Preoccupied, a little sad, but calm*) Hunh? (*Puts her hand out for his*) Hey, give me a hand, will ya, sweetie? This just ain't a good day. Old Malcolm's gonna die. He's gonna leave us.

HELIODORO

(*Quiet surprise*) Yeah? (*They exit*)

SCENE NINE

(Malcolm's bedroom. MALCOLM *propped up on pillows, pale, half-conscious. The room in near-darkness.* MADAME GIRARD *enters, hesitantly, comes to the bed)*

MADAME GIRARD

Malcolm? Malcolm? Can I help?

MALCOLM

(Little boy) Is it . . . true? Am I going to die?

MADAME GIRARD

(Not looking at him; softly) Well . . . who is to say?

MALCOLM

(Home truth) You.

MADAME GIRARD

I . . . suspect it may be so.

MALCOLM

(Sits up in bed, says, with great force) BUT I'M NOT EVEN TWENTY! IT'S . . . NOT BEEN TWENTY YEARS!

MADAME GIRARD

(Easing him back to the pillows) Malcolm . . . please.

MALCOLM

(Lying back, a little delirious) I've . . . lost so much, I've . . . lost so very much. (MADAME GIRARD *gets up, moves a little away, doesn't look at* MALCOLM) And . . . everyone has . . . swept by . . . Kermit and, and Mr. Girard . . .

(MADAME GIRARD *stiffens a little*) . . . and even Mr. Cox
. . . *(She thinks to speak; does not)* . . . and . . . my father . . . my FATHER! . . . What . . . *(softly)* what have I
not lost?

MADAME GIRARD
*(Waits, expecting more, nodding. Waits, suddenly realizes,
turns)* No . . . *(shakes her head)* . . . no . . . PRINCE!
(Goes to the bed, touches him, takes her hand away) Say
. . . say more. . . . There's more. *(Begins to cry)* There's
. . . much, much more. More, Oh, Malcolm . . . oh, child.
My Malcolm. What have you not lost? . . . And I . . .
And all . . . What have *we* not lost? What, indeed. Did
none of us ever care? *(The others start coming on, will group
near, around, behind the bed)* You, my poor husband, with
that woman you choose to call your wife? Or you? Or you?
Or even you. Malcolm is dead.

KERMIT
Malcolm? Dead?

LAUREEN
Dead?

ELOISA
Just like that?

JEROME
(Quiet awe) Wow.

MADAME GIRARD
No, not just like that.

COX
I suppose he didn't have the stuff, that's all. God knows,
I tried.

MADAME GIRARD

Oh, yes, we tried . . . we all tried.

MALCOLM

I'm . . . I'm cold.

MADAME GIRARD

And you, my husband? Silent?

GIRARD GIRARD

(*Considerable pain*) Let it go, my dear. He . . . he passed through so quickly; none of us could grasp hold.

LAUREEN

We tried.

ELOISA

Sure; we tried.

JEROME

Sure.

LAUREEN

He was a sweet kid.

KERMIT

I tried . . . as much as I could.

COX

He didn't have the stuff, that's all.

MADAME GIRARD

None of you . . . ever cared. (*She senses they want to leave*) I shall have a funeral for him! A silver casket? Banks of roses and violets? Thousands and thousands of . . . and a gilded hearse? With black-plumed horses?

GIRARD GIRARD

Let it go, my dear.

LAUREEN

Yes, let it go.

MADAME GIRARD

None of you . . . ever cared. None of you. *(They begin to
fade)*

ELOISA

We cared, dear.

JEROME

Sure, we cared.

LAUREEN

Of course we did, dear.

KERMIT

I cared . . . as much as I could.

GIRARD GIRARD

Let it go, my dear.

COX

He . . . he didn't have the stuff . . . that's all.

MADAME GIRARD

(Isolated now) You . . . you can come and see his portrait
. . . if you care. It's . . . not much. But . . . it will have to
do. That's all that's left. Just that. Nothing more. Nothing
more. Just that.

(As the lights fade on MADAME GIRARD *and the dead* MAL-
COLM, *they rise on the golden bench, high on a platform,
above and behind. The bench is suffused in a golden light for
a few moments, then all fades to blackness)*

THE PLAY

THE BALLAD
OF THE
SAD CAFE

CARSON
MCCULLERS'
NOVELLA
ADAPTED TO
THE STAGE BY
EDWARD
ALBEE

This adaptation to the stage
of THE BALLAD OF THE SAD CAFE
is dedicated to Carson McCullers,
of course, with great love.

EDWARD ALBEE

October 30, 1963, New York City, Martin Beck Theatre

THE NARRATOR	ROSCOE LEE BROWNE
RAINEY 1	LOUIS W. WALDON
RAINEY 2	DEANE SELMIER
STUMPY MAC PHAIL	JOHN C. BECHER
HENRY MACY	WILLIAM PRINCE
MISS AMELIA EVANS	COLLEEN DEWHURST
COUSIN LYMON	MICHAEL DUNN
EMMA HALE	ENID MARKEY
MRS. PETERSON	JENNY EGAN
MERLIE RYAN	ROBERTS BLOSSOM
HORACE WELLS	WILLIAM DUELL
HENRY FORD CRIMP	DAVID CLARKE
ROSSER CLINE	GRIFF EVANS
LUCY WILLINS	NELL HARRISON
MRS. HASTY MALONE	BETTE HENRITZE
MARVIN MACY	LOU ANTONIO
HENRIETTA FORD CRIMP, JR.	SUSAN DUNFEE
TOWNSPEOPLE	ERNEST AUSTIN
	ALICE DRUMMOND
	JACK KEHOE

Directed by ALAN SCHNEIDER

Set by BEN EDWARDS
Lighting by JEAN ROSENTHAL
Music by WILLIAM FLANAGAN
Production Stage Manager, JOHN MAXTONE-GRAHAM

THE BALLAD
OF THE
SAD CAFE

THE SET

One set: MISS AMELIA'S *house (later the cafe) taking most of the stage, not centered, though, but tending to stage-right, leaving a playing area, stage-left, for the battle, which will take place out-of-doors.* MISS AMELIA'S *house must be practical, in the sense that its interior will be used, both upstairs and down, and, as well, we must be able to see its exterior without entering it. The main street of the town runs before the porch of the house, parallel to the apron of the stage.*

THE BALLAD OF THE SAD CAFE

is meant to be played without an intermission

Noon sun; street deserted; house boarded up;
nothing moves, no one is to be seen; heat; quiet.
Music: under all or some of the following.

THE NARRATOR

The Ballad of the Sad Cafe. The Beginning.

This building here—this boarded-up house—is twice distinguished; it is the oldest building in town . . . and the largest. Of course, the town is not very old—nor is it very large. There isn't much to it, except the cotton mill, the two-room houses where the workers live, a few peach trees, a church with two water-colored windows, and a miserable main street only a hundred yards long. The town is lonesome—sad—like a place that is far off and estranged from all other places in the world. The winters here are short and raw . . . the summers—white with glare, and fiery hot. If you walk along the main street on an August afternoon, there is nothing whatever to do. (*Pause*) There is heat . . . and silence. (*Pause*) Notice that window up there; notice that second-story window; notice that shuttered window. There's someone living up there. (*Short pause*) These August afternoons there is absolutely nothing to do; you might as well walk down to the Fork Falls Road and watch the chain gang . . . listen to the men sing. Though . . .
   (*Here, the upstairs window mentioned before, slowly*
   opens, and MISS AMELIA's *appearance at the window*
   is described as it occurs)

. . . look now; watch the window. (*Pause*) Sometimes, in
the late afternoon, when the heat is at its worst, a hand will
slowly open the shutter there, and a face will look down at
the town . . . a terrible, dim face . . . like the faces known
in dreams. The face will linger at the window for an hour
or so,

> (*Silence for a moment or two, then, as the shutters
> are slowly closed*)

. . . then the shutters will be closed once more, and as likely
as not there will not be another soul to be seen along the
main street.

> (*Silence; a lighting change begins*)

But once . . . once, this building—this boarded-up house—
was a cafe. Oh, there were tables with paper napkins, colored
streamers hanging from the lamps, and great gatherings on
Saturday nights.

> (*Perhaps an echo of such sounds here*)

It was the center of the town! And this cafe . . . this cafe
was run by a Miss Amelia Evans . . . who lives up there
even now . . . whose face, in the late afternoons, sometimes,
when the heat is at its worst, can be seen peering out from
that shuttered window.

> (*Now we are shifting to an April evening, eight years
> previous. The boarded-up house will become a gen-
> eral store, its interior and exterior both visible*)

We are going back in time now, back even before the opening of the cafe, for there are two stories to be told: How the
cafe came into being . . . for there was not always a cafe
. . . and how the cafe . . . died. How we came to . . . silence.

> (*By now it is night; the lights are dim in the general
> store, the interior of which is visible. During the fol-
> lowing paragraph, three townsmen saunter onstage,
> move to the porch in front of the store; two sit on
> the steps, one leans against a porch post or the build-
> ing itself*)

It is toward midnight; April . . . eight years ago. Most people are in bed, but several men of the town, for reasons we shall see directly, prefer the front steps of Miss Amelia's general store. It is the kind of night when it is good to hear from far away, across the dark fields, the slow song of a field hand on his way to make love; or when it is pleasant to sit quietly and pick a guitar, or simply to rest alone, and think of nothing at all. Talk . . . or stay silent.

(*The focus of the scene is now on the general store. Brief tableau, held chord under it*)

The men are STUMPY MACPHAIL, *and the* RAINEY TWINS, RAINEY 1 *and* RAINEY 2. THEY *are silent; then a figure is seen coming in the shadows from stage-right.*

MACPHAIL

Who is that? (*The figure continues advancing*) I said, who is that there?

RAINEY 1 (*A high, giggly voice*)

Why, it's Henry Macy; that's who it is.

RAINEY 2 (HE, *too*)

Henry Macy; Henry Macy.

MACPHAIL

Henry?

HENRY MACY
(*In view now, by the porch. Nods*)

Stumpy; evening. (*Then, to the twins*) Boys?

RAINEY 2

How you, Henry? And how is Marvin, Henry? How is your brother?

(RAINEY 1 *giggles*)

MACPHAIL
Now, now.

RAINEY 1
How is he enjoying his stay, Henry? How is he enjoying the
penitentiary?

MACPHAIL
Quiet, you!

HENRY MACY *(Placating)*
Now, Stumpy . . .

MACPHAIL
You got no sense at all? You *all* foolish in the head? Talk
about Marvin Macy, Miss Amelia nearby, maybe, God knows?
(RAINEY 2 *giggles*)
Miss Amelia hear that name, she knock you clear to Society
City.
(Both RAINEYS *giggle)*

HENRY MACY *(A weary sigh)*
That true, Lord knows.

MACPHAIL
Knock you clear to Society City.

RAINEY 2
Miss Amelia ain't back. She at the still.

MACPHAIL
It don't matter.

RAINEY 1

You here for liquor, Henry?

HENRY MACY *(Distant)*

I just come by; just . . . by.

RAINEY 2

You not waiting on liquor, Henry?

MACPHAIL

He said he come by.

HENRY MACY *(To* MACPHAIL)

Miss Amelia digging up a barrel?

RAINEY 2 *(Giggling)*

He just come by.

HENRY MACY

I thirst for good liquor like any man; I thirst for Miss Amelia's liquor.

RAINEY 1 *(To* RAINEY 2)

We all waiting on liquor
      (RAINEY 2 *giggles.*
      A door in the rear of the general store opens; MISS
      AMELIA *enters, carrying several dark glass bottles.*
      SHE *is dressed in Levis and a cotton work shirt
      (red?), boots.* SHE *kicks the door shut with a foot.
      The sound is heard)*

MACPHAIL

Hm?

RAINEY 1

It Miss Amelia; it Miss Amelia back.

HENRY MACY *(Rising)*

That so?

RAINEY 2

Why, sure, less we got prowlers . . . thieves, people break-
ing in t'houses like some people . . .
(Both RAINEYS *go into smothered giggles.* MISS
AMELIA *carries the bottles to the store counter,
puts them down, comes out onto the porch)*

HENRY MACY

Evening, Miss Amelia.

MACPHAIL

Miss Amelia.

RAINEY 1 & 2

Evening, Miss Amelia.

MISS AMELIA

*(Nods; grunts. Not unpleasantly, though; it is her
way)*

HENRY MACY

I come by. I thought . . . I come by.

RAINEY 1

. . . We said you been to the still.

MISS AMELIA *(Very deliberately)*

I been *thinking.*

RAINEY 2

*(*MISS AMELIA's *remark is a known quantity)*

Oh-oh.

(RAINEY 1 *giggles*)

You been thinking on a new medicine? You making improvements on your Croup Cure?

MISS AMELIA *(Shakes her head)*

No.

RAINEY 1

You figuring on someone to sue, Miss Amelia? You found somebody you can bring suit against, Miss Amelia?

MISS AMELIA

No. *(Pause)* I been thinking on some way to get some silence out of you; I been figuring up a nice batch of poison to stop your foolish mouth.

(The RAINEY TWINS *giggle, laugh.* MACPHAIL *roars.* HENRY MACY *shakes his head, smiles)*

MISS AMELIA

(Pushing RAINEY 1 *roughly, but not angrily with her boot)*

That's what I been doing.

RAINEY 1

Oh, Miss Amelia, you wouldn't do that with me.

MACPHAIL

Best thing ever happen round here.

RAINEY 2

Poison me; you poison my brother, you poison me.

MISS AMELIA

Oblige you both.

MACPHAIL

Better idea yet.
            (A *chuckle or two; a silence*)

MISS AMELIA
            (A *silence.* To THEM *all*)
You come to buy liquor?

MACPHAIL

If you'd be so kind . . .

RAINEY 1

We all thirsty from the lack of rain.
            (RAINEY 2 *giggles*)

            MISS AMELIA (*After a long pause*)
I'll get some liquor.

HENRY MACY
            (*Just as* MISS AMELIA *starts to turn, halting her*)
I see something coming.
            (THEY *all look off, stage-left, where nothing is yet to
            be seen*)

RAINEY 1

It's a calf got loose.
            (THEY *keep looking*)

MACPHAIL

No; no it ain't.
            (THEY *keep looking*)

RAINEY 2

No; it's somebody's youngun.
            (THEY *keep looking*)

HENRY MACY
(As a figure emerges from stage-left)
No . . . no.

MISS AMELIA *(Squinting)*
What is it then?
(COUSIN LYMON *moves into the lighted area near the porch; his clothes are dusty; he carries a tiny battered suitcase tied with a rope.* HE *is a dwarf; a hunchback.* HE *stops, suitcase still in hand;* HE *is out of breath)*

COUSIN LYMON
Evening. I am hunting for Miss Amelia Evans.
(The group neither replies nor nods; merely stares)

MISS AMELIA *(After a long pause)*
How come?

COUSIN LYMON
Because I am kin to her.
(The group looks at MISS AMELIA *to see her reaction)*

MISS AMELIA *(After a long pause)*
You lookin' for me. How do you mean "kin"?

COUSIN LYMON
Because . . . *(Uneasily, as if* HE *is about to cry, setting the suitcase down, but keeping hold of the handle)* Because my mother was Fanny Jesup and she came from Cheehaw. She left Cheehaw some thirty years ago when she married her first husband.
(RAINEY 1 giggles)

COUSIN LYMON

. . . and I am the son of Fanny's first husband. So that
would make you and I . . . *(His voice trails off. With quick,
bird-like gestures* HE *bends down, opens the suitcase)* I have
a . . . *(Brings out a photograph)* . . . this is a picture of my
mother and her half-sister.

> (HE *holds it out to* MISS AMELIA, *who does not take
> it.* MACPHAIL *does, examines it in the light)*

MACPHAIL
(After squinting at the photograph)
Why . . . what is this supposed to be! What are those . . .
baby children? And so fuzzy you can't tell night from day.
*(*HE *hands it towards* MISS AMELIA *who refuses it, keeping her
gaze on* COUSIN LYMON. HE *hands the photograph back to the
hunchback)* Where you come from?

COUSIN LYMON *(Uncertainly)*
I was . . . traveling.
> *(*RAINEY 2 *giggles contemptuously.* HENRY MACY *gets
> up, starts to leave)*

HENRY MACY
Night, Miss Amelia.

RAINEY 1
Where you going, Henry? Ain't you going to wait on your
liquor?

RAINEY 2
Oh, no; Henry will sacrifice his thirst cause he is too squeam-
ish; he don't want to be here when Miss Amelia boot this
kind off her property. He don't want to be here for that.

HENRY MACY *(As* HE *exits)*
Night, Miss Amelia.

RAINEY 1

That right, Henry? You don't want to see Miss Amelia send this one flying?

(HENRY MACY *exits, without commenting or turning.* COUSIN LYMON, *who has been waiting, apprehensively, finally sits down on the steps and suddenly begins to cry. No one moves;* THEY *watch him*)

RAINEY 2 *(Finally)*

Well, I'll be damned if he ain't a . . . look at him go! . . . I'll be damned if he ain't a regular crybaby.

RAINEY 1

He is a poor little thing.

MACPHAIL

Well, he is afflicted. There is some cause.

(RAINEY 2 *loudly imitates* COUSIN LYMON'S *crying.* MISS AMELIA *crosses the porch slowly but deliberately.* SHE *reaches* COUSIN LYMON *and stops, looking thoughtfully at him. Then, gingerly, with her right forefinger,* SHE *touches the hump on his back.* SHE *keeps her finger there until his crying lessens. Then,* SHE *removes her finger from his hump, takes a bottle from her hip pocket, wipes the top with the palm of her other hand, and offers it to him to drink*)

MISS AMELIA

Drink. *(Brief pause)* It will liven your gizzard.

RAINEY 1 *(To* COUSIN LYMON*)*

Hey there, you; better get your money up; Miss Amelia don't give liquor free. Unh-unh, you get your money up.

MISS AMELIA *(To* COUSIN LYMON*)*

Drink.

(COUSIN LYMON *stops crying and, rather like a snuf-*
fling child, puts the bottle to his mouth and drinks.
When HE *is done,* MISS AMELIA *takes the bottle,*
washes her mouth with a small swallow, spits it out,
and then drinks. This done, SHE *hands the bottle*
back to COUSIN LYMON. HE *takes it enthusiastically*
To the others, as SHE *moves to the store door)*
You want liquor? You get your money up.
(SHE *goes inside, takes three bottles from the counter.*
The three men watch COUSIN LYMON *as* HE *drinks.*
MISS AMELIA *returns with the liquor, gives a bottle to*
each of the men, takes money. The men open the
bottles—which are corked—and take long, slow swal-
lows. MISS AMELIA *near to* COUSIN LYMON)

MACPHAIL *(Music beginning)*
It is smooth liquor, Miss Amelia; I have never known you to
fail.

RAINEY 1
Yeah.

RAINEY 2
Yeah, sure is.

THE NARRATOR
(Music under this speech. Maybe the lighting on
the scene alters slightly. The players drink, laugh,
ad lib, but softly under the following paragraph)
The whiskey they drank that evening is important. Otherwise, it would be hard to account for what followed. Perhaps
without it there would never have been a cafe. For the liquor
of Miss Amelia has a special quality of its own. It is clean and
sharp on the tongue, but once down a man, it glows inside
him for a long time afterward. And that is not all. Things
that have gone unnoticed, thoughts that have been harbored

far back in the dark mind, are suddenly recognized and com-
prehended.

> (*Laughter from the group here, more noticeable than usual*)

A man may suffer, or he may be spent with joy—but he has
warmed his soul and seen the message hidden there.

> (*Music ending; focus now back on porch scene*)

RAINEY 1
> (*Leaning back; a quiet sound of deep satisfaction*)

Ohhhh—Whooooooo . . .

MACPHAIL (*After a pause*)

Yes; that *is* good.

MISS AMELIA
> (*To* COUSIN LYMON, *after a pause*)

I don't know your name.

COUSIN LYMON

I'm Lymon Willis.

RAINEY 2 (*Softly, to no one*)

I am warm and dreamy.

MISS AMELIA
> (*Rising, to* COUSIN LYMON)

Well, come on in. Some supper was left in the stove and you
can eat.

> (*The three* TOWNSMEN *look at* MISS AMELIA *and* COUSIN LYMON. RAINEY 1 *nudges* RAINEY 2. COUSIN LYMON *does not move*)

MISS AMELIA

I'll just warm up what's there.
> (*As before, more or less*)

There is fried chicken; there are rootabeggars, collards and sweet potatoes.

COUSIN LYMON
(Stirring, shy and coy, almost like a young girl)
I am partial to collards—if they be cooked with sausage.

MISS AMELIA *(Pause)*
They be.

(RAINEY 2 giggles softly)

COUSIN LYMON
(Rising, facing MISS AMELIA)
I am partial to collards.

MISS AMELIA
(Moving toward the door)
Then bring your stuff.
(COUSIN LYMON closes his suitcase, picks it up, stands on a step, looking at MISS AMELIA, still hesitant)

COUSIN LYMON
(Softly, as if describing a glory)
. . . with sausages.

MISS AMELIA
There is a room for you upstairs . . . where you can sleep . . . when you are done eating.
(COUSIN LYMON follows MISS AMELIA into the store, the interior of which fades, the front wall of the building takes its place.
The three TOWNSMEN sit for a moment. Music, softly)

MACPHAIL *(Stirring)*
Well . . . *(Pause)* . . . home *(Rises)*

RAINEY 1
(To MACPHAIL *in some awe)*
I never seen nothing like that in my life. What she up to?
Miss Amelia never invite people into her house . . . eat
from her table. What she up to?

MACPHAIL *(Puzzled)*
Don't know.
(Begins to cross, stage left. The RAINEY TWINS *follow
after)*

RAINEY 1
What is she up to, Stumpy? Hunh?

MACPHAIL *(Speeding up, exiting)*
Don't know.
*(*THE TWINS *stop, toward stage left, look back to the
building)*

RAINEY 1
What is she up to? She never done a thing like that since . . .

RAINEY 2
Shhh! *(Giggles)* Can't talk about that.

RAINEY 1
Maybe . . . maybe she think there something in that suitcase of his. *(With some excitement)* Maybe she going to rob
him! And then . . . and then kill him!

RAINEY 2 *(Giggles)*
Oh . . . hush. *(Giggles again)*

RAINEY 1
(As THEY *move off, stage left)*
I don't know . . . I don't know what she up to.

RAINEY 2 *(Expansively)*
I am warm and dreamy!

RAINEY 1 *(Shaking his head)*
I don't know.
*(Lights slowly down to black, music under. Black
for five seconds, chord held under, then lights up to
bright day; brief, brisk morning music)*

HENRY MACY *enters, stage-left, stays there.* MISS
AMELIA *comes out from the building, looks at the
sky, goes to the pump in front of the building,
washes her head, arms; does not dry—shakes off her
arms; spies* HENRY MACY, *pauses; does not speak or
nod.*

HENRY MACY
(A greeting that is a question)
Morning, Miss Amelia?
(SHE nods, waits. HE takes a step or two closer)
You . . . you opening the store?

MISS AMELIA *(Squinting)*
You here to buy?

HENRY MACY
Why, no now; I just . . .

MISS AMELIA
Then I am closed.

HENRY MACY
Well . . . I just . . .

MISS AMELIA *(Fixing a sleeve)*

I am off to tend to some land I bought . . . up near Fork Falls Road.

HENRY MACY *(Shyly)*

Land, Miss Amelia?

MISS AMELIA

Cotton. *(Pause)* You don't want nothing?
(Pause. HENRY MACY *shakes his head)*

MISS AMELIA

Then I am off.
*(*SHE *turns, moves stage-right. Two Townsladies,* EMMA *and* MRS. PETERSON *enter from stage-right)*

EMMA *(In a portentous way)*

Morning, Miss Amelia.

MRS. PETERSON
(Timid; breathless)

Morning, Miss Amelia.
*(*THEY *stand;* MISS AMELIA *stands. The two* LADIES *cannot help but steal glances toward the building.* THEY *stand silently;* MISS AMELIA *scratches her leg)*

MISS AMELIA
(Not unfriendly, but not friendly)

You two want something?

MRS. PETERSON

Why . . . why whatever do you mean?

EMMA *(Significantly again)*

Just passing the time of day, Miss Amelia.

MISS AMELIA
You here to buy?

EMMA *(As before)*
Why, are you open today, Miss Amelia?

MISS AMELIA
Yes . . . or no?

MRS. PETERSON *(Flustered)*
Why . . . no; no.

MISS AMELIA
(Striding past them exiting)
I got business to tend to.

EMMA
(After her, but so SHE *cannot hear; really for* MRS.
PETERSON *and* HENRY MACY*)*
Oh! I'll bet you do. Have you foreclosed on someone, Miss
Amelia? You grabbed some more property on a debt? You
drove another poor, luckless soul out of his land?
                    (MRS. PETERSON *tsks, rapidly, softly)*
Bet that's what she done.

HENRY MACY
Morning, ladies.
          (The THREE *meet toward center stage)*

EMMA
Henry Macy! Is it true? Is it true what I hear?

HENRY MACY *(Drawled)*
Why, I don't know, Emma. What is it you hear?

EMMA

Don't you sport with me! You know perfectly well what I hear . . . what the whole town hear.

HENRY MACY (*A small smile*)

Well, now, people hear a lot.

EMMA

Two nights ago? Here? You all sitting around, late, you men?

HENRY MACY

Well that is true; yes; we was sitting.

MRS. PETERSON (*Exasperated*)

Ohhhhhhhhhh.

EMMA

. . . and then up the road, out of the dark, come this broke-back, this runt? Some tiny thing claim to be kin to Miss Amelia?

HENRY MACY

Now is that what you hear?

EMMA

. . . and this twisted thing claim to be kin?

MRS. PETERSON

(*Almost whispered*)

. . . and he was took upstairs . . . and he ain't been seen since?

(HENRY MACY *shakes his head; laughs softly*)

EMMA (*Officiously*)

Well?

HENRY MACY *(Calmly; slowly)*
A brokeback come by . . . two nights ago . . . he claim to
be kin to Miss Amelia . . . Miss Amelia take him in . . .
feed him . . . offer him a bed.
     (MRS. PETERSON *gasps with enthusiasm*)

EMMA *(To nail it down)*
And he ain't been seen since.

MRS. PETERSON
I knew it; I knew it.

HENRY MACY
You knew what?

MRS. PETERSON *(Helplessly)*
I . . . knew it.
     (STUMPY MACPHAIL *enters, from stage-left, carrying a
     lunch pail*)

EMMA *(To MACPHAIL)*
. . . And he ain't been seen since; morning.

MACPHAIL
Morning. Who ain't? Morning, Henry.

EMMA
Why, you know . . .

HENRY MACY
Morning, Stumpy.

MACPHAIL *(To MRS. PETERSON)*
Morning. *(To EMMA)* Who ain't?

EMMA *(Exasperated)*

Why, you know! That brokeback . . . that kind claim to be
kin to Miss Amelia.

MACPHAIL
(Scratching his head, looking toward building)

Oh . . . yeah, yeah.

MRS. PETERSON *(Proudly)*

And he ain't been seen since.

EMMA

Two days . . . no sign of . . . whatever it is.

HENRY MACY *(Weary)*

Oh, Emma . . .

MACPHAIL

Well, now; he may have took ill. He is afflicted.

EMMA *(Mysteriously)*

May. May not.

MRS. PETERSON

May not.

MACPHAIL

It ain't natural.

EMMA

It sure ain't.

HENRY MACY

He say he is kin.

EMMA

Miss Amelia got no kin!

MACPHAIL

Who can have kin like what come 't'other night? That be
kin to no one.

EMMA

Whatever he be, Miss Amelia been took in.

HENRY MACY

Miss Amelia ain't known to be soft-hearted.

EMMA *(Triumphantly)*

In the head, then!

MACPHAIL

I say she fed him, sent him on.

HENRY MACY

You told me she give him a bed.

MACPHAIL

She *say*. That don't mean nothing.
> (*Enter* RAINEY 1, *he, too, with a lunch pail. Trailing
> behind him,* MERLIE RYAN.
> *To* RAINEY 1)
That don't mean nothing; do it?

RAINEY 1

What don't mean nothing?

MACPHAIL

Miss Amelia *say* she give the brokeback a bed don't mean he
stay.

RAINEY 1 (*With great relish*)
Ain't nobody seen him, hunh? Well now, where could he be?

EMMA
(*To* MRS. PETERSON, *who breathes agreement*)
Just what I *say.*

MERLIE RYAN
I know what Miss Amelia done.

EMMA (*Dismissing him*)
Hunh, you—you queer-headed old thing.

MACPHAIL
(*With a gesture to quiet* EMMA: *very interested*)
What; what she done?
(RAINEY 1 *giggles*)

MERLIE RYAN
I know what Miss Amelia done.
(RAINEY 1 *giggles again*)

EMMA
Well, what?

MRS. PETERSON
What?

MERLIE RYAN
(*As if remembering a message to be given*)
I know what Miss Amelia done: She murdered that man for
something in that suitcase.
(HENRY MACY *snorts dismissal;* RAINEY 1 *giggles;*
MACPHAIL *whistles; the* LADIES *gasp*)
She murdered that man for something in that suitcase. She

cut his body up, and she bury him in the swamp. (*As before from the* OTHERS) I know what Miss Amelia done?
   (*Maybe the* LADIES *stare at the building, move back from it*)

HENRY MACY
(*Ridiculing the idea*)

Oh, now . . .

MRS. PETERSON

I knew it; I knew it . . .

EMMA
(*With great, slow nods of her head*)

So that what she done.

MERLIE RYAN (*Sing-song*)

That what she done; that what she done.
   (RAINEY 1 *giggles*)

HENRY MACY (*To* RAINEY 1)

You tell him this? You put these things in his head?

RAINEY 1
(*So we do not know if* HE *is serious or not*)

Me? Tell a thing like that to Crazy Merlie here? Why, Henry; you know me better'n that.

EMMA

Buried him in the swamp.

MACPHAIL

It ain't beyond reason.

HENRY MACY (*Angry*)

It ain't likely!

MERLIE RYAN

I know what Miss Amelia done.

(RAINEY 1 *giggles*)

(*Barely audible chatter from those on stage during the following*)

THE NARRATOR (*Music under it*)

And so it went that whole day. A midnight burial in the swamp, the dragging of Miss Amelia through the streets of the town on the way to prison . . .

(THREE OTHER TOWNSMEN *enter, join in*)

. . . the squabbles over what would happen to her property —all told in hushed voices and repeated with some fresh and weird detail.

(*Lighting moves toward evening:* MISS AMELIA *enters, stage-right, takes brief note of the townspeople, moves into the building*)

And when it came toward evening, and Miss Amelia returned from her business, and they saw that there were no bloodstains on her anywhere, the consternation grew.

MISS AMELIA

Well, quite a gathering.

(*It becomes dark, now. The townsmen*—HENRY MACY, MACPHAIL, THE RAINEY TWINS, MERLIE RYAN *and the* THREE TOWNSMEN, RAINEY 2 *having entered from stage-left at the beginning of this lighting change*—*have moved to the porch of the building, are sitting or standing with* HENRY MACY *off to one side of the group . . . stage-right.* EMMA *and* MRS. PETERSON *have been joined by two other women, and are in a group, stage-left, watching the porch, watching the men*)

THE NARRATOR

And dark came on. It was just past eight o'clock, and still

nothing had happened. But there was silent agreement
among the men that this night would not pass with the
mystery still unsolved. There is a time beyond which questions may not stay unanswered. So, the men had gathered
on Miss Amelia's porch, and Miss Amelia had gone into the
room she kept as an office.

(*Lights on* MISS AMELIA *in the office*)

FIRST TOWNSMAN (*To* SECOND)

What she doin'?

SECOND TOWNSMAN

Don't know. I don't know.

MERLIE RYAN

I know what she done. She murdered that man for somethin' . . .

MACPHAIL

Shhh.

HENRY MACY

Hush, Merlie!

(BOTH RAINEYS *giggle*)

FIRST TOWNSMAN

What we gonna do?

RAINEY 1

We goin' in?

MACPHAIL (*Rising portentously*)

Yup; we goin' in. Henry?

HENRY MACY (*After a pause*)

All right.

(*The* MEN *rise, file slowly into the store; the* WOMEN, *taking this as a sign, move, with sotto voce comments, toward the porch. The* MEN *move silently, keeping fairly close to the walls, keeping a distance from both* MISS AMELIA's *office and from the stairs, stage-center-rear.*

Maybe there is a high, soft sustained chord of music here, ending abruptly with a sound from the top of the stairs. The MEN *turn toward the sound.*

COUSIN LYMON *descends the stairs, slowly, one at a time—imperiously, like a great hostess.* HE *is no longer ragged;* HE *is clean;* HE *wears his little coat, but neat and mended, a red and black checkered shirt, knee breeches, black stockings, shoes laced up over the ankles, and a great lime green shawl, with fringe, which almost touches the ground. The effect is somehow regal . . . or papal. The room is as still as death.* COUSIN LYMON *walks to the center of the room; the* MEN *move back a little.* HE *stares at them, one after the other, down to up, slowly, craning his neck to see their faces.* RAINEY 2 *giggles, but there is some terror in it*)

COUSIN LYMON

(*After* HE *has examined the* MEN; *as if* HE *had heard some piece of unimportant news, which* HE *dismisses*)

Evenin'.

(HE *seats himself on a barrel, quite center, and takes from a pocket a snuff-box. There is an intake of breath from* SOME *of the* MEN)

MACPHAIL

(*Daring to move a step closer*)

What is it you have there?

FIRST TOWNSMAN

Yeah; what is that, Peanut?

SECOND TOWNSMAN

Why, that is Miss Amelia's snuffbox . . . belonged to her
father.

MACPHAIL

What is it you have there?

COUSIN LYMON
(Sharply; mischievously)

What is this? Why, this is a lay-low . . . to catch meddlers.

SECOND TOWNSMAN

It *is* her snuffbox. Belonged to her father.

COUSIN LYMON *(After taking snuff)*

This is not proper snuff; this is sugar and cocoa.
   (Silence from the MEN; MISS AMELIA *can be heard*
   whistling softly to herself)
The very teeth in my head have always tasted sour to me;
that is the reason why I take this kind of sweet snuff.

MACPHAIL *(To get it straight)*

It *is* Miss Amelia's snuffbox.

COUSIN LYMON *(Almost arrogantly)*

Yes?

HENRY MACY

It is natural enough.

COUSIN LYMON
(Swinging on him; not unfriendly—objective)

Who are you?

HENRY MACY *(Kindly)*

I am Henry Macy.

COUSIN LYMON

I remember; when I come. How old are you?
> *(An exchange of glances among the* OTHER MEN; *one or two words)*

HENRY MACY

I am forty-seven.

COUSIN LYMON *(Swinging his legs)*

Where you work?

HENRY MACY

The mill.

COUSIN LYMON *(To* MACPHAIL*)*

And you!

MACPHAIL

I . . .

COUSIN LYMON

Who are *you?*

RAINEY 2

That Stumpy MacPhail.
> *(Giggles)*

COUSIN LYMON

How old are you?

MACPHAIL

I am . . . thirty-eight.

RAINEY 1

He work in the mill, too.

COUSIN LYMON
(*Igoring* RAINEY 1; *to* MACPHAIL)
You married, Stumpy MacPhail?

RAINEY 2

Oh, is he!
(A COUPLE *of the* MEN *laugh gently*)

MACPHAIL (*Retaining his dignity*)
I am married. Yes.

COUSIN LYMON
(A *small, pleased child*)
Is your wife fat?
(*Whoops of laughter from the* MEN, *which bring
the* WOMEN *hovering to the door*)

MACPHAIL
(*Embarrassed, but by the attention, not the fact*)
She is . . . ample.
(*More laughter*)

COUSIN LYMON (*To* RAINEY TWINS)
And you two giggling things . . . who are *you*?

FIRST TOWNSMAN
Them is the Rainey twins . . .

SECOND TOWNSMAN
(*Indicating* MERLIE RYAN)
And this here is Merlie Ryan . . .

COUSIN LYMON
(*With a sweep of his hand*)

Come in, ladies!

(*The* TOWNSWOMEN *enter, the introductions become general, simultaneous. The* THREE TOWNSMEN *use names such as* HASTY MALONE, ROSSER CLINE, *and* HENRY FORD CRIMP. EMMA *is* EMMA HALE. *The chatter is general; and while there is a lot of talk and some laughter, there is still tension, and people tend to look at* COUSIN LYMON *out of the corners of their eyes and keep a formal distance—as if* HE *were a Martian, a friendly Martian, but still a Martian. There are now* TWELVE TOWNSPEOPLE *in the store. Through the general chatter we hear, specifically, things like the following*)

RAINEY 1

When you come up the road t'other night . . . I swore it were a calf got loose.

RAINEY 2 (*Qualifying*)

It were so dark.

HENRY MACY

It is a pleasure to have you visiting.

EMMA

This lime green scarf is pretty.

MRS. PETERSON

Oh, yes; yes, it look well on you.

COUSIN LYMON
(*To* MRS. PETERSON)

I will not bite you. (*Snaps his teeth at her*) Grrr!

MRS. PETERSON (*Almost fainting*)
Oh! Oh!

MERLIE RYAN
Know what I thought she done? . . . Know what I thought
happened to the brokeback? . . .

HENRY MACY & MACPHAIL
Hush. You be still.

RAINEY 2
. . . and I thought it were someone's youngun . . .

RAINEY 1
It were so dark.

COUSIN LYMON
Well, it were not.

RAINEY 2
No; it were not.
(*Giggles*)

RAINEY 1
It were dark.
(*Groups have formed, and the conversation does not
hinge solely on* COUSIN LYMON. *Perhaps music has
been used judiciously throughout this ad lib scene.
The door to the office swings open, and* MISS AMELIA
enters the store. As the TOWNSPEOPLE *see her, their
conversation trails off, until there is silence.* MISS
AMELIA *stands for a moment, taking everything in,
glances at* COUSIN LYMON *and smiles, briefly, shyly,
then leans her elbows back on the counter*)

MISS AMELIA (*Quietly*)

Does anyone want waiting on?

    (*A brief pause, which* HENRY MACY *breaks*)

HENRY MACY

Why, yes, Miss Amelia . . . if you have some liquor . . .

    (*This serves as a dam-break, and* SEVERAL *of the* MEN
    ad lib agreement, and the general chatter starts
    again.
    Music from now until the end of the scene.
    MISS AMELIA *turns, goes behind the counter, gets*
    bottles, serves the MEN, *takes money*)

THE NARRATOR (*Over the talk*)

What happened at this moment was not ordinary. While the
men of the town could count on Miss Amelia for their liquor,
it was a rule she had that they must drink it outside her
premises—and there was no feeling of joy in the transaction:
after getting his liquor, a man would have to drink it on the
porch, or guzzle it on the street, or walk off into the night.
But at this moment, Miss Amelia broke her rule, and the
men could drink in her store. More than that, she furnished
glasses and opened two boxes of crackers so that they were
there hospitably in a platter on the counter and anyone who
wished could take one free.

    (*Suitable action under the above, general chatter*
    continuing)

Now, this was the beginning of the cafe. It was as simple as
that. There was a certain timidness, for people in this town
were unused to gathering together in any number for the sake
of pleasure. But, it was the beginning.

    (*The sounds continue.* MISS AMELIA *moves to where*
    COUSIN LYMON *is sitting*)

MISS AMELIA

Cousin Lymon, will you have your liquor straight, or warmed
in a pan with water on the stove?
(*A slight lessening in the general conversation in attention to this*)

COUSIN LYMON

If you please, Amelia . . . if you please, I'll have it warmed.
(*Some general consternation*)

EMMA

(*A half-whisper, to anyone, as* MISS AMELIA, *smiling
secretly, moves off to do* COUSIN LYMON's *bidding*)
Did you hear that? He called her *Amelia!* He said *Amelia!*

MRS. PETERSON
(*Breathless, as usual*)
Why, it is *Miss* Amelia to . . . to everyone.

EMMA

And *he* called her *Amelia.*

THIRD TOWNSMAN
Her Daddy called her . . . Little. He called her Little.
(RAINEY 2 *giggles*)

RAINEY 1
Some Little!

EMMA (*Unable to get over it*)
Did you hear it? He called her Amelia.
(*In another area,* HENRY MACY, MACPHAIL *and* MERLIE
RYAN *are gathered*)

MACPHAIL

I ain't see Miss Amelia like this. There is something puzzling to her face.

HENRY MACY
(*Looking at her;* SHE *is oblivious to all but* COUSIN
LYMON)
Well . . . it may be she is happy.

MACPHAIL (*Uncertain*)

It may be.

MERLIE RYAN

I know; I know what it is.

HENRY MACY

Oh, now, Merlie . . .

MERLIE RYAN

I know what it is . . . Miss Amelia in love. That what it is.
(*Only* HENRY MACY *and* MACPHAIL *have heard this*)

MACPHAIL
(*As if* HE *is being joshed*)

Ohhhhhhhh . . .

HENRY MACY

Hush, now, Merlie . . .

MERLIE RYAN

Miss Amelia in love. Miss Amelia in love.
(*Music and* CROWD *louder, general party. Interior of
the store dims, becomes invisible during the next
speech, the exterior becoming visible, in the darkness and moonlight*)

THE NARRATOR

And so it went. This opening of the cafe came to an end at
midnight. Everyone said goodbye to everyone else in a friendly
fashion . . . and soon, everything—all the town, in fact—
was dark and silent. And so ended three days and nights in
which had come the arrival of a stranger, an unholy holiday,
and the start of the cafe.

(Dim to blackness. MUSIC *holds)*

*Daylight—toward evening—comes up; only the ex-
terior of the cafe is visible save directly below, as
indicated. No one, narrator excepted, is on stage.
Music up and under.*

THE NARRATOR

Now time must pass. Four years . . . Time passes quickly in
this section of the country; you breathe in and it is summer;
out, and it is autumn; in again, out, and a year has gone by.
Only the seasons change, but they are so regular in their turning that four years can pass . . . *(Pause)* . . . like that. The
hunchback continued to live with Miss Amelia. The cafe ex-
panded in a gradual way, and Miss Amelia began to sell her
liquor by the drink, and some tables were brought into the
store, and there were customers every evening, and on Saturday nights a great crowd. The place was a store no longer but
had become a proper cafe, and was open every evening from
six until twelve o'clock. Things once done were accepted.

*(*MISS AMELIA *and* COUSIN LYMON *emerge, sit on the
steps)*

And Cousin Lymon's presence in Miss Amelia's house, his
sleeping in her dead father's room, was passed by, save by a
few, women mostly, whose minds had darker corners than
they dared dream of. And the cafe was welcomed by every-

one but the minister's wife, who was a secret drinker and felt more alone than ever. Four years have passed . . .

COUSIN LYMON
(As MISS AMELIA *massages his shoulders)*
Slowly, Amelia, slowly.

MISS AMELIA *(Amused tolerance)*
Yes, Cousin Lymon.

COUSIN LYMON
That do feel good, Amelia.

MISS AMELIA
You have not grown stronger; you are still so pitiful.

COUSIN LYMON
I am not a big person, Amelia.

MISS AMELIA
Now, I think your head *has* got bigger . . . and your hunch, too . . .

COUSIN LYMON *(Pulls away; surly)*
Leave me be.

MISS AMELIA
But your legs, as thin as ever . . . grasshopper . . .

COUSIN LYMON
(A tone of command)
Amelia! *(A sudden giggle)* Course, you could always figger up a new medicine for me . . . one turn me into a giant; you could do that.

MISS AMELIA *(Affectionately)*
You enough trouble big as you are. Don't know what I'd do
with you normal size.

COUSIN LYMON *(Greatly amused)*
Though there be a danger you make me a growin' medicine,
since you so particular with your remedies you try 'em out on
yourself first . . .

MISS AMELIA *(Laughs)*
Hush, you.

COUSIN LYMON
. . . you make me a growin' medicine, an' it work we gonna
have you in the treetops, birds nestin' in you, an' . . .

MISS AMELIA *(Gently)*
Ain't no medicine gonna make you grow, Cousin Lymon.

COUSIN LYMON *(Briefly serious)*
I know that, Amelia. *(Giggling again)* Only thing happen,
you make up a new remedy be you try it out on yourself an'
you spend the next two days hustlin' to the privy . . .

MISS AMELIA *(To stop him)*
Well, you gotta try your medicine on yourself first, you be
any good at doctorin'.

COUSIN LYMON *(Giggles)*
I know . . . but it's funny.

MISS AMELIA
An' all ailments is centered in the bowel.

COUSIN LYMON
Oh?

MISS AMELIA

Yes.

COUSIN LYMON
(Mischievous scoffing)

Do that be so, Amelia?

MISS AMELIA

Yes.

COUSIN LYMON

Well, your remedies *do* affect the bowel, no doubt there. Surprisin' anyone die in these parts.

MISS AMELIA

People die here same as anywhere.

COUSIN LYMON *(Still mischievous)*

What do they die of, Amelia? Ain't your medicine, now . . .

MISS AMELIA

People die of natural causes. Like anywhere.

COUSIN LYMON

What is the natural cause, Amelia?

MISS AMELIA
(At a loss first; then . . .)

. . . dyin'.

COUSIN LYMON
(As if a great truth has been revealed)

Oh.

COUSIN LYMON
(A tone of command)
Amelia! *(A small silence, then* HE *continues in a cajoling tone)* As tomorrow is Sunday, Amelia, you gonna drive us into Cheehaw to the movie show? Or, maybe we can go to the fair. There is a fair which is out beyond . . .

MISS AMELIA
We will go . . . we will go . . . somewhere.

COUSIN LYMON
To the fair, Amelia.

MISS AMELIA
We will go . . . somewhere.
        (COUSIN LYMON *pulls away again, dead-spoiled, pout-
        ing, moves a few feet away)*
Cousin Lymon?

COUSIN LYMON *(Imperiously)*
Your father's bed is too big for my size, Amelia; I am not comfortable in a bed that size.

MISS AMELIA *(Laughing)*
Oh, now . . .

COUSIN LYMON *(Greatly petulant)*
I said I am not at ease in a ten acre bed. Have one made for me; have a bed made for me that I can sleep comfortable in.

MISS AMELIA
(Attempting a light tone)
I will have a bed made for you, Cousin Lymon, just to your size, and it can be used for you as a coffin some day.

COUSIN LYMON
(Rising; furious; screaming)

I AM SLEEPING IN A COFFIN NOW! I AM SLEEPING IN YOUR FA-
THER'S COFFIN. *(Softer, whining again)* I want a small bed,
Amelia. I want a bed my size.

MISS AMELIA *(Placating)*

Yes; yes.

COUSIN LYMON

And . . . and I want to go in the Ford tomorrow . . . to
Cheehaw . . . to the movie show, and . . .

MISS AMELIA
(Quietly correcting him)

You want to go to the *fair*.

COUSIN LYMON *(Imperious again)*

Either way; don't matter.

MISS AMELIA *(A slightly sad smile)*

No; don't matter.

COUSIN LYMON
(Mysterious and intensely curious)

Amelia . . . in the parlor upstairs there is that curio cabinet
that had that snuff-box you gave me I admired so when I first
came.

MISS AMELIA *(Affirming this)*

Yes, Cousin Lymon, there be.

COUSIN LYMON

Well, that cabinet has in it some *other* things that I have
become curious about, and I would like to ask you about
them.

MISS AMELIA
(Suddenly defensive, her eyes narrowing)
You go in there? You rummage about in that curio cabinet?

COUSIN LYMON
(His eyes narrowing, too)
Why, Amelia, it is a curio cabinet, and I am a curious little
person; besides, Amelia, you got no secrets from me. You got
secrets from me, Amelia?

MISS AMELIA
No.
(Music out)

COUSIN LYMON
No. Well Amelia, I have found something I would like to ask
you about (HE *fishes into a pocket and brings up an acorn*) I
found this: an acorn. What does it signify?

MISS AMELIA
Why, it's just an acorn, just an acorn I picked up on the
afternoon Papa died.

COUSIN LYMON
How do you mean?

MISS AMELIA
I mean it's just an acorn I spied on the ground that day. I
picked it up and put it in my pocket. But I don't know why.

COUSIN LYMON
What a peculiar reason to keep it.

MISS AMELIA
Do you want *it*, Cousin Lymon?

COUSIN LYMON
(After a brief, almost unkind hesitation; gifting her)
Why no, Amelia, you may have it. It were your father's and
he were dear to you.

MISS AMELIA
(With a remembering smile)
He were. Law, I remember when I were little, I slept and
slept. I'd go to bed just as the lamp was turned on and sleep
—why, I'd sleep like I was drowned in warm axle grease.
Then come daybreak Papa would walk in and put his hand
down on my shoulder. "Get stirring, Little," he would say.
Then later he would holler up the stairs from the kitchen
when the stove was hot. "Fried grits," he would holler.
"White meat and gravy. Ham and eggs." And I'd run down
the stairs and dress by the hot stove while he was washing up
out at the pump. Then off we'd go to the still, or maybe . . .

COUSIN LYMON
The grits we had this morning was poor; fried too quick so
that the inside never heated.

MISS AMELIA
And when Papa would run off the liquor in those days . . .

COUSIN LYMON
You know I don't like grits lest they be done exactly right.
You know I have told you many times, Amelia . . .

MISS AMELIA
. . . or when he would take me with him when he buried the
barrels . . .

COUSIN LYMON
I say: the grits we had this morning was poor.

MISS AMELIA

. . . an' we would go, an' . . . all right, Cousin Lymon; I
will take more care with them.

COUSIN LYMON

You loved your poppa, didn't you, Amelia?

MISS AMELIA

I . . .

COUSIN LYMON

You can say it.

MISS AMELIA *(Finally)*

Course I loved my poppa. Momma dyin' as she did, birthin'
me . . .

COUSIN LYMON

You were normal size, Amelia? You a regular baby size when
you born?

MISS AMELIA
(Laughing amazement)

Course I was, Cousin Lymon.

COUSIN LYMON

Course you were.

MISS AMELIA

. . . an' . . . an' poppa an' me, we'd take long trips together . . .

COUSIN LYMON

Into Cheehaw? Or to the fair sometimes?

MISS AMELIA

Yes . . . an' sometimes beyond. Way beyond. We'd take long trips.

COUSIN LYMON

And I found this Amelia—
> (HE *goes into a pocket, takes out a small velvet box,*
> *at the sight of which* MISS AMELIA *makes a half grab,*
> *but* COUSIN LYMON *moves away*)

I have found this tiny velvet box, and if I open it up . . . *(Does so)* . . . what do I see?

MISS AMELIA *(Blushing)*

You give that here.

COUSIN LYMON

What do I see? *(Pause)* Hmm? What do I see?
> (*Looks to* MISS AMELIA, *who still blushes and will*
> *not look at either him or the box*)

I see two small little grey stones, and I wonder to myself "What do they be? Why has Amelia kept these stones?" What do they be, Amelia?
> (MISS AMELIA *mumbles something at last, which we*
> *cannot hear*)

Hmm? I did not hear you, Amelia.

MISS AMELIA *(Shyer than ever)*

They be . . .

COUSIN LYMON *(Enjoying it greatly)*

Yes? Yes?

MISS AMELIA *(Finally)*

They be . . . I were in great pain, years back, and I went into Cheehaw, to the doctor there—I couldn't figure the pain, and none of my remedies worked for it—and I went to the

doctor there and . . . *(In great embarrassment)* . . . those
be my kidney stones. *(A fair silence)* Now, give 'em here.

COUSIN LYMON
(Examining the stones)
So that is what they be.

MISS AMELIA
Give them here, now.

COUSIN LYMON
I admire these, Amelia. You ain't given me a present in the
longest time now. You give me these as a present. Yes?

MISS AMELIA
(Can't help but laugh)
But what would you do with them Cousin Lymon?

COUSIN LYMON
I have always admired . . . I have always wanted a great
gold chain across my vest, and you could get me a great gold
chain for across my vest, and you could have these hung from
it. Oh, Amelia, I would love that so. I would so love that.
(MISS AMELIA *laughs blushingly)*
Oh, I would.

MISS AMELIA
Unh-hunh; yes, if you want it, Cousin Lymon.

COUSIN LYMON
(Quite coldly)
Oh, Amelia, I do love you so.

MISS AMELIA
*(With some awkward gesture: kicking the dirt off a
boot, maybe)*

Humf! Those are words I don't wanna hear. (*Pause*) Understand?

COUSIN LYMON
(*A too-eager schoolboy*)
Yes, Amelia!

MISS AMELIA (*After a silence*)
I am fond of you, Cousin Lymon.
(*Music begins here, softly*)

THE NARRATOR
Ah, Amelia, I do love you so. Now, was that true? Well, we will find out. But it is true that Miss Amelia loved Cousin Lymon, for he was kin to her, and Miss Amelia had, for many years, before the arrival of Cousin Lymon, lived a solitary life. And, too, there are many kinds of love . . . as we shall find out. But this is how they talked, and was one of the ways in which Miss Amelia showed her love for Cousin Lymon . . . her fondness. In fact, there was only one part of her life that she did not want Cousin Lymon to share with her . . . to know about; and it concerned a man named Marvin Macy. It was a name that never crossed her lips . . . a name that no one in the town dared mention in her presence . . . the name Marvin Macy.

The scene changes slowly to dark. MISS AMELIA *and* COUSIN LYMON *rise, go indoors. Under* THE NARRATOR's *next speech the lights rise on the interior of the cafe, revealing it full of* TOWNSPEOPLE, *sitting around tables, drinking, or standing, buying, etc. Saturday night is in full swing. Everyone is there.* STUMPY MACPHAIL *and one of the* TOWNSMEN *are*

playing checkers; the RAINEY TWINS *are at separate
places, and* THEY *glower at each other occasionally.*
HENRY MACY *is at a table by himself, downstage;* HE
is drinking and HE *does not look happy.*
Music continues.

THE NARRATOR

We come now to a night of terrible importance, the beginning of a series of events which will result in calamity and
great sadness. It looks to be a Saturday night like any other
since the cafe has opened, but the great and terrible events of
a person's life occur most often in the most commonplace of
circumstances.

(Music out.

Cafe scene up full, general chatter. COUSIN LYMON
mills around the GUESTS. MISS AMELIA *enters, from
the kitchen, bearing a handwritten sign with the
legend, "Chicken dinner tonite—twenty cents")*

MISS AMELIA
(Tacking the sign up)

For them of you as can't read . . . Chicken dinner tonight
. . . twenty cents.

(General approval; SOME PEOPLE *move to the kitchen
to be served. It must be understood that there is ad
lib conversation all throughout this scene)*

It's in the kitchen. Pay on the bar and get it yourselves.

(SHE *moves to where* HENRY MACY *sits)*

What ails you?

HENRY MACY *(Half rising)*

Miss Amelia?

MISS AMELIA

What ails you tonight, Henry?

HENRY MACY *(Obviously lying)*

Why . . . why, nothing, Miss Amelia. Nothing.

MISS AMELIA

Then you better eat.

HENRY MACY

No, no; I got a drink here, Miss Amelia; I will sit with it.

MISS AMELIA
(Still sits, regarding him)

Suit yourself.

COUSIN LYMON
(To STUMPY MACPHAIL*)*

And I walked to Rotten Lake today to fish, and on the way I stepped over what appeared at first to be a big fallen tree. But then as I stepped over I felt something stir and I taken this second look and there I was straddling this here alligator long as from the front door to the kitchen and thicker than a hog.

(STUMPY MACPHAIL *and* SEVERAL *of the* OTHERS *laugh goodnaturedly)*

STUMPY MACPHAIL

Sure you did, peanut. Sure.

COUSIN LYMON

I did. I did. And . . . and I looked down at him, and I . . .

MACPHAIL

. . . and you picked him up by his big ugly tail, and you swung him around your shoulder, and you flung him over the . . .

COUSIN LYMON (*Superior*)

All right, you just go look over at Rotten Lake sometime, smarty!

MISS AMELIA
(*Smiling over to* COUSIN LYMON)

You tell 'em.
                (*Now back to* HENRY MACY)
Still not talkin'? Not eating? An' nothin' ails you, and you're just gonna sit there drinkin'. Right?

HENRY MACY

That's right, Miss Amelia.

MISS AMELIA
(*Nods knowingly again*)

All right.

COUSIN LYMON
(*Having moved to where* RAINEY 1 *is sitting*)

And how are you tonight?

RAINEY 1
(*Glowering at* RAINEY 2, *who returns his glower*)

Just dandy.

COUSIN LYMON
(*Determined to make mischief*)

Ohhhhh, and I see your brother is just dandy, too.

RAINEY 1

I don't know who you mean.

COUSIN LYMON

Why, I mean your lookalike.

RAINEY 1 *(Greatly indignant)*

Humf! That one!

RAINEY 2

(To COUSIN LYMON; HE *too indignant)*

Don't you go talkin' to that noaccount. He rob the hump off your back quick as look at you.

COUSIN LYMON

(Marches over to RAINEY 2; *swipes at him, snarls, almost)*

You mean to say your brother is some kind of wizard? That what you mean to say?

MISS AMELIA

(Still sitting, but concerned)

Cousin Lymon . . . ?

COUSIN LYMON

(Stamping back to RAINEY 1*)*

That what he mean to say? That what your noaccount brother saying? He some kind of wizard?

RAINEY 2 *(So* ALL *will hear)*

I don't mean that. I mean that thievin' nogood over there'll steal you blind before you know it.

RAINEY 1 *(Rising)*

I ain't no thief!

COUSIN LYMON

(Mischief again, coming between the BROTHERS*)*

Oh, now now now. You talked to him; I caught you: you talked to your own brother.

RAINEY 1 (*Angry*)

I talked *on* him; I said I ain't no thief. I didn't talk *to* him.

COUSIN LYMON

My, my; two years now you two ain't spoke a word to each other; not a word in two whole years.

RAINEY 2

HE STOLE MY KNIFE!

RAINEY 1

I NEVER STOLE NOBODY'S KNIFE!
          (THEY *glare, subside.* COUSIN LYMON *moves to* MISS
          AMELIA)

COUSIN LYMON

Now, ain't that something, Amelia: These two not speaking to one another for more'n two years now over six inches of sharp steel? Ain't that something?

MISS AMELIA

Some people been killed for less.
          (COUSIN LYMON *chases* HENRIETTA FORD CRIMP JR.
          around a table)

MISS AMELIA

Leave that kid be. She been sick. (*Rises*) I'm eatin'. Cousin Lymon, can I bring you your dinner?

COUSIN LYMON

My appetite is poor tonight; there is a sourness in my mouth.

MISS AMELIA

Just a pick: the breast, the liver and the heart.

COUSIN LYMON
(Sweet-spoiled; sitting at the table with HENRY
MACY*)*
All right, Amelia, if you will do that for me.

MISS AMELIA
Henry?

HENRY MACY
No, Miss Amelia . . . thank you. I will stay with your good
liquor.

MISS AMELIA
(Walking to the kitchen)
Ain't like you, Henry.

COUSIN LYMON
(Imitating MISS AMELIA*)*
Ain't like you, Henry. What ails you, Henry Macy?

HENRY MACY
Nothin'! Now don't you start in, too!

COUSIN LYMON
Oooohhhh . . . Law!

HENRY MACY
Just . . . leave it be.

COUSIN LYMON
Now, that ain't polite, Henry . . .

HENRY MACY
(A quiet warning; a little drunk)
Look, runt; go pick on someone your own size, hear?

MACPHAIL

Yeah, go back fight another flock o' alligators or whatever they was.

COUSIN LYMON
(To STUMPY MACPHAIL)

You go on out to Rotten Lake now, and you see!
(EMMA *and* MRS. PETERSON *emerge from the kitchen, carrying plates; call back to* MISS AMELIA *in the kitchen)*

EMMA *(Her mouth full)*

Real fine chicken, Miss Amelia!

MRS. PETERSON

Oh, yes, a good bird . . . it is, Miss Amelia.

EMMA *(Still shouting)*

Real fine. *(Then sotto voce, to* MRS. PETERSON) Probably stole them chickens off some poor tenant farmer out near . . .

MRS. PETERSON

Ooooohhhh, *Emma* . . .

EMMA

. . . or maybe somebody behind on a loan to her, she walk in an' say, "I'll take all your birds." That's what. Somethin' like that.

MRS. PETERSON *(Whispering)*
Emma.

EMMA *(Loud)*

Wouldn't put it past her.

COUSIN LYMON
(*As* THEY *pass him, barks at* EMMA)
WARF! WARF!

(SEVERAL PEOPLE *laugh*)

EMMA
(*As* MRS. PETERSON *squeals, jumps*)
You stop that, runt. I'll knock you clear into next week!

COUSIN LYMON
(*Raises his hands like a puppy's paws, whimpers a moment; then*)
FATTY! You fat thing!

EMMA
(*Looming above* COUSIN LYMON, *as* MISS AMELIA *emerges from the kitchen with two plates*)
FAT: Well, fat is better'n twisted you miserable little runt . . . !

MISS AMELIA (*A command*)
EMMA HALE!

(EMMA *subsides, moves to a table*)

EMMA
(*Not to* MISS AMELIA, *but for her ears*)
They is some good cafes in these parts, I hear, where they is not monkeys crawling around the floor; where the owners' pets is not . . .

MISS AMELIA
(*Setting a plate down before* COUSIN LYMON *and one at her own place*)
That'll do now.

MRS. PETERSON
(Whispered, breathless)
Emma, you *know* you mustn't . . .

MISS AMELIA
Them people oughta go to them cafes; if they ain't careful
they won't be welcome no more in *this* cafe.
(To COUSIN LYMON*)*
Eat.

COUSIN LYMON
(Sweet in victory and vindication, looking toward
EMMA*)*
Thank you, Amelia. And they is *some* cafes, I hear, where
they do not allow just *any*body to come in an' . . .

MISS AMELIA
(Silencing him, too, but kindly)
All right now. Eat.
*(*THEY *fall to; the general cafe conversation continues, lessens a bit, perhaps, for our attention should
move outside, stage-left, where the figure of a man
appears. It is* MARVIN MACY. HE *stands, gazing at the
cafe, begins whittling, all the while staring at the
cafe, and whistling softly.*
(To COUSIN LYMON*)*
You was hungry after all.

COUSIN LYMON
(Shovelling food into his mouth)
It would seem. But only for the delicacies. Like you choose
'em.
*(*HENRY MACY *clears his throat, makes as if to speak
of something difficult, but stops)*

MISS AMELIA

Henry Macy, if you gonna sit here all night, and drink liquor, and . . .

COUSIN LYMON *(Gleefully)*

Bet he got a secret.
> *(Throughout the following, the cafe conversations grow quiet; eventually, when indicated, cease entirely)*

MISS AMELIA

You got a secret, Henry?

COUSIN LYMON

Bet he do.

HENRY MACY *(Finally)*

I . . . I got a letter last week, Miss Amelia.

MISS AMELIA

> *(After a brief pause; unsurprised at the news)*

Yeah?

HENRY MACY

It were . . . it were a letter from my brother.
> *(Noticeable lessening in the cafe conversation)*

MISS AMELIA

> *(After a silence, leaning to* HENRY MACY, *saying, with great force)*

You are welcome to it. *(Pause)* You hear?

HENRY MACY

He . . . he is on parole. He is out of the penitentiary. I got this letter last week, an' he is on parole.
> *(The cafe is very quiet now.* COUSIN LYMON *senses*

something extraordinary; HE gets up, moves about,
speaks to the OTHERS)

COUSIN LYMON

Who? . . . Who? . . . What?

MISS AMELIA
(Slamming her fist down on the table)
You are welcome to any letter you get from him, because
your brother is a . . . because he belong to be in that penitentiary the balance of his life!

COUSIN LYMON

Who? . . . Who is this about?

MERLIE RYAN

Marvin Macy comin' back? Is Marvin Macy . . .

MACPHAIL

Hush, you!

COUSIN LYMON (To HENRY MACY)
You got a brother? Hunh? What is all this?

MISS AMELIA

Marvin Macy belong to be in that penitentiary the balance
of his life!

COUSIN LYMON
(Beside himself with curiosity and a strange excite-
ment)
WHO IS MARVIN MACY? Parole? What . . . what did he do?

MISS AMELIA
(Still to HENRY MACY)
You hear me?

COUSIN LYMON
(*To* STUMPY MACPHAIL)
What did he do?

MACPHAIL
(*With embarrassment, not looking up*)
Well, he . . . well, he robbed three filling stations . . . for
one . . .

MERLIE RYAN
Do Miss Amelia know Marvin Macy comin' back?
(SEVERAL *quiet him*)

HENRY MACY
(*With great difficulty*)
He don't say much . . . his letter don't say much . . .
'cept . . .
(HE *stops*)

MISS AMELIA (*Her fists clenched*)
. . . 'Cept?
(*Dead silence*)

HENRY MACY (*Finally*)
'Cept he is comin' back here.
(*Flurry of excitement*)

MISS AMELIA
(*A commandment*)
He will never set his split hoof on my premises! Never. That
is all!
(*Swings around to the* OTHERS)
Get back to your drinkin', all of you!
(*Self-conscious and half-hearted return to normalcy.
But* COUSIN LYMON *will not be put by*)

COUSIN LYMON
(*Turning to* FIRST TOWNSMAN)
Tell me about Marvin Macy; tell me what he done!

FIRST TOWNSMAN (*Moving away*)
Let it be.

COUSIN LYMON
Who is Marvin Macy?

SECOND TOWNSMAN
Go on about your business, now.

COUSIN LYMON
(*To no one; to the center of the room*)
Who is . . . who is . . .
(*Sees* MISS AMELIA *moving to the porch; runs after her*)
Who is he? Amelia, who is Marvin Macy?

MISS AMELIA
(*Going on to the porch*)
Finish your dinner.

COUSIN LYMON
(*Following her on to the porch*)
Amelia, who is Marvin Macy? I want to know who this man is! Who is . . . ?
(MISS AMELIA *and* COUSIN LYMON *see* MARVIN MACY *simultaneously. Tense silence*)

MISS AMELIA
(*As* COUSIN LYMON *takes a couple of tentative steps toward* MARVIN MACY, *stops*)
You clear outa here! You get on!
(*Silence for a second, then* MARVIN MACY *laughs*,

turns, exits. MISS AMELIA *stares after him, turns to
go in, goes, leaving* COUSIN LYMON *alone on the
porch)*

COUSIN LYMON *(Alone)*

WHO IS MARVIN MACY?

(Stays where HE *is)*

THE NARRATOR

Who is Marvin Macy? Who is Marvin Macy? Now, while
no one would tell Cousin Lymon about Marvin Macy
that night in the cafe . . . *(Lighting shift to day here)*
. . . people are braver in the daylight, and the next day it
was not hard at all for him to learn what he wanted to know.
And what he found out was this . . . that many years ago,
back when Miss Amelia was nineteen years old, there occurred in her life a singular and awesome event: Miss Amelia
had been married. Back when Miss Amelia was nineteen years
old there were, at the same time, two brothers, the living re-
mainder of a brood of seven children. The brothers were
Marvin and Henry Macy, and Marvin was ten years younger
than his brother, Henry. And Marvin Macy was a loom-fixer
at the mill, and he was the handsomest man in the region
. . . and the wildest.

*(*COUSIN LYMON *stays on stage, way to one side.
Music out.*

MARVIN *and* HENRY MACY *come on)*

HENRY MACY

The Tanner girl . . .

MARVIN MACY

What about the Tanner girl?

HENRY MACY

She gone off to Society City.

MARVIN MACY (*Challenging*)

So?

(*No response from* HENRY)

So, let her go; she be happy there, give her some free space to run about in.

HENRY MACY
(*Sitting;* MARVIN *stays standing*)

I hear she left on account of you.

MARVIN MACY

Who says? . . . Hunh?

HENRY MACY

Mrs. Tanner. She stops me comin' back from the mill . . . yesterday . . . she say Laura go off to Society City on account of you . . .

MARVIN MACY

On account of me *what* . . . ?

HENRY MACY

Land, Marvin, *you* know.

MARVIN MACY
(*Intentionally transparent pretense of innocence*)

I don't know.

HENRY MACY

Ain't the first young girl you take out to the woods with you, ain't the first young girl you forced to leave home . . . you ruined. Ain't the first . . .

MARVIN MACY (*Bored impatience*)

I know what I *do*. (*Leers*) I know who I take walkin' in

the moonlight with me, goes out little girls comes back women . . .

HENRY MACY

It ain't right!

MARVIN MACY *(Suddenly ugly)*

Don't you tell me what's right! God damn, for a brother you act one hell of a lot like you was my father!

HENRY MACY
(Softer, but still to the point)

It ain't right.

MARVIN MACY

Them young girls . . . ? Them young girls you talk about . . . *(Cruel imitation)* . . . "it ain't right" . . . *(His face close to* HENRY's*)* . . . you know what they want? Hunh? How you know what they do out there in the woods, drive a man half out of his mind; what d' you know about that? *(Sneers)* The kinda moonlight walks *you* take, Henry, them solitary walks at night, that . . . *(Chuckles)* . . . that ain't the same thing . . . ain't, at all. *(An afterthought; still not kind)* 'Sides, don't think a walk in the woods with Laura Tanner do you any harm . . . might do you some good!

HENRY MACY *(To avoid)*

She ain't the first you take out there! They ain't all pressing theirselves up against you, free for all. They be a legal word for what you do out there, Marvin!

MARVIN MACY *(Quietly amused)*

Yeah? What be it?

HENRY MACY

Never . . . never mind.

MARVIN MACY

They be a word for what you do out there in them woods, too, Henry.

HENRY MACY
(Embarrassed, but still brother)

You . . . you gonna get yourself in big trouble one day.

MARVIN MACY *(Sneering bravura)*

I been in trouble. Oooh, I am evil, Henry.

HENRY MACY

Carryin' marijuana around with you, and . . .

MARVIN MACY
(Pretending to fish into a pocket)

Want some, Henry? Want some marijuana?

HENRY MACY *(Vacant)*

It is for them who are discouraged and drawn toward death.

MARVIN MACY *(A great laugh)*

And you ain't? *(Pause)* It is also for little girls who would be women; makes their heads whirl, gives 'em that floating feelin' . . .

(Laughs again, softer)

HENRY MACY

And aside from that, all your drinkin', and you not savin' any money, an' . . .

MARVIN MACY *(Angry)*

I got steady work, an' I make good money! I spend it as I like! I don't need you tellin' me . . .

HENRY MACY *(Softly)*

All right. *(Loud)* ALL RIGHT!

MARVIN MACY *(Muttering)*

I don't need you tellin' me anything 'bout how to go about livin'. I make good money . . .

HENRY MACY *(Weary impatience)*

. . . you make good money, an' you don't need me . . . yeah, I know all about it.

MARVIN MACY

Yeah.

HENRY MACY

Yeah. Don't change nothin', though.

MARVIN MACY *(Almost whining)*

Oh, Henry.

HENRY MACY

Man like you oughta settle down, oughta get married, raise some kids.

MARVIN MACY *(Suddenly furious)*

For what! Raise kids, have 'em a life like what we had? For what!

HENRY MACY

They is no need for kids to grow up like we had to; they is . . .

(MISS AMELIA *enters, near them;* SHE *wears a dress.* SHE *looks younger—maybe her hair is down.* THEY *do not see her)*

MARVIN MACY

For what!

HENRY MACY

All right now.

MARVIN MACY

Kids better off not born!

HENRY MACY

All right.

MARVIN MACY

Damn fool idea!

MISS AMELIA *(Irony)*

Afternoon.
        (HENRY MACY *rises*; MARVIN MACY *does not*)

HENRY MACY

Afternoon, Miss Amelia.

MARVIN MACY

Afternoon, Miss Amelia.

MISS AMELIA *(To* MARVIN MACY*)*

Your legs broke?

MARVIN MACY

Miss Amelia?

MISS AMELIA

I say: your legs broke?

MARVIN MACY *(Lazily)*

Why, no, Miss Amelia; my legs fine.

MISS AMELIA *(Snorts)*

I wondered. *(Purposefully, to* HENRY MACY*)* Whyn't you sit on back down, Henry?

HENRY MACY *(Resits)*

Thank you, Miss Amelia.

MARVIN MACY

Ohhhhhh.

(Slowly rises, mock-bows to MISS AMELIA*)*

Half the time I forget you're a girl, Miss Amelia . . . you so big; you more like a man.

MISS AMELIA

Yeah?

*(*SHE *swings backhand at* MARVIN MACY, *who ducks, laughs, sits again)*

MARVIN MACY

Temper, Miss Amelia.

MISS AMELIA *(Only half a joke)*

Don't you worry about temper. I'll knock you across the road.

MARVIN MACY

Bet you'd try.

MISS AMELIA

Bet I would. Do it, too.

MARVIN MACY

Well, you might *try*, Miss Amelia . . .

MISS AMELIA

Stand back up; I'll give you a sample.

HENRY MACY

Now, why don't you two just . . .

MISS AMELIA (*Smiling*)

Stand back up.

MARVIN MACY (*Gently*)

I don't go 'round hittin' girls, now.

MISS AMELIA

I didn't say nothin' about you hittin' me; I said I knock you across the road, an' I could do it.

MARVIN MACY (*Pleased*)

Well, maybe you could, Miss Amelia; maybe you could, at that.

MISS AMELIA

'Course, you could always pull a razor on me, like I hear you done to that man over in Cheehaw you fought.

MARVIN MACY (*Mock shock*)

Miss Amelia!

MISS AMELIA

I hear about it.

MARVIN MACY

Now, what did you hear?

MISS AMELIA

I hear. I hear you take a razor to that man, an' you cut his ear off.

HENRY MACY

Oh, now.

MISS AMELIA
An' you know what else I hear?

MARVIN MACY *(Greatly amused)*
No. What else you hear?

MISS AMELIA
I hear you got that man's ear salted and dried an' you carry it around with you.

HENRY MACY *(Dogmatically)*
That ain't true.

MARVIN MACY
Now, do you think I'd do a thing like that?

HENRY MACY
That ain't *true.*

MISS AMELIA *(To* HENRY MACY*)*
You know? You got proof it ain't?
(To MARVIN MACY*)*
You got proof you ain't got that man's ear?

MARVIN MACY
(Leans back lazily)
You want proof, Miss Amelia? You wanna search me? I'll lay back real quiet and let you go through my pockets, if you have a mind to. I'll lay back real quiet.

MISS AMELIA
(Finally, after a moment's noticeable embarrassment and confusion)
Clear across the road! I'll knock you clear across the road.
*(*MARVIN MACY *laughs;* HENRY *joins in)*

MARVIN MACY

Uhhh-*huh!*

MISS AMELIA
(Embarrassment back a little, begins to move to-ward her house)
I'll . . . I'll let you two go on back to whatever caused all that shoutin' you two were at . . . yellin' at each other . . .

MARVIN MACY

Why, you know what we were talkin' about, Miss Amelia? Shoutin', you say? We were talkin' about how it time for me to get a wife, that's what.

MISS AMELIA *(Snorts)*

Who marry you?

MARVIN MACY *(Mock seriousness)*

Why, Miss Amelia, I thought you would. Don't you want to marry me, Miss Amelia?

MISS AMELIA
(Confused for a moment, then)
In a pig's ear!
(Strides to and into her house)

MARVIN MACY
(To her retreating form)
Why, I thought you'd like that, Miss Amelia.

HENRY MACY

Bye, Miss Amelia.

MARVIN MACY

Thought you'd like that.

HENRY MACY
(After MISS AMELIA *has gone)*
Some jokes ain't in the best taste, Marvin.

MARVIN MACY
Hm?

HENRY MACY
Some jokes ain't in the best taste.

MARVIN MACY
(After momentary puzzlement)
Oh . . . no . . . that be a point, Henry . . . some jokes
ain't.

HENRY MACY
No; they ain't.

MARVIN MACY
Hey, you know I be right about somethin': Miss Amelia ain't
no girl; she be a woman already.

HENRY MACY
Yes, she be. Sure ain't right for you, Marvin; she be grown
up.

MARVIN MACY
(Gets up, wanders toward the door to the house)
No. Sure ain't.

HENRY MACY
(Gets up, prepares to leave)
Well . . .

MARVIN MACY
Hey, Henry . . . ?

HENRY MACY

Yeah?

MARVIN MACY

A real grown-up woman.

HENRY MACY

Marvin . . .

MARVIN MACY

Hey, Henry . . . if I *was* gonna get a wife . . .

HENRY MACY

You crazy?

MARVIN MACY

Some say.

HENRY MACY

You ain't serious, Marvin. She laugh in your face.

MARVIN MACY

Hmmm? Oh, yeah, bet you right.

HENRY MACY

You ain't serious, Marvin.

MARVIN MACY

(*After a moment; smiles at* HENRY MACY)

No. I ain't serious.

(THEY *hold positions*)

THE NARRATOR

Oh, but he was; Marvin Macy was dead serious. He had, at
that moment, without knowing it, chosen Miss Amelia Evans

to be his bride. He had chosen her to be his bride, and when he realized that astonishing fact he was dismayed. For while he knew he loved her, had probably loved her for some time without knowing it, he also knew he did not deserve her. He was sick with dismay at his unworthiness. So, for two full years, Marvin Macy did not speak to Miss Amelia of his love for her, but spent that time in bettering himself in her eyes. No man in the town ever reversed his character more fully. And finally, one Sunday evening, at the end of two years, Marvin Macy returned to Miss Amelia and plighted his troth.

(MARVIN MACY *enters from stage-left, bearing a sack of chitterlins, a bunch of swamp flowers and, in the pocket of his dressy suit, a silver ring.* HE *approaches slowly, his eyes on the ground;* HE *stops a number of feet from where* MISS AMELIA *is sitting)*

MARVIN MACY
(Still not looking at her)
Evenin' Miss Amelia. *(No response)* Sure is hot.

MISS AMELIA *(After a pause)*
It so hot, what you all dressed up for a funeral for?

MARVIN MACY
(After a blushing laugh)
Oh, I . . . I am come callin'.
(Let it be understood here that there are, unless otherwise stated, varying pauses between speeches in this scene)

MISS AMELIA
Yeah? On who?

MARVIN MACY
Oh . . . on you . . . Miss Amelia.

MISS AMELIA *(Restating a fact)*

On me.

MARVIN MACY *(Laughs briefly)*

Yep . . . on you.

MISS AMELIA *(Considers it; then)*

Somethin' wrong?

MARVIN MACY

I . . .
> (HE *makes a sudden decision, hurriedly brings the bag of chitterlins and the flowers over to where* MISS AMELIA *is, puts them on the ground below where* SHE *is sitting, the flowers on top of the bag, and returns to his position)*

. . . I brought you these.

MISS AMELIA *(Stares at them)*

What be these?

MARVIN MACY *(Terribly shy)*

Flowers.

MISS AMELIA

I can see that. What be in the bag?

MARVIN MACY *(As before)*

They be . . . chitterlins.

MISS AMELIA *(Mild surprise)*

Chitterlins.

MARVIN MACY

Yep.

(MISS AMELIA *descends the stairs, picks up the flowers as though they were a duster*)

MISS AMELIA (*Reseating herself*)

What for?

MARVIN MACY

Miss Amelia?

MISS AMELIA

I say: what for? Why you bring me chitterlins and flowers?

MARVIN MACY
(*Bravely taking one or two steps forward*)
Miss Amelia, I am . . . I am a reformed person. I have mended my ways, and . . .

MISS AMELIA

If you are come to call, sit down. Don't stand there in the road.

MARVIN MACY

Thank . . . Thank you, Miss Amelia.
(HE *comes onto the porch and seats himself, but four or five feet from* MISS AMELIA)
I have mended my ways; I am, like I said, a reformed person, Miss Amelia . . .

MISS AMELIA
(*Looking at the flowers*)
What are these called?

MARVIN MACY

Hunh? . . . Oh, they . . . they be swamp flowers.

MISS AMELIA

But what are they *called?*

MARVIN MACY *(Shrugs, helplessly)*

Swamp flowers.

MISS AMELIA

They got a name.

MARVIN MACY

I . . . I don't know.

MISS AMELIA

I don't neither. *(Pause)* They got a name in some *language*; all flowers do.

MARVIN MACY

I don't know, Miss Amelia.

MISS AMELIA

I don't neither. *(Smells them)* They don't smell none.

MARVIN MACY

I'm . . . sorry.

MISS AMELIA

Don't have to smell; they pretty.

MARVIN MACY *(Blurting)*

Miss Amelia, I have mended my ways; I go to church regular, and I have . . .

MISS AMELIA

I see it. You go to church now, services an' meetings . . .

MARVIN MACY

. . . yes, an' I have learned to put money aside . . .

MISS AMELIA

. . . you have learned thrift; that good . . .

MARVIN MACY

. . . an' I have bought me some land, I have bought me ten acres of timber over by . . .

MISS AMELIA

. . . I hear so; timber is good land . . .

MARVIN MACY

. . . an', an' I don't drink none no more . . .

MISS AMELIA

. . . don't drink? . . .

MARVIN MACY *(Blushes)*

. . . well, you know what I mean . . .

MISS AMELIA

Man don't drink none ain't natural.

MARVIN MACY

Well, I don't squander my wages away on drink an' all that I used to . . .

MISS AMELIA

Uh-huuh.

MARVIN MACY

. . . an' . . . Miss Amelia? . . . an' I am less sportin' with the girls now . . . I have reformed my character in that way, too . . .

MISS AMELIA *(Nods slowly)*

I know; I hear.

MARVIN MACY

. . . an'; an' I have stopped pickin' fights with folks . . .

MISS AMELIA

You still got that ear? You still got that ear you cut off that man in Cheehaw you fight? . . .

MARVIN MACY *(Embarrassed)*

Oh, Miss Amelia, I never done that.

MISS AMELIA *(Disbelieving)*

I *hear*.

MARVIN MACY

Oh, no, Miss Amelia, I never done that. I . . . I let that story pass 'round . . . but I never done that.

MISS AMELIA
(The slightest tinge of disappointment)

Oh. That so.

MARVIN MACY

So, you see, I have reformed my character.

MISS AMELIA *(Nods)*

Would seem.
(A long pause between them)

MARVIN MACY

Yes.

MISS AMELIA

Land is good to have. I been dickerin' over near Society City to pick up thirty-five acres . . . timber, too . . . man there near broke, an' he wanna sell to me.

MARVIN MACY
Miss . . . Miss Amelia . . . *(Brings the ring from his pocket)* I brought somethin' else with me, too . . .

MISS AMELIA *(Curious)*
Yeah?

MARVIN MACY
I . . .
(Shows it to her)
. . . I brought this silver ring.

MISS AMELIA
(Looks at it; hands it back)
It silver?

MARVIN MACY
Yep, it silver. Miss Amelia, will you . . .

MISS AMELIA
Bet it cost some.

MARVIN MACY
(Determined to get it out)
Miss Amelia, will you marry me?

MISS AMELIA
(After an interminable pause, during which she scratches her head, then her arm, then very offhand)
Sure.

MARVIN MACY
(Almost not having heard)
You . . . Yes?! . . . You will?

MISS AMELIA
(Narrowing her eyes, almost unfriendly)
I said sure.

MARVIN MACY
*(Not rising, begins sliding himself across the step
to her)*
Oh, Amelia . . .

MISS AMELIA *(Sharply)*
What?

MARVIN MACY
(In a split second studies what HE *has said wrong,
realizes it, keeps sliding)*
Oh, *Miss* Amelia . . .
*(*HE *reaches her, begins the gesture of putting one
arm behind her back, the other in front, prepara-
tory to kissing her.* MISS AMELIA *reacts swiftly, leans
back a bit, swings her right arm back, with a fist,
ready to hit him)*

MISS AMELIA
Whoa there, you!

MARVIN MACY
(Retreats some, slides back a few feet)
Wait 'til I tell Henry; wait 'til I tell *everybody*. (*Very hap-
py*) Oh, Miss Amelia.

MISS AMELIA *(Rises, stretches)*
Well . . . g'night.

(MARVIN MACY, *momentarily confused, but too happy to worry about it, rises, also, backs down the porch steps, begins backing off, stage left*)

MARVIN MACY

G' . . . G' . . .G'night, Miss Amelia. (*Reaches the far side of the stage, then just before turning to run off, shouts*) G'night, Miss Amelia.

(*Exits*)

MISS AMELIA
(*Standing on the porch, alone; long pause*)
G'night . . .

(*Pause*)

Marvin Macy.

(MISS AMELIA *goes indoors*)

NARRATOR
And the very next Sunday they were married. It was a proper church wedding, performed by the Reverend Potter, and Miss Amelia had held a bouquet of flowers, and Henry was there to give Marvin away, and it was, indeed, a proper wedding. Now it is true that some of the townspeople had misgivings about the match, but no one—not even the most evil-minded—had foreseen what was to happen: for the marriage of Marvin Macy and Miss Amelia Evans lasted only ten days . . . ten unholy days which became a legend, a whispered legend in the town.

(*Interior of store visible.* MISS AMELIA *and* MARVIN MACY *alone.* MISS AMELIA *wears a wedding dress, carries a wedding bouquet.* MARVIN MACY *has a flower in his coat*)

MARVIN MACY (*Shyly*)
Well, Miss Amelia . . .

MISS AMELIA
(Picking at her dress)
Don't know why a person's supposed to get all up in this
stuff . . . just to get married.

MARVIN MACY
I think it look . . . nice.

MISS AMELIA *(Studying the dress)*
Belong to my mother.

MARVIN MACY
It look . . . nice.

MISS AMELIA
Too short.

MARVIN MACY
It look . . . nice. You . . . you pass it on down to . . .

MISS AMELIA
Hm?

MARVIN MACY
You pass it on down to our kids . . . our daughters.

MISS AMELIA
(Looks at him, snorts)
Hunh! *(Laughs briefly, sardonically)* If you hungry, go eat.

MARVIN MACY
I ain't hungry, Miss Amelia.

MISS AMELIA
No? Suit yourself. I got some figgerin' to do.

MARVIN MACY *(Shyly)*
Figgerin' . . . Miss Amelia?

MISS AMELIA
(Totally oblivious of his surprise)
Yeah, I got a bargain goin' on some kindlin' I want, an' I gotta figger. I think I figgered a way to get that kindlin' good an' cheap. That farmer owe me a favor: once I fixed boils for him, an' he ain't never paid a bill he owed papa when he were alive. I kin get it good an' cheap. What you think?

MARVIN MACY
I think . . . I think it be time . . . ain't it time for bed, Miss Amelia?

MISS AMELIA
Ain't ten. You tired?

MARVIN MACY
(Sitting gently, to wait)
No. I . . . ain't tired.

MISS AMELIA
You wanna smoke a pipe? Before sleep? Ain't no pockets in this dress. Thought I had my clothes on.

MARVIN MACY
No, I don't need a pipe. Miss Amelia, it . . . time for bed.

MISS AMELIA
(Stretching; off-hand)
Yeah . . . well, c'mon . . . I'll show you where your room is.

MARVIN MACY
My . . . room . . . Miss Amelia?

MISS AMELIA
(Going toward the stairs)
C'mon.

MARVIN MACY *(Moving to her)*
Kin I . . . kin I take your arm?

MISS AMELIA
(Looks at him as though HE *were crazy. Laughs in his face)*
What for?

MARVIN MACY
Well, it is . . . proper for a groom . . . to take his bride by the hand, an' . . .

MISS AMELIA
(Annoyed by the impracticality of his suggestion)
I got a lamp. You want it to spill?
*(*MISS AMELIA, *followed by* MARVIN MACY, *climb the stairs, disappear. It becomes dark in the store, but the interior stays visible)*

THE NARRATOR
And what happened next, what happened that wedding night of Miss Amelia and Marvin Macy, no one will ever truly know. But part of it—part of it—was witnessed by Emma Hale, who had watched it, her nose pressed against the downstairs window of the store. And she could not wait to tell what she had seen.

EMMA HALE *(To* HENRY MACY*)*
An' it weren't no more'n a half hour after they'd gone upstairs, him followin' after her . . .

(*Pantomime from* MISS AMELIA *and* MARVIN MACY *to this*)

Miss Amelia come thumpin' back down those stairs, her face black with anger? An' she'd changed outa that dress o' hers, an' she were got up like she usually be now, an' she went into her office . . .

(*Pauses for effect*)

. . . and she stayed there 'till *dawn*. She stay there the whole night! He stayed up *there*, an' she stayed down *there*, in her office. (*Proudly*) An' how do you like that for a weddin' night?

HENRY MACY

I . . . I . . . didn't know.

EMMA HALE

All I can say is: a groom is in a sorry fix when he is unable to bring his well-beloved bride to bed with him. An' the whole town know it. There is some question there—specially a man like Marvin, his reputation: up-ending girls from here to Cheehaw an' back. Somethin' funny there.

HENRY MACY

Marvin?

MARVIN MACY
(*His attention only on* HENRY)

Henry . . . she . . .

HENRY MACY (*Gently*)

I know; I know.

MARVIN MACY (*A child*)

Henry, she don't like me . . . she don't . . . want me.

HENRY MACY

Well, now, Marvin, sometime it takes a while to . . .

MARVIN MACY

What'd I do wrong, Henry? She don't want me.

HENRY MACY *(Helplessly)*

Well, Marvin . . .

MARVIN MACY

We get upstairs, an' . . .

HENRY MACY

It take time, Marvin.

MARVIN MACY

I don't know; I don't know, Henry.

HENRY MACY *(Vaguely)*

Well . . .

MARVIN MACY
(An idea coming to him, enthusiasm growing)
Hey! Henry, maybe . . . maybe it 'cause I didn't give her
no . . . no weddin' gifts . . . you know, women like to have
them things. Hey, Henry? Maybe that it, huh?

HENRY MACY *(Cautious)*

Well, now . . .

MARVIN MACY

That's what I'll do, Henry: I'll go in to Society City an' . . .
an' I'll get her a bunch of stuff.
                    (HE *leaves the porch, heads off*)
That'll do it, Henry! I bet!
                    (HE *exits, happily*)

HENRY MACY *(After him)*

Maybe . . . might be.

(Stays on stage)

THE NARRATOR

And off he went to Society City, and he brought her back all kinds of things; a huge box of chocolates which cost two dollars and a half, an enamel brooch, an opal ring, and a silver bracelet which had, hanging from it, two silver lovebirds. And he gave these presents to her . . . and she put them up for sale . . . all save the chocolates . . . which she ate. And, sad to tell, these presents did not soften her heart toward him.

MISS AMELIA

Oh, by the way, I gonna drag a mattress down from upstairs; you can sleep on *it*, in front of the stove, down here in the store.

(SHE waits for some reaction, gets none, goes inside)

MARVIN MACY

(By himself; the night has deepened a little. In a soft plaintive voice)

Henry? . . . Henry?

HENRY MACY

(From far off to one side)

Yes, Marvin.

MARVIN MACY

(To the night, not to HENRY's voice)

Henry, I don't know what to do.

HENRY MACY *(Helpless, himself)*

Well, now, Marvin . . .

MARVIN MACY

I love her, Henry. I don't know what to do.

HENRY MACY

Time, Marvin. Time?

MARVIN MACY *(Pause)*

Yeah. *(Pause)* Sure, Henry.
>   *(It comes up to daylight again now,* MARVIN MACY
>   *staying where* HE *is)*

MARVIN MACY

>   *(Gets up, shouts at the upstairs of the house, both a*
>   *threat and a promise)*

I be back!

HENRY MACY

>   *(As* MARVIN MACY *passes him, exiting)*

Marvin? Marvin, where you . . .

MARVIN MACY *(Pushing past)*

I goin' into Cheehaw; I be back.
>   *(Exits)*

THE NARRATOR

There was, of course, speculation in the town on the reason
Miss Amelia had married Marvin Macy in the first place. No
one doubted that *he* loved *her,* but as to why she had accepted his proposal in the first place there were myriad opin-
ions. And while some people were . . . confused by the
course of events, no one could honestly say he was surprised.

MARVIN MACY
(Reenters, moves inside to MISS AMELIA; SHE *looks up at him with a cool curiosity)*
Miss Amelia?

MISS AMELIA
You doin' a lot of travelin', I notice.

MARVIN MACY
I . . . I been to Cheehaw today.

MISS AMELIA *(Indifferent)*
Yeah? What you do there?

MARVIN MACY
I went into Cheehaw, an' . . . an' I saw a lawyer.

MISS AMELIA
(Suddenly on her guard)
Yeah? What you seein' a lawyer about?

MARVIN MACY *(Shy; embarrassed)*
Well, now . . .

MISS AMELIA *(Smelling trouble)*
What you know about lawyers?

MARVIN MACY
Well, I got me a lawyer . . . *(Takes out the paper)* . . . an'
I got this paper drawn up . . .

MISS AMELIA *(Belligerently)*
Yeah, an'? . . .

MARVIN MACY
(*Shy, but enthusiastic*)
An' what I done, I got this paper drawn up, an' I had the
deed to my timber land . . . the . . . the ten acres of timber
land I bought with my savin's the past couple years . . . an'
I had the deed to my timber land turned over to you, Miss
Amelia. I had it put in your name; it all yours.
(HE *eagerly holds the paper out to* MISS AMELIA)

MISS AMELIA
(SHE *looks at him for a moment, no expression on
her face, then* SHE *takes the paper from him, not
snatching it, but not taking a gift, either.* SHE *studies it*)
Hm!

MARVIN MACY
It all legal, Miss Amelia; I seen to that.

MISS AMELIA (*Still studying it*)
Hm.

MARVIN MACY
Them ten acres all yours now.

MISS AMELIA (*Still studying*)
Unh-hunh.

MARVIN MACY (*Shy*)
I . . . I thought you'd be pleased . . . Miss Amelia.

MISS AMELIA
(*Folding the paper, putting it in her jeans, rising*)
Yeah; it all legal.

MARVIN MACY

It is everything I have in the world.

MISS AMELIA
(Moving toward the door)

It legal.

MARVIN MACY

It is everything I have in the world, an' . . . I thought it would please you to have it.

MISS AMELIA

It adjoin *my* timber land, *my* acres; it make a nice spread.

MARVIN MACY *(Bewildered)*

Miss Amelia . . .

MISS AMELIA *(Daring him)*

Yeah?

MARVIN MACY
(His eyes on his feet)

I am not . . . as comfortable as I might be, sleepin' down in the store, in front of the stove, like I am.

MISS AMELIA *(No compassion)*

Oh no?

MARVIN MACY

No, I am not too comfortable sleepin' there.
(There is a pleading in this)

MISS AMELIA *(Considers it)*

Oh. *(Then)* Well, in that case then, why don't you pull your

mattress out onto the porch, sleep there, or move over into
the smoke house? Plenty of places you can sleep.
> (SHE *waits, challengingly, for his reply*)

MARVIN MACY
> (*Too pitiable to be pitied*)
I'd . . . you know where I'd rather sleep, Miss Amelia.

MISS AMELIA
Or why don't you just move back with your brother Henry?
> (SHE *turns, goes indoors*)

MARVIN MACY
> (*Sits for a moment, contemplates his hopelessness;
> speaks to himself, gathering resolve*)
I am your husband; you are married to me, Miss Amelia
Evans.
> (HE *gets up, follows her into the store, says to her
> with firmness and bravura*)
Where is your likker?

MISS AMELIA (*Preoccupied*)
Hm?

MARVIN MACY
Gimme some likker!

MISS AMELIA
> (*With some distaste*)
You takin' up drinkin' again? High noon drinkin'?

MARVIN MACY
Gimme some likker!

MISS AMELIA
(Her eyes narrowing)
You want some likker, you get your money up like anybody
else.

MARVIN MACY
(Digging into his pocket)
I got my money; you give me that likker!
(HE slams the money down on the counter)
*(SHE reaches under the counter, brings up a bottle
and slams it down on the counter. The two glower
at each other)*
(Murderously)
Thank you.

MISS AMELIA *(The same)*
You welcome.

MARVIN MACY
(Taking the bottle)
Now, I think I'll just take me off into the swamp an' have
me a few drinks, an' then I think I'll just come back here
an' . . .

MISS AMELIA
You get yourself full of likker you don't set your foot in my
house!

MARVIN MACY
We see about that . . . Mrs. Macy!

MISS AMELIA *(A threat)*
You come back here drunk you wish you never born.

MARVIN MACY
We see about that! I love you, Miss Amelia.

MISS AMELIA

OUTA HERE!!

MARVIN MACY
(Still coming toward her)
You my bride, an' I gonna make you my wife.

MISS AMELIA
(Her fist cocked)
One step more, you!

MARVIN MACY
(At her now, tries to embrace her)
I love you, Miss Amelia.
(At this, MISS AMELIA swings at him, cracks him right in the jaw, with such force that HE staggers back and crashes, hard, against a wall; slumps there a little, one hand to his mouth)

MISS AMELIA
(Her fists still cocked)
OUT! OUT!

MARVIN MACY
(Surprised and hurt)
You . . . you broke my tooth; you . . . you broke one of my teeth.

MISS AMELIA
(Beginning to advance on him)
I break your head you don't get outa here!

MARVIN MACY
(Scrambling to get out, keeping as far from her advancing form as HE can)
You . . . you broke my tooth.

MISS AMELIA *(Advancing)*

OUT!

MARVIN MACY
(Backs out onto the porch, down the steps)
You . . . you hit me.

MISS AMELIA
(Towering above him)
You stay out, an' don't you never come back!

MARVIN MACY
(Still unable to believe it)
You hit me.

MISS AMELIA
You hear me? Don't you never come back! (MISS AMELIA
goes back into the store)
   *(MARVIN MACY gets up, moves front and center,
   broods at the footlights.)*
   *(HE reconsiders, marches up the steps, pauses mo-
   mentarily, then, with renewed resolve, gets to the
   door. Forcefully:)*
Miss Amelia?
   *(SHE turns around where SHE is, behind the counter,
   perhaps, looks at him)*
Miss Amelia, I comin' back in.
         (SHE moves to another area of the store)
You hear me? I got rights to be in here, as you is my wife an'
what's yours is mine, too. So, I comin' in!
   *(MISS AMELIA picks up her shotgun, breaks it,
   reaches for shells, loads it, begins to walk toward
   MARVIN MACY)*
I got my rights now, an' I'm comin' in there, an' I'm
gonna . . . (HE *sees the gun in her hand)*

(SHE *keeps advancing, pointing the gun at him,*
holding it at hip level)
You . . . you can't do that, now . . . you . . .
(HE *retreats from the door, as* MISS AMELIA *keeps advancing*)
I got my rights, an' . . .
(HE *backs down the steps as* MISS AMELIA *comes out*
on the porch, stony-faced, the shotgun still pointed
at him)
You . . . you keep that thing off me!
(HE *keeps backing off, finally stops*)
Miss Amelia . . .
(*So plaintively*)
I love you.

MISS AMELIA
(*Sits on the porch, the gun is still on him*)
You come one step closer, I blast your head off. You step one
foot on my property again, I shoot you.

MARVIN MACY
(*Stands stock still for a moment, then breaks, moves*
off past HENRY MACY)
I'm leavin', Henry, I can't take no more; I can't take no more
of this, Henry.
(*Exits*)

HENRY MACY
(*Moving to where* MISS AMELIA *is*)
Miss . . . Miss Amelia?

MISS AMELIA
(*In a rage, but abstracted*)
Yeah? Whadda ya want?

HENRY MACY

Miss Amelia, Marvin say he leavin'.

(SHE *does not react*)

He say he gonna take off from you.

MISS AMELIA

(*Finally*)

What this I hear 'bout a bridge gonna be built . . . ten mile up, or so. What about that? I hear they gonna have prison labor put it up. Gonna have the chain gang work on it.

HENRY MACY

He say he gonna . . . leave town.

MISS AMELIA

Been thinkin' . . . been thinkin' of havin' the prison farm bring some trusties work my cotton. It cheap labor.

HENRY MACY

I . . . You could do that, Miss Amelia.

MISS AMELIA

(*Belligerently, almost a dare*)

I know I could.

HENRY MACY

I . . .

(*Decides to say nothing, moves away*)

Well . . .

(*Touches two fingers to his forehead*)

Miss Amelia.

MISS AMELIA

Henry.

(*Dusk begins to fall now.* MISS AMELIA *stays sitting on her porch, the gun across her knees.* MARVIN

MACY *comes back on stage, carrying his tin suitcase.*
NOTE: *While it is true that on stage the* MACY
BROTHERS *and* MISS AMELIA *will be in fairly close
proximity, the following scene must give the im-
pression that* MISS AMELIA *cannot overhear what is
being said)*

MARVIN MACY *(Quietly)*

I'm leavin', Henry.

HENRY MACY

Are you, Marvin?

MARVIN MACY

Yep.

(Almost tearful)

I can't take no more.

HENRY MACY

No. I don't figger so.

MARVIN MACY

So I'm takin' off.

HENRY MACY

Where you goin', Marvin?

MARVIN MACY

I don't *know.* I go somewhere; I get away from *here.*

HENRY MACY

It best . . . I suppose.

MARVIN MACY

You write me a letter?

HENRY MACY

Why, sure I write you, Marvin, you tell me where you
are . . .

MARVIN MACY

No. I don't mean that.
(Takes paper and a pencil from his pocket)
You write a letter *for* me, you put down what I tell you.

HENRY MACY

Oh!
(Takes the paper and pencil from MARVIN MACY,
takes the tin suitcase to use as a writing table)
All right, Marvin; I ready.

MARVIN MACY

You take down just what I tell you.

HENRY MACY *(Quietly, patiently)*

Yes, Marvin.

MARVIN MACY
*(*HENRY MACY *always writing)*
Dear Miss Amelia, my wife. Underline wife.

HENRY MACY

Yes, Marvin.

MARVIN MACY

Dear Miss Amelia, my *wife*. I hate you.

HENRY MACY

Marvin . . .

MARVIN MACY

Put it down! I hate you. I love you.

HENRY MACY

Marvin . . .

MARVIN MACY

Do what I tell you! I love you. I have loved you for two
years, an' I have reformed my ways to be worthy of you. I
hate you. You gettin' all this?

HENRY MACY

Yes, Marvin.

MARVIN MACY

I . . . I hate you with all the power of my love for you. I
woulda been a good husband to you, an' I loved you for two
years 'fore I even dared speak my love for you, you . . . you
no-good rotten . . .

HENRY MACY

Slow down, Marvin . . . you no-good rotten . . .

MARVIN MACY

. . . you no-good rotten cross-eyed ugly lump!

HENRY MACY

Miss Amelia's eyes don't cross . . .

MARVIN MACY

When she mad! When she mad one eye bang right into her
nose. Yes.

HENRY MACY

I . . . I never noticed.

MARVIN MACY

I . . . I reformed my character, an' I made myself worthy of
you, an' the night you said yes you marry me no man ever

been happier . . . ever. I gonna come back some day an' kill
you!

HENRY MACY

Marvin, you don't mean that, now . . .

MARVIN MACY

You put it down! I gonna come back some day an' kill you.
I gonna . . . I gonna bust your face open, I gonna . . . I
gonna tear your arms outa your body like they bug wings.

HENRY MACY

Slow down, now.

MARVIN MACY

Write fast!

HENRY MACY

I writin' fast. You want it readable, don't you?

MARVIN MACY

Yes. No. I don't care.

HENRY MACY

I doin' the best I can.

MARVIN MACY

I . . . I give you my land, land I worked hard for, 'cause I
thought it'd please you; I . . . I bought you jewels, I bought
you jewelry, an' you put it up for *sale*. You treated me like
nothin', an' I *loved* you. I . . . I love you, Miss Amelia; I
love you. An' . . .

HENRY MACY
(As MARVIN MACY *pauses)*

Go on, Marvin.

MARVIN MACY *(Almost tearfully)*

An' I goin' away now, I goin' away an' I never comin' back *(A rush)* An' when I come back I gonna fix you, I gonna kill you!

HENRY MACY
(As MARVIN MACY *pauses again)*

Yeah?

MARVIN MACY
(In a sort of disgusted, sad rush)

With all my love very truly yours your husband Marvin Macy.

HENRY MACY *(As* HE *finishes)*

You . . . you wanna sign it?

MARVIN MACY

No, you write my name down, but I gonna sign it special.
> (HE *takes out his knife and gingerly jabs his thumb, drawing blood)*

Here, gimme that.
> (HE *bends down, bloods the bottom of the letter with his thumb)*

That make it all official.

HENRY MACY

You . . . you want me give her this?

MARVIN MACY

After I go; I goin' now.
> (HE *picks up his tin suitcase)*

HENRY MACY *(Gets up)*

I take care of it.

MARVIN MACY
(*Almost not wanting to go*)
Well, Henry . . .

HENRY MACY
Marvin, you take care now.

MARVIN MACY
I'll . . . (*Shrugs*) take care of myself.

HENRY MACY
Don't go . . . gettin' in any trouble.

MARVIN MACY
(*A brief, rueful laugh*)
You know, Henry? I wouldn't be surprised one bit if I did?
Wouldn't surprise me I turned into one of the worst people
you ever saw?

HENRY MACY
You . . . stay good now.

MARVIN MACY
(*A sudden, sick violence*)
WHY?

HENRY MACY
You . . . you take care.

MARVIN MACY
Well . . . (*Pause*) . . . Goodbye, Henry.

HENRY MACY
(*As* MARVIN MACY *exits*)
Goodbye . . . Marvin.

(HENRY MACY *watches after* MARVIN MACY *for a moment, looks at the letter in his hand, turns, slowly walks to the foot of the steps, where* MISS AMELIA *is sitting)*

HENRY MACY *(Quietly)*

Miss Amelia.

MISS AMELIA

That loom-fixer take off? Your brother finally clear out?

HENRY MACY *(As before)*

Yeah. He gone.

MISS AMELIA
(After a brief silence)

Good riddance.

HENRY MACY

He . . .
(Hands her the letter)
. . . He want you to have this.

MISS AMELIA
(Glances at it only long enough to realize it is a letter)
Good riddance.

HENRY MACY

Well . . . 'night, Miss Amelia.

MISS AMELIA *(Pause)*

'Night, Henry.
(HENRY MACY *exits,* MISS AMELIA, *left alone on stage, begins to read the letter.*
(Music up, if not used throughout so far)

THE NARRATOR

And so ended the ten days of marriage of Miss Amelia Evans and Marvin Macy and answers the question that Cousin Lymon asked some years later. Who is Marvin Macy? Who is Marvin Macy?

MISS AMELIA *and* COUSIN LYMON *alone on the porch.*

COUSIN LYMON

Amelia!

MISS AMELIA

Yeah?

COUSIN LYMON

I been learnin' some things, Amelia.

MISS AMELIA

Yeah? What?

COUSIN LYMON
(After a long pause; quietly, seriously, with no trace of sport in it)
Amelia? Why you never tell me you married?
(This startles MISS AMELIA; *maybe she rises, walks a few steps, kicks a post, does not look at* COUSIN LYMON)

MISS AMELIA
(Finally; hoarsely, angrily)

I ain't!

COUSIN LYMON
(Quietly, persistently)
Yes, you be. You married Marvin Macy, years an' years ago.
You married.

MISS AMELIA *(A pretense)*
No!

COUSIN LYMON
Why you never tell me that?

MISS AMELIA
(Convincing herself)
I ain't married!

COUSIN LYMON
Why you never tell me you married, Amelia?

MISS AMELIA
(Finally turning, facing him)
I *were* married. I were married, to that no-account loom-fixer
. . . but that is past . . . over! . . . done!

COUSIN LYMON
(The same quiet insistence)
You ever divorce from him?

MISS AMELIA
He run off; he run off years ago; I ain't married to him no
more!

COUSIN LYMON
You ever divorce from him?

MISS AMELIA *(Furious)*
HE RUN OFF!! *(Then, finally, softer)* I ain't married no more.

COUSIN LYMON
(Quietly, logically)
Oh, yes you be. You still married to him. Why you never tell me about that, Amelia?

MISS AMELIA
(Returning to him, sitting, quieter)
It . . . it long ago; it . . . it way in the past.
(As COUSIN LYMON *just looks at her)*
It . . . It don't have nothin' to do with . . . nothin'.

COUSIN LYMON
I find it mighty strange you never tell me about that, Amelia.

MISS AMELIA
(Strangely shy)
Ain't . . . weren't nothin' to tell. I . . . I married him . . . he run off. *(Almost pleading)* He . . . he no good, Cousin Lymon. He never were a good man.

COUSIN LYMON
You married him.

MISS AMELIA *(Shyer yet)*
We were . . . we never really . . . *married.*

COUSIN LYMON
You promise you never have secrets from me, Amelia. Give me a real funny feelin', . . . knowin' you keep things from me; give me a feelin' I don't like.

MISS AMELIA
It weren't no real secret, Cousin Lymon. I don't . . . I don't like you to worry none about things; I like you to be comfortable, an' . . . an' happy.

COUSIN LYMON
It give me a feelin' I don't like.

MISS AMELIA
It were nothin' for you to know.

COUSIN LYMON
(*Turning on her; almost savage; yes, savage*)
It were nothin' for me to *know!?!*

MISS AMELIA
I . . . I don't keep much from you, Cousin Lymon; you
know my business, my . . . my accounts; I told you all
about my poppa, an' all . . .

COUSIN LYMON (*Accusing*)
All 'cept Marvin Macy.

MISS AMELIA (*Acquiescing*)
All 'cept Marvin Macy.

COUSIN LYMON
(*A change begins to come over him;* HE *is through
chastising* MISS AMELIA: *an excitement has come
into his voice*)
An' Marvin Macy, he . . . he is, what I hear tell, such a
man!

MISS AMELIA
(*Still wrapped in thought*)
Huuh! A no good.

COUSIN LYMON
You . . . you keep from me the most . . . the most excitin'
thing in your life.

MISS AMELIA *(Still half-hearing)*
Never been no good, that one.

COUSIN LYMON
An' you keep the fact of him from me, the most important
fact of all in your whole life . . .

MISS AMELIA
(Becoming aware of what HE *is saying)*
Cousin Lymon . . . ?

COUSIN LYMON
(Caught up with it now)
. . . a man like Marvin Macy, who has been *everywhere,*
who has seen things no other man never seen, who . . .

MISS AMELIA *(Disbelief)*
Cousin Lymon!
(Music begins here)

COUSIN LYMON
. . . who has . . . who has *(Wonder comes into his voice)*
been to *Atlanta!*

MISS AMELIA
(Trying to gather what is going on)
Atlanta ain't much.

COUSIN LYMON
Who has been to *Atlanta,* an' . . . *(Religious awe enters his
voice now)* an' who has had to do with the *law* . . . an'
(This is the ecstasy) who has spent time in the *penitentiary.*
Oh, Amelia! You have kept this from me!

MISS AMELIA
(Anger coming through)
He is a common criminal, that's all!

COUSIN LYMON
Oh, Amelia, he has been in the penitentiary, an' . . . an' I
bet he spent time on the chain gang. Oh, Amelia!

MISS AMELIA *(Confused)*
You . . . you seen the chain gang, Cousin Lymon.

COUSIN LYMON
Yes!

MISS AMELIA
A bunch of common criminals, chained together by the an-
kle, workin' on the roads in the broilin' sun, a guard standin'
over 'em with a gun.

COUSIN LYMON
Yes! Yes! Yes! Amelia!

MISS AMELIA *(Pleading)*
Cousin Lymon . . . they common criminals, they . . . they
got no freedom.

COUSIN LYMON
I know, Amelia . . . but they *together*.

MISS AMELIA
(After a long pause; shyly)
We together . . . Cousin Lymon.

COUSIN LYMON *(Dismissing it)*
Yes, Amelia, we together.

MISS AMELIA
An' . . . an' we got a good life together.

COUSIN LYMON *(Same)*
Oh, yes, of course, Amelia. *(The ecstasy returns)* An' they are together, those men, an' . . . an' how they *sing*, Amelia! You hear them sing, Amelia?

MISS AMELIA
(Retreating into her mind)
Yes, I hear them sing.

COUSIN LYMON
An' . . . an' they . . . *together.*
(Silence.
Music stops abruptly. MARVIN MACY *enters from stage-left, stays there, leans against the proscenium, maybe, whittling on a piece of wood.* MISS AMELIA *and* COUSIN LYMON *see him simultaneously.* MISS AMELIA *rises, stiffens, her fists clenched.* MARVIN MACY *stays lounging.* COUSIN LYMON *gets up, moves slowly, cautiously toward* MARVIN MACY)

MISS AMELIA *(To* MARVIN MACY)
You clear outa here!
*(*COUSIN LYMON *continues his slow move toward* MARVIN MACY)

MARVIN MACY
(Throws his head back, laughs contemptuously at MISS AMELIA. COUSIN LYMON *continues moving toward him, is quite near him now.*
To COUSIN LYMON, *contemptuously)*
Whatta you want, bug?

MISS AMELIA

Cousin Lymon!

COUSIN LYMON (*Waving her off*)

Leave it be, Amelia.
   (*Approaches* MARVIN MACY)
You . . . you be Marvin Macy.
  (*With this,* COUSIN LYMON *begins small, involuntary
  spasms of excitement, little jumps from the ground,
  strange jerks of his hands*)
You be Marvin Macy.

MARVIN MACY
  (*To* MISS AMELIA, *but staring at* COUSIN LYMON)
What ails this brokeback?

MISS AMELIA (*Not moving*)

You clear out!

COUSIN LYMON
  (*His spasms continuing*)
You been . . . you been to Atlanta, an' . . . an' . . .
an' . . .

MARVIN MACY

Is the runt throwin' a fit?

COUSIN LYMON (*As before*)

An' . . . an' . . . an' you been to the penitentiary?
  (MARVIN MACY *backhands* COUSIN LYMON *a sharp
  cuff on the ear which sends him sprawling backwards toward center-stage.* HE *falls, scrambles up*)

MARVIN MACY

That'll learn you, brokeback, starin' at me!

COUSIN LYMON

(On his feet, staring at MARVIN MACY, *but with a hand stopping signal to* MISS AMELIA *who has taken a step down the porch steps)*

Leave it be, Miss Amelia . . . just . . . leave . . . it . . . be . . .

MISS AMELIA

I'll fix that no-good!

COUSIN LYMON

(His eyes firmly on MARVIN MACY: *a command to* MISS AMELIA*)*

Leave me alone, Amelia! Just leave it be!

MISS AMELIA *(A hopeless call)*

Cousin Lymon!

COUSIN LYMON

Leave off, Amelia; leave off.

MARVIN MACY *(Laughs, turns)*

Bye . . . Mrs. Macy.

(Exits)

COUSIN LYMON

Marvin Macy!

MISS AMELIA

(As COUSIN LYMON *follows* MARVIN MACY *off-stage)*

Cousin Lymon?

COUSIN LYMON *(From off-stage)*

Marvin Macy! Marvin Macy! Marvin Macy!

*(*MISS AMELIA *is left alone on stage in the deepening night . . .*

Music holds)

Music begins.
Tableau: MISS AMELIA *on the porch, one step down.*

THE NARRATOR

The time has come to speak about love. Now consider three
people who were subject to that condition. Miss Amelia,
Cousin Lymon, and Marvin Macy.

But what sort of thing is love? First of all, it is a joint experience between two persons, but that fact does not mean
that it is a similar experience to the two people involved.
There are the lover and the beloved, but these two come
from different countries. Often the beloved is only the stimulus for all the stored-up love which has lain quiet within the
lover for a long time hitherto. And somehow every lover
knows this. He feels in his soul that his love is a solitary
thing. He comes to know a new, strange loneliness.

Now, the beloved can also be of any description: the most
outlandish people can be the stimulus for love. Yes, and the
lover may see this as clearly as anyone else—but that does
not affect the evolution of his love one whit. Therefore, the
quality and value of any love is determined solely by the
lover himself.

It is for this reason that most of us would rather love than
be loved; and the curt truth is that, in a deep secret way, the
state of being beloved is intolerable to many; for the lover
craves any possible relation with the beloved, even if this
experience can cause them both only pain.

But though the outward facts of love are often sad and ridiculous, it must be remembered that no one can know what
really takes place in the soul of the lover himself. So, who
but God can be the final judge of any love? But one thing
can be said about these three people—all of whom, Miss
Amelia, Cousin Lymon, and Marvin Macy, all of whom were
subject to the condition of love. The thing that can be said
is this: No good will come of it.

Music still holding.

MISS AMELIA *rises right at the end of* THE NARRATOR'S *speech, goes indoors, leaving the stage momentarily empty. It is still evening*

Music out; MISS AMELIA *has gone inside.* MARVIN MACY *and* HENRY MACY *come on stage together, with* COUSIN LYMON *trailing after them, peripheral, but hovering*

MARVIN MACY
(To COUSIN LYMON: *ugly)*
You quit followin' me!? You hear!?

HENRY MACY
Oh, let him be. He don't do no harm.

MARVIN MACY *(To* HENRY MACY*)*
Followin' me around like some damn dog . . . yippin' at my heels. *(Falsetto)* "Marvin Macy; hello there, Marvin Macy; Marvin Macy, Marvin Macy." *(Natural voice again)* Drive a man crazy.
(Back to COUSIN LYMON*)*
Whyn't you get on back to your friend . . . jabber at her?

COUSIN LYMON
(Shy, but almost flirtatious)
Oh, now, I ain't no trouble.

HENRY MACY
Marvin, he don't do no harm.

MARVIN MACY
Damn brokeback, trailin' after me.
(To COUSIN LYMON, *loud)*
What you want, anyway!?

COUSIN LYMON *(Shy)*

Oh . . . I, I don't want nothin'.

MARVIN MACY *(To himself)*

Damn bug.

HENRY MACY

You . . . you passin' through, Marvin? You on your way somewhere?

MARVIN MACY
(With a mean grin)

Oh, I don't know, Henry; don't got no plans. I, uh . . . I might settle a spell.

HENRY MACY *(Sorry)*

Oh, I thought you might be on your way through.

MARVIN MACY *(Ugly)*

Whatsa matter, Henry, don't you want me 'round here?

COUSIN LYMON

Stay, Marvin Macy. Don't go on nowhere.

MARVIN MACY *(To COUSIN LYMON)*

You shut up, you damn little . . .
(Switches his attention to HENRY MACY)
You see? You see? That brokeback want me to stay. Whatsa matter with you, Henry? Why you so eager to have me move on?

HENRY MACY *(Hesitant)*

It just . . . it just that things all settled down now, now you been gone so long, an' . . . I figgered you might be plannin' to stir up . . . you know . . . some trouble.

MARVIN MACY
(After a great laugh)
Me? Stir up trouble? Why, whatever could you mean?
    (COUSIN LYMON *giggles in support of* MARVIN MACY)
Look you!
            (This to COUSIN LYMON*)*
You been followin' me around near a week now, wigglin'
your ears at me, flappin' around, dancin' . . . you don't
go home 'cept for your eats an' bed. What you expectin' me
to do . . . *adopt* you?

COUSIN LYMON
(With exaggerated longing)
Oh, Marvin Macy . . . *would* you? Would you do that?

MARVIN MACY
(Takes a swipe at him which COUSIN LYMON *ducks
    expertly, laughs)*
Damn little lap dog.
            (But there is kindness in the contempt)

HENRY MACY
An' . . . an' I hoped you wasn't plannin' to stir up no trouble.

MARVIN MACY
Maybe just you tired of havin' me move in on you. That
house of yours half mine, just like this place here, half mine
you know, but I 'spect you got so used to livin' there all by
yourself you got a little selfish in your middle-age.

HENRY MACY *(Quietly)*
You welcome to stay long as you like.

MARVIN MACY *(Unrelenting)*
Or maybe you don't want no ex-convict hangin' around you.

Well, I tell you somethin', Henry: I ain't quite sure why I come back, not that there ain't no scores to settle, but I ain't quite sure *why* I come back; just thought I'd have a look around.

HENRY MACY

Miss Amelia is . . .

MARVIN MACY *(Suddenly harsh)*

Who said anythin' bout *her?* Hunh? I bring her up?

HENRY MACY

Miss Amelia is . . . settled down, now; she is . . . she have Cousin Lymon with her.
                              (Cousin LYMON giggles)
. . . an' she got her cafe, an' . . . an' everythin' is quiet an' settled.

MARVIN MACY

Yeah, she got quite a business goin' for herself, hunh? She takin' in good money, I bet, hunh?

HENRY MACY *(Defensively)*

Miss Amelia run the cafe for . . . us, for all of *us*: it be . . . it be a good place to come. It be a special place for us. Important.

MARVIN MACY

Yeah, an' it half mine, ain't it?

HENRY MACY
(Disappointed in his brother)

Oh, Marvin!

MARVIN MACY

She still my wife; don't you forget that!

HENRY MACY

Oh, Marvin! That were years ago.

MARVIN MACY

I know how long ago it were; I had lots of time to think about it! Lots of time rottin' in that penitentiary . . . all on account of her! On account of that one!!!

HENRY MACY

That . . . that kinda thing you can't blame on no one person, Marvin.

MARVIN MACY

The hell I can't!! Who says?!

HENRY MACY (*Weakly*)

It . . . it all long past now.

MARVIN MACY

Yeah, but you got a lotta time to think on things when you in the penitentiary, Henry.
(COUSIN LYMON *giggles*)
Ain't that right, peanut?

COUSIN LYMON (*Hopefully*)

Oh, I ain't never been in the penitentiary.

MARVIN MACY (*Ironically*)

Well, maybe you will be someday, peanut.
(*Back to* HENRY MACY)
Yeah, you get a lotta time to brood on things, Henry. An' . . . you know? You start makin' *plans*? Oh, all kindsa plans.

HENRY MACY

Leave . . . leave everythin' be, Marvin. Let it all rest.

MARVIN MACY
(Concluding an interview)

Well, you just keep to your own business, Henry, an' you let me worry on mine. All right?

(HE rises)

HENRY MACY *(Still sitting)*

You . . . you always done what you wanted, Marvin.

MARVIN MACY *(Proudly)*

Damn right, Henry; so you just let me go about my business.

(Looks at COUSIN LYMON, *smiles at him)*

You just let *us* go about *our* business. Right, peanut?

COUSIN LYMON *(Beside himself)*

Oh, yes, yes; oh, yes.

THE NARRATOR

It was the beginning of the destruction. And the things that happened next were beyond imagination.

*(*MARVIN MACY *and* COUSIN LYMON *move off-stage,* COUSIN LYMON *second, leaving* HENRY MACY *alone on stage.*

The interior of the cafe becomes visible; a usual evening is in progress. Most of the TOWNSPEOPLE *are there.* HENRY MACY *remains stationary where* HE *was, to one side of the stage. Drinking and general conversation in the cafe, though there seems to be a curious expectant quietness which* EMMA HALE *feels* SHE *must comment on from time to time, by talking too loud)*

EMMA *(Too loud)*

My, it sure is cheerful in here tonight . . . considerin' everythin'.

MACPHAIL

Oh, Emma.

EMMA *(Undaunted)*

Well, it do seem strange to me.

MISS AMELIA *(No nonsense)*

What seem strange to you, Emma?
(The group becomes quieter at this)

MRS. PETERSON
(A whispered warning)

Now, Emma, watch yourself now.

MISS AMELIA *(Louder; sterner)*

What seem strange to you, Emma?

EMMA

(Flustered at first, but regaining her composure as
SHE *goes on)*

Why, it seem strange to me that . . . uh, that everybody
sittin' here so cheerful . . .

MISS AMELIA

Why! Why that strange?

EMMA

Why . . . uh . . . *(Her eyes narrowing)* . . . it seem strange
to have everybody here save one. *(Murderously solicitous)* I
mean when poor Cousin Lymon ain't here to join in the
merriment, an' have his little supper, an' be such an enter-
*tain*ment for us all, an' to keep you *company*, Miss Amelia?
(Transparently false innocence) Where is Cousin Lymon,
Miss Amelia? Why, I hardly don't see him *ever* no more.
Where do he keep himself these days Miss Amelia?

MRS. PETERSON *(Whispered again)*
Emma!

MISS AMELIA *(Clenching her fists)*
Emma!? *(Pause as the cafe falls silent)* You shut your mouth!!

EMMA *(Feigned shock)*
But, Miss Amelia, I was just askin' to find out the where-
abouts of poor cousin . . .

MISS AMELIA
SHUT IT I SAID!!

EMMA
*(Her face back to her dinner plate, mortally of-
fended)*
Well, of course if you gonna talk *that* way I . . . I just
won't bother myself about the little runt no more, that's
all.

MISS AMELIA
Eat an' get out, Emma.

MRS. PETERSON
Oh, now, Miss Amelia, all she meant was . . .

MISS AMELIA
You, too. Both of you. Eat an' git.

EMMA *(Great dignity)*
We will do that, Miss Amelia, lest we choke to death first
on whatever this is you servin'.

MISS AMELIA
Better'n your cookin'. My pigs wouldn't eat the slop you set
before yourself in your own kitchen.

MACPHAIL
(A *little drunk; genial*)

Ladies. Now, *please.*

MISS AMELIA (*Grumpily*)

She can't talk that way about the food in this cafe.
(HENRY MACY *enters*)
Evenin', Henry.

HENRY MACY

(*As several say evening to him, chooses his solitary
table*)
Evenin', Miss Amelia.

MISS AMELIA

(*Comes up to him; tries to take care none of the
others overhear*)
You, uh . . . have you, uh . . . seen Cousin Lymon?

HENRY MACY
(*Not looking at her*)

Yeah, I have, Miss Amelia. He with Marvin. He with Marvin again.

MISS AMELIA (*After a pause*)

Eats, or likker?

HENRY MACY (*Very polite*)

I . . . I think I will just have a bottle, Miss Amelia.

MISS AMELIA (*Preoccupied*)

Suit yourself.

HENRY MACY

They not far off, I wouldn't guess; they somewhere near here
together.

MISS AMELIA
(A stab at unconcern)
Huuh; couldn't care less. Don't make no matter to me.
*(MARVIN MACY and COUSIN LYMON reappear on
stage, stay lurking to one side until it is time for
them to enter the cafe)*

HENRY MACY *(Embarrassed)*
I . . . I know.

EMMA *(Loud)*
What I find so remarkable is the way no one ain't allowed
to talk about nothin' in this cafe, which is a public gatherin'
place.

FIRST TOWNSWOMAN
(Weary of it all)
Oh, Lord.

MACPHAIL
Emma Hale, you been told to eat up an' get out.

EMMA
(With the speed of a copperhead)
Stumpy MacPhail, you go back to your boozin, an' keep
outa this. *(Same loud tone)* What I find so remarkable is
that now Marvin Macy back in town our little Cousin
Lymon spend all his time with *him* . . . 'stead of with
Miss Amelia.
(Dead silence in the cafe)

MISS AMELIA
Emma? You remember that lawyer cheated me six—seven
years back? The one tried to cheat me outa some land on a
deed? You remember what I did to him?

EMMA *(Pretending forgetfulness)*

Why, now . . .

MACPHAIL *(To EMMA: helpful)*

Why, you remember, Emma. Miss Amelia went at him, beat him up within an inch of his life. Broke his arm? An' he were big; an' he were a *man.*

MISS AMELIA *(To EMMA)*

Don't let it be said I wouldn't take my fists to a woman, either . . . if she didn't keep her place.

(MARVIN MACY *and* COUSIN LYMON *start moving toward the steps,* COUSIN LYMON *leading the way*)

MERLIE RYAN *(Cheerfully)*

Miss Amelia gonna kill Emma? She gonna kill her?

SECOND TOWNSMAN

No, Merlie; 'course not.

MERLIE RYAN *(Disappointed)*

Don't see why not.

EMMA

(To MISS AMELIA; *uncertainly)*

I . . . I ain't afraid of you.

(COUSIN LYMON *and* MARVIN MACY *are up the steps now*)

MACPHAIL *(Great slow wisdom)*

Why don't you all simmer down.

EMMA

(To MRS. PETERSON *and one of the* TOWNSWOMEN*)*

I ain't afraid of her.

MRS. PETERSON

You crazy if you ain't.

TOWNSWOMAN

That sure.

EMMA

I put my faith in God!

MRS. PETERSON *(Very unsure)*

Well . . . Amen.

MERLIE RYAN *(Waving a glass)*

Amen! Amen!
> (COUSIN LYMON, *having waved* MARVIN MACY *out of
> the light from the door, enters.* MISS AMELIA *smiles
> to see him)*

EMMA *(Her assurance back)*

Well, here the little cockatoo now.

MACPHAIL

Evenin', Cousin Lymon.

HENRY MACY

Cousin Lymon.
> (And, as well, a chorus of greeting. COUSIN LYMON
> ignores them all, marches directly up to MISS AME-
> LIA)

COUSIN LYMON
(Mockingly formal)

Evenin', Amelia.

MISS AMELIA

Well, where you been, Cousin Lymon; I about give you up.

COUSIN LYMON

Ooohhh . . . been about; been wanderin' around. Havin' a little stroll an' a talk.

(Waits very briefly to see if MISS AMELIA *reacts to this; she does not)*

My! Supper do smell good! What we havin'?

MISS AMELIA *(Preoccupied)*

Uh . . . what, Cousin Lymon?

COUSIN LYMON

I say: what we havin' for supper!

MISS AMELIA

Oh! Oh, well, there be ham, an' winter peas, an' hominy grits, an' I brung out the peach preserves.

RAINEY 1 *(His mouth full)*

It be good.

RAINEY 2 *(The same)*

Yeah, it awful good.

COUSIN LYMON

Well, ain't that nice.

MISS AMELIA

You . . . you hungry now, Cousin Lymon?

COUSIN LYMON

I mean ain't that nice . . . since we have a guest for dinner tonight.

(The cafe becomes silent)

I have invited a special guest for dinner tonight.

*(*HE *can hardly keep still waiting for* MISS AMELIA'S *reaction)*

MISS AMELIA
(Her reaction is slow in coming; finally, tonelessly)
Yeah?

COUSIN LYMON
Yeah.
(Calls to outside)
C'mon in, now; Miss Amelia waitin' on you.
(Absolute silence as MARVIN MACY *enters, silence
except an audible intake of breath here and there.*
MARVIN MACY *surveys the scene briefly, smiles wick-
edly at* MISS AMELIA, *who is immobile, moves to an
empty table, kicks the chair out, sits down. Still
silence)*

MARVIN MACY
Hey! Brokeback! Bring me my dinner.

MERLIE RYAN
Hey, Miss Amelia; Marvin Macy back. Miss Amelia!

MACPHAIL
Shut up, you damn fool!

EMMA
(As MISS AMELIA *is still silent, immobile)*
I never thought I'd live to see it. I tell you, I never thought
I'd live to see it.

MERLIE RYAN
Miss Amelia? Marvin Macy back.
*(*RAINEY 1 *chokes on his food, has a brief choking
fit;* RAINEY 2 *slaps his back.* MISS AMELIA *doesn't
move)*

MARVIN MACY

Hey, brokeback! My dinner!

COUSIN LYMON
(Moving to do his bidding)

Yes; yes, Marvin.

MISS AMELIA *(Barring his way)*

Keep outa there.

COUSIN LYMON

Marvin want his dinner!

MARVIN MACY *(To MISS AMELIA)*

Let him through!!

MISS AMELIA
(Advancing on MARVIN MACY)

Look you!

MARVIN MACY

Yeah?
*(THEY face each other, MARVIN MACY having risen;
perhaps his chair has fallen over. THEY both clench
their fists, but near their sides; they begin to circle
each other. The tension is immense)*

COUSIN LYMON
(From behind the counter)

You like grits, Marvin?

MARVIN MACY
(His eyes never off MISS AMELIA)

Pile 'em on.

MISS AMELIA
(To COUSIN LYMON, *her eyes never off* MARVIN MACY)
There some rat poison under the counter while you at it; put a little on for flavor.

MRS. PETERSON
I gonna faint.

EMMA
Hush!

MARVIN MACY
(As THEY *continue circling each other)*
I found that trap you set for me in the woods where I hunt. That woulda killed me good, wouldn't it?

MISS AMELIA
It woulda done the job.

MARVIN MACY *(Murderously)*
You watch yourself.

COUSIN LYMON
(Appearing with a heaping plate)
Dinner! Dinner!
*(*MISS AMELIA *suddenly swings around and stalks out of the cafe to the porch steps, sits. Action continues inside, though maybe the interior lights dim a little; certainly the interior conversation, such as it is, lessens in volume.* HENRY MACY *waits a moment, then follows* MISS AMELIA *out on to the porch)*

HENRY MACY
Miss Amelia? *(No reply)* Miss Amelia?

MISS AMELIA (*Finally*)

Leave me be.

HENRY MACY

He . . . he gonna move on soon. I know it.

MISS AMELIA (*Doubting*)

Yeah?

HENRY MACY (*Soothing*)

Sure, he move on; ain't no place for him here.

MISS AMELIA (*With deepest irony*)

You sure, huuh?

HENRY MACY (*Unsure*)

Sure.

(*Music up.*

During THE NARRATOR'S *speech,* MISS AMELIA *and* HENRY MACY *return inside the cafe, where life goes on,* COUSIN LYMON *waiting on* MARVIN MACY, MISS AMELIA *staying off to one side. Maybe there is barely audible conversation under this speech*)

THE NARRATOR

Oh, but Henry Macy was wrong, for Marvin did not move on. He stayed in the town, and every night the cafe was open he would arrive for dinner, and Cousin Lymon would wait on him, and bring him liquor for which he never paid a cent. And during these nights, which stretched into weeks, Miss Amelia did nothing. She did nothing at all, except to stand to one side and watch.

(*Appropriate action for the following*)

But every night one thing would be sure to happen. Once every night, sometimes for no reason at all that anyone could see, Miss Amelia and Marvin Macy would approach each

other, their fists clenched, and they would circle one another, and it was during these rituals that the townspeople
expected blows to be struck . . . but it never happened.
All that ever happened was they would circle one another,
and then move apart. Everyone knew that one time they
would finally come to blows, that sooner ro later Marvin
Macy and Miss Amelia would fight, would set upon one
another in a battle that would leave one of them brutally
beaten or dead. But everyone also knew that it was not yet
time.

One night, though, nearly three months after Marvin Macy
returned to town, there occurred an event which set the sure
course to calamity.

(*Music out.*
Cafe scene back)

MISS AMELIA

You finally movin' on.

MARVIN MACY

Yeah?

MISS AMELIA

Well, you all packed.

COUSIN LYMON
(*From his throne on the barrel*)
Amelia!
(*Brief silence; she looks to him*)
Marvin Macy is goin' to visit a spell with us.

MISS AMELIA
(*After quite a pause, shakes her head as if to clear it*)
I don't understand you, Cousin Lymon.

COUSIN LYMON

I said: Marvin Macy is goin' to visit a spell with us. *(Slowly, distinctly)* He is goin' to move in here. *(Pause, as nothing seems to have registered)* He is gonna live here. With us.
(*A stock-still silence, broken by*)

MISS AMELIA
(*Finally: to* MARVIN MACY)

Ain't no room.

MARVIN MACY *(Mocking)*

Ain't no room, huuh?

MISS AMELIA

This ain't no flop house . . . for convicts.

MARVIN MACY
(*His eyes still on* MISS AMELIA)

Cousin Lymon? They ain't no room for me?

COUSIN LYMON *(Imperious)*

Amelia!
(SHE *turns her sad attention to him*)

Amelia, I think I told you Marvin Macy is gonna live here with us.

MISS AMELIA
(*Surprisingly helpless before his tone*)

But . . . but, Cousin Lymon . . .

COUSIN LYMON
(*Giving orders, but taking a childish pleasure in the power of it*)

Marvin Macy will sleep in your Papa's big bed, an' we will

move what you have referred to as my coffin—my tiny bed—
into your room . . . an' you . . .
              (HE *pauses here for full effect*)
. . . an' you, Amelia . . . well, you can pull up a mattress,
an' sleep by the stove down here.
       (*More silence, broken only by* MARVIN MACY'S *soft,
       throaty chuckle*)

                    HENRY MACY
       (*Quietly, to the bottle in front of him on the table*)
Lord God in heaven.

                    MISS AMELIA
       (*Tries to speak, but all that emerges is*)
Arrggh . . . uh, uh, arrggh.

                    COUSIN LYMON
              (*Oblivious to her attempted reply*)
So, you see, Amelia, there *is* room, after all. It merely a
question of makin' space.

                    MACPHAIL
              (*Rises, but does not move*)
I think I goin' home.

                  MRS. PETERSON
                 (*Not moving at all*)
Yes; me, too.

              SECOND TOWNSWOMAN
Think you right.

                    COUSIN LYMON
                 (*Jumping off the barrel*)

So! Now I think Marvin an' I move upstairs an' get things arranged comfortable. Marvin?

MARVIN MACY
(Picking up his tin suitcase)

Comin'.

(MISS AMELIA has not moved; will not look at any-one. MARVIN MACY follows COUSIN LYMON up the stairs; THEY vanish. All the TOWNSPEOPLE, save HENRY MACY slowly exit now, all of them, save MERLIE RYAN, who just sort of drifts out, pausing briefly by MISS AMELIA, either to say goodnight, or touch her by the elbow, or just stop, then move on. When THEY have all left the cafe and are nearly off-stage, MISS AMELIA rouses herself slightly from her leth-argy, looks slowly around the cafe, and moves out on to the porch, where SHE sits, staring vacantly off.
Music here, maybe a move back.
The lights go down on the cafe, its interior van-ishes, and then HENRY MACY comes out the door and sits fairly near MISS AMELIA)

MISS AMELIA *(After a pause)*

Henry?

HENRY MACY

Yes, Miss Amelia.
(All the speeches slowly responded to now)

MISS AMELIA

I gotta do it now.

HENRY MACY

Do . . . what, Miss Amelia?

MISS AMELIA

I gotta get your brother.

HENRY MACY

Yes.

MISS AMELIA

I gotta drive him off, or kill him, or . . .

HENRY MACY

I know.

MISS AMELIA

But if I do that . . .

HENRY MACY

If you do that, what?

MISS AMELIA

If I drive him off then . . . then Cousin Lymon go off with him.

HENRY MACY

Oh, Miss Amelia . . .

MISS AMELIA

He would! I'd 'a done it long before now . . . 'cept . . .

HENRY MACY

'Cept you think Cousin Lymon go off too; go off with him?

MISS AMELIA

Unh-hunh.

HENRY MACY

But . . . but do it matter that much?

MISS AMELIA
(Looking at him finally)
Cousin Lymon go off . . . I all alone.

HENRY MACY

He ain't . . . much comfort, Cousin Lymon.

MISS AMELIA

He some. He been some. I gonna get your brother, Henry.

HENRY MACY
(Thinks; acquiesces to it)
All right. *(Pause)* Night, Miss Amelia.

MISS AMELIA

Night, Henry.

HENRY MACY
(Starting to walk off; stops, makes a statement)
Ain't nothin' I can do, is there.

MISS AMELIA
(Rising, starting to go indoors)
No. Ain't nothin', Henry.

HENRY MACY

No. Well . . . night.
(HE moves off exits)

MISS AMELIA

Night, Henry.
(SHE goes indoors)

Music up.
Lights up to daylight. Only the outside of the cafe
is seen.

THE NARRATOR

And the fight, which everybody had expected but nobody had known exactly when it would happen, took place, when it finally occurred, on Ground Hog's Day.

(Appropriate action for the following)

And it was at the same time both a solemn and a festive occasion. Bets had been placed—with Emma Hale's money going on Marvin Macy, of course. And Miss Amelia had lay flat down on her porch to rest her strength for the fight, and Marvin Macy sat nearby with a tin can of hog fat between his knees and carefully greased his arms and legs. Everybody knew, and they did not need Cousin Lymon as their clarion —though of course they could not stop him.

COUSIN LYMON *(To* MARVIN MACY*)*

You grease up good, now; you be real slippery she can't get a good grip on you.

MARVIN MACY *(Greasing his arm)*

That what I doin'; don't you worry.

COUSIN LYMON

(To some of the TOWNSPEOPLE *who are beginning to saunter in)*

Today! It gonna be today!

STUMPY

Yeah, we know; we know.

THIRD TOWNSMAN

Yeah, don't worry, now; we know.

COUSIN LYMON
(Beside himself with excitement, stops briefly at
MARVIN MACY)
You grease real good now.
(Darts off toward MISS AMELIA)

MARVIN MACY
(As HE *greases the other arm)*
Yeeessssss!!

COUSIN LYMON
(On his way to MISS AMELIA, *spies other* TOWNS-
PEOPLE *entering from the other side)*
The fight startin'! It about to begin.
(Moves toward MISS AMELIA *again)*

HENRY MACY *(Sadly; impatiently)*
We *know!* We know!

EMMA
An' I gonna win me a dollar today, too.

MRS. PETERSON *(Stuck-up)*
Don't see how that can be, since *I* gonna win one.

EMMA *(A gay laugh)*
You see.

COUSIN LYMON
(Now by where MISS AMELIA *is lying)*
Amelia?

MISS AMELIA
*(Not moving; staring at the sky; little expression in
her voice)*
Yes, Cousin Lymon?

COUSIN LYMON (*All excitement*)
You . . . you restin' for the fight, huuh?

MISS AMELIA
Yes, Cousin Lymon.

COUSIN LYMON
An' . . . an' . . . you eat good?

MISS AMELIA
Yes, Cousin Lymon; I had me three helpings of rare roast.

COUSIN LYMON
Marvin ate *four*.

MISS AMELIA
Good for him.

COUSIN LYMON
(*A tentative finger out to touch her*)
He . . . Marvin all greased up. You . . . you greased, Amelia?

MISS AMELIA
Yes, Cousin Lymon.

COUSIN LYMON
(*Takes a step or two back, looks around the crowd, seems to be pleading*)
Then . . . then you both about ready, I . . . I'd say.
(*To* STUMPY MACPHAIL)
I'd say they both about ready.
(EVERYBODY *is on stage, now, the* TOWNSPEOPLE *still peripheral*)

MACPHAIL *(Piqued)*

I'll decide on that.

COUSIN LYMON
(Moving to one side, a curved smile on his lips)
I just tryin' to be helpful.

HENRY MACY
You be more help you go hide under a log, or somethin'.

MACPHAIL
(Moves over to MARVIN MACY*)*
You all fixed an' ready, Marvin?

MARVIN MACY
(Rises, rubs a little more grease into his arms)
Never be readier!

MACPHAIL
(Moving toward where MISS AMELIA *is lying;* SHE
sits up)
You . . . you all ready, Miss Amelia?

MISS AMELIA
I been ready for years.

MACPHAIL
(Moves front and center)
Well, then, you two c'mere.

MERLIE RYAN
What . . . what gonna happen?
*(*MISS AMELIA *and* MARVIN MACY *slowly approach
front and center)*

EMMA (*Answering* MERLIE RYAN)
Marvin Macy gonna kill Miss Amelia, Merlie; that what
gonna happen.

MRS. PETERSON
Other way 'round!

MERLIE RYAN
Why . . . why they gonna fight?

SECOND TOWNSMAN
Hush, you.

MERLIE RYAN (*A lonely child*)
I wanna know why. I wanna know why Marvin an' Miss
Amelia gonna kill t'other.

THIRD TOWNSMAN (*Laughing*)
'Cause they know each other, Merlie.
    (*A couple of people laugh at this, but mostly there
    is tense silence*)

MERLIE RYAN (*Same*)
'T'ain't no good reason.

EMMA
It gonna have to do.

MACPHAIL
(*To* MARVIN MACY *and* MISS AMELIA, *who come and
stand, one to either side of him.* MARVIN MACY *is
stripped to the waist, his trouser legs folded up to
above the knees;* MISS AMELIA *has her sleeves rolled
up to the tops of her shoulders, her jean legs pulled
up, too*)
Got knives, either of you?

MISS AMELIA & MARVIN MACY

Nope.

MACPHAIL

I gotta check anyway. (HE *feels into* MARVIN's *back pockets*)
You clean.

MARVIN MACY *(Vicious)*

What you think I be . . . a liar?

MACPHAIL *(Stony)*

Knives has a way of slippin' into pockets sometimes without
a person knowin' about 'em, Marvin. You musta seen a lot of
that in your time.

MARVIN MACY
(Ugly, but not about to argue further)

Yeah?

MISS AMELIA *(Impatiently)*

Come on!

MARVIN MACY
(At MISS AMELIA; *soft and wicked)*

Oh, I can't wait.

MACPHAIL *(To quiet them)*

All right! All right, now.
(Tense silence from everyone; MISS AMELIA *and* MAR-
VIN MACY *move a bit apart, stand in boxing poses,
ready)*
All right! Begin!
*(*THE FIGHT: *They circle for a moment, and then
both strike out simultaneously, without warning.
Both blows land well and stun both fighters for a
little.* THEY *circle more, then* THEY *join and mix in*

vicious in-fighting. MISS AMELIA *gets hit, staggers backwards, almost falls, rights herself.* THEY *in-fight again.* MARVIN MACY *gets struck a hard blow, staggers back.* THEY *in-fight again. Suddenly the fight shifts from boxing to wrestling. At this, the crowd comes in closer. The fighters battle muscle to muscle hip-bones braced against each other; gradually* MISS AMELIA *gains the advantage, and inch by inch* SHE *bends* MARVIN MACY *over backwards, forcing him to the ground.* COUSIN LYMON *is extremely agitated. Finally,* MISS AMELIA *has* MARVIN MACY *to the ground, and straddles him, her hands on his throat. The crowd presses closer, to watch the kill)*

MRS. PETERSON *(Shrieking)*

Kill him! Kill him!

MERLIE RYAN *(Taking it up)*

Kill him! Kill him!

COUSIN LYMON
(Half a shriek, half a word, howled)

NNNNNNOOOOOOOOOOOOO!

*(*COUSIN LYMON *races from where* HE *has been standing, mounts* MISS AMELIA'S *back and begins choking her from behind)*

HENRY MACY

Stop him!

EMMA

Get her; get her!

*(*COUSIN LYMON *continues choking* MISS AMELIA, *and this is enough to shift the balance of the fight.* MARVIN MACY *manages to get* MISS AMELIA'S *hands from his throat, forces her down.* COUSIN LYMON *backs off*

a few steps. MARVIN MACY *straddles* MISS AMELIA, *beats her senseless, furiously, excessively, as the crowd gasps, yells.*
All becomes silence. Music stops. The crowd moves back a bit. MARVIN MACY *rises from the prostrate form of* MISS AMELIA; *he breathes heavily, stands over her, barely able to stand, himself)*

HENRY MACY *(Very quietly)*

Oh, Lord, no.
(All is very still, the loudest sound MARVIN MACY'S *breathing. Some of the* TOWNSPEOPLE *begin to wander dreamily off)*

EMMA

(Moving toward MISS AMELIA; *great solicitude)*
Oh, poor Miss Amelia, poor . . .

HENRY MACY

Leave her be.
*(*EMMA *obeys, exits, leaving, finally, only* MISS AMELIA, MARVIN MACY, COUSIN LYMON *and* HENRY MACY *on stage.*
MISS AMELIA *slowly pulls herself up on one arm, crawls slowly, painfully from where* SHE *has been lying to the steps, up them, collapses again on the porch.*
COUSIN LYMON *walks slowly, shyly over to* MARVIN MACY *who puts his arm around him, still breathing hard, still looking at* MISS AMELIA.
HENRY MACY *takes a few tentative steps toward* MISS AMELIA, *changes his mind, begins to exit)*

MARVIN MACY

'Bye, Henry.

HENRY MACY *(Continuing out)*
'Bye Marvin.

COUSIN LYMON
'Bye, Henry.
>   (HENRY MACY *exits, as if* HE *had not heard* COUSIN
>   LYMON)
>   *(Music up)*

THE NARRATOR
>   *(Tableau, with* MARVIN MACY, COUSIN LYMON *to-*
>   *gether,* MISS AMELIA *sprawled on the porch)*
Marvin Macy and Cousin Lymon left town that night, but
before they went away, they did their best to wreck the store.
They took what money there was in the cafe, and the few
curios and pieces of jewelry Miss Amelia kept upstairs; and
they carved vile words on the cafe tables. After they had done
all this . . . they left town . . . together.
>   (MARVIN MACY *and* COUSIN LYMON *stand for a mo-*
>   *ment,* MARVIN MACY *breathing a little less hard,*
>   *laughing a little)*

MARVIN MACY
>   *(With a small chuckle)*
C'mon, peanut; let's go.
>   *(The two exit,* MARVIN MACY'S *arm still over* COUSIN
>   LYMON'S *shoulder.* MISS AMELIA *is left alone on stage)*

>   SHE *rights herself to a sitting position, howls once,*
>   *becomes silent.*
>   *Music continues to the end of the play.*

THE NARRATOR
And every night thereafter, for three years, Miss Amelia sat

out on the front steps, alone and silent, looking down the road and waiting. But Cousin Lymon never returned. Nothing more was ever heard of Marvin Macy or Cousin Lymon. The cafe, of course, never reopened, and life in the town was that much drearier.

(MRS. PETERSON *comes on, timidly, advances to where* MISS AMELIA *is sitting*)

And Miss Amelia closed the general store, as well, or it would be more correct to say that she discouraged anyone from coming there anymore.

MRS. PETERSON *(Quietly)*

Miss Amelia?

(MISS AMELIA *looks at her after a moment, says nothing*)

I . . . I wondered . . . I thought I would buy a coke.

MISS AMELIA

(No expression, save some vague loss)

Sure. *(Not moving)* That will be a dollar and five cents.

MRS. PETERSON

(Still quiet, but flustered)

But . . . but a coke be a nickel.

MISS AMELIA

(Looking steadily at her; blank voice)

Yes. *(Pause)* Five cents for the coke, and a dollar for seein' me. A dollar for lookin' at the freak.

MRS. PETERSON

(Moving away, slowly at first, then fleeing)

Oh . . . Miss Amelia . . .

(MISS AMELIA *alone on stage. Gets up, goes indoors, closes the door after her. Lights up to opening of the play*)

THE NARRATOR

And at the end of three years Miss Amelia went indoors one night, climbed the stairs, and never again left her upstairs rooms.

The town is dreary. On August afternoons the road is empty, white with dust, and the sky above is bright as glass. If you walk along the main street there is nothing whatsoever to do. Nothing moves—there are no children's voices, only the hum of the mill.

(The upstairs window opens and closes as in the be-
ginning of the play, accompanying the below)

Though sometimes, in the late afternoon, when the heat is at its worst, a hand will slowly open the shutter of the window up there, and a face will look down at the town . . . a terrible, dim face . . . like the faces known in dreams. The face will linger at the window for an hour or so, then the shutters will be closed once more, and as likely as not there will not be another soul to be seen along the main street. Heat . . . and silence. There is nothing whatsoever to do. You might as well walk down to the Fork Falls Road and watch the chain gang. The twelve mortal men . . . who are together.

The Ballad of the Sad Cafe . . . the end.

(Music holds for four seconds, stops. Silence for four
seconds)

CURTAIN

Edward Albee

Edward Albee was born March 12, 1928, and be-
gan writing plays thirty years later. His plays are,
in order of composition: THE ZOO STORY; THE DEATH
OF BESSIE SMITH; THE SANDBOX; THE AMERICAN
DREAM; WHO'S AFRAID OF VIRGINIA WOOLF?;
BALLAD OF THE SAD CAFE (adapted from Carson
McCuller's novella); TINY ALICE; MALCOLM
(adapted from James Purdy's novel); A DELICATE
BALANCE; EVERYTHING IN THE GARDEN (adapted
from a play by Giles Cooper); BOX AND QUOTATIONS
FROM CHAIRMAN MAO TSE-TUNG; ALL OVER; SEA-
SCAPE; LISTENING; COUNTING THE WAYS; THE LADY
FROM DUBUQUE; and LOLITA (adapted from Vladi-
mir Nabokov's novel).